Dancing in the Sea

Catherine Hill was born in Watford in 1959. After studying and working in Leeds and London, she travelled to Italy and now lives in Milan, where she works as an English Language teacher for multinational companies.

DANCING IN THE SEA

Once The Hijack Was Over

Catherine Hill

MAINSTREAM
PUBLISHING

EDINBURGH AND LONDON

For my mother, Christine.

ACKNOWLEDGEMENTS

THERE ARE MANY people whose invaluable help I have received over the years following the terrorist attack and I would love to publicly thank them all. However, the list would be so long and I know that I would inevitably leave a name out, which would be unpardonable. I therefore thank you all with all my heart. You know who you are.

Some of those have also helped me with my book, so I would like to acknowledge their support and belief in the project, despite the fact that this story has taken so long to come to light.

My thanks go to Pat Bradsen and Phil Bristow for their robust enthusiasm; Cameron Hill for his reading and constructive criticism; Stephen and Gloria Vizinczey for their encouragement; Rosemary Wells for the first reading and criticism outside my family; Moira Coleman, my English teacher when I was at school, who told me it was better 'to show not tell'; and Silvia Daino, the technology whizz who helped me communicate with the publishers on my computer. My gratitude also goes to Peter George and, of course, Ailsa Bathgate, my editor, who has taught me a great deal about the craft of writing, and without whom I would have been lost.

CONTENTS

1

THE HIJACK

ON 5 SEPTEMBER 1986, my boyfriend Picci and I touched down in Karachi en route home to Milan after five weeks travelling around India. We had boarded the plane in Bombay and had now stopped in Pakistan to pick up some more passengers. As we waited for them to board our Europe-bound flight, we fantasised about food back home in Italy. Throughout our travels, the only meat we had tasted had been mutton, accompanied by watery vegetables or curried pulses. No whiff of alcohol had eased the culinary horrors, so now that we were homeward-bound we felt we could safely drool over images of pasta, pizza and a good T-bone steak.

We had been asleep, but now that we had landed we laughed and joked as we thought of our future and all the plans we had made. How very happy I was in that instant as I thought about how our Indian adventures had brought us closer together and how this man intrigued and attracted me.

When the door in front of our row of seats flew open and security guards burst into the cabin with machine guns at the ready, I was not so much alarmed as annoyed. 'Trust this to happen. Now it will be hours before take-off. They must be looking for a wanted criminal or escaped convict,' I thought. Far from my mind was the possibility of this being something more serious, and it was not until an air stewardess spoke into the microphone that I understood what was happening.

'This is a hijack. Hold your hands up over your head and don't move. These men are armed and will use their weapons when and where necessary. Please keep calm and as still as you can.'

Staring blankly ahead in disbelief, I could think of nothing further than the headrest in front of me. Brusque Arabic shouts and rough gestures brought our arms up over our heads and knots in our solar plexi. Terror hit me as I realised I couldn't even look at Picci for support let alone speak to him.

There was an uncanny silence all around me as each one of us took in the horror of what was happening. My peripheral vision rapidly shut down, blocking out awareness of anyone or anything else, and the ringing in my ears further isolated me from a normal world with normal noises and normal expectations.

For the next hour, my brain raced from one seemingly inconceivable possibility to another, covering a series of alternative scenarios. This huge American jumbo parked on the runway at Karachi Airport would surely now be featuring on every news programme around the world, bringing us into people's homes. That much I could well imagine, given the airline's name and the dramatic nature of such an incident. It was too good a piece of headline news not to be immediately captured on TV, although I couldn't actually see any film crews in the vicinity. The fact that we were probably being watched bothered me, as I felt we were so near to others and yet so far from them.

In those first moments, Picci watched what was happening with a cool detachment few people would be able to achieve. Not immobilised by fear as I was, he made a tentative move to tell me what was going on. Incredibly, this was the second time he'd been taken hostage and he was marginally more prepared for the shock than me. He had been held, along with other employees, in the toilets of the company where he worked in Milan by the extreme left-wing organisation the Italian 'Red Brigade' in the late 1970s. The hostages had been locked away for the afternoon and later been found unharmed by the police. Because of that experience, he was confident that hostages were usually released and was not unduly worried by the situation. His eyes flickered round the confines of our space, checking out the exit doors and assessing how the hijackers had positioned themselves. Picci was familiar with terrorists' body language and the threatening atmosphere they created. He didn't have the same outlook on Pakistan, or indeed the Arab world, as I did. He had been brought up in Italy, where foreign policy was not as clear-cut as that of the US or indeed Great Britain, and he was, therefore, less aware of the implications of the hijack.

We were told to lower the window blinds and our communication possibilities, slight though they had been, were cut off. The people in the rows behind us were made to stand up and disperse into seats in front, to give our guard the necessary room to control his group of passengers. We were the first lot of seats in his line of vision.

I wondered if my family had heard or seen the news, and whether they would connect the event with me. Fran, my sister, might. I tried to think back to our brief pre-vacation phone call. Had I told her where we were going? If the family didn't know I was on the plane, then they might not take much notice of the news, and they wouldn't get to know I'd been involved in the hijack unless I was hurt, of course, or killed.

My arms ached. How I wished we could lower them. I hoped the terrorists wouldn't expect us to keep them up like that for the duration of the hijack. I didn't dare move, however. Our captors would in all probability be very unpredictable, likely to do anything without hesitation.

I stole a look at one of them, who could only have been about 17 with acne scars on his jaw and neck. He held his machine gun over us, ready to fire off a round should the need arise. What tension there was in his body: it was electric, near breaking point. Better not look any longer. My gaze returned to the headrest in front of me, my arms crying out with fatigue. Perhaps I could rest them on the seat in front. I began my journey. The seconds went by as my muscles began to tremble under the strain.

'Don't move. The next person to move will be shot.'

I jumped and sweat broke out across my back. I could hear the fear in the stewardess's voice and I was shaking from having been caught, because, of course, out of all the hostages I was the only one moving, wasn't I? How could they have seen me? I'd barely started to go forward.

Terror is such an efficient guardian and immobilises each and every one of us to varying degrees. I tried to glance at Picci, but he was slightly further back than me in his seat and I didn't dare turn my head. My resolve was ebbing as I felt tears of panic pricking my eyes. The voice over the intercom continued as the hostess repeated instructions to keep our hands above our heads and not to move. She retained the same detached voice she used on more routine flights, but the message was very different.

That word 'shot' was so onomatopoeic, it was surreal hearing it and it triggered a stream of word association. Shot, shoot, dead, death, dying. Would I end up dying? Would it hurt if I died? My eyes burned from concentrating, and I clung to more positive ideas so as not to lose control. I wouldn't think of death any more, only of life, for Picci and I had too much to live for. We'd get through this. Of course, it was dramatic now at this precise moment, but it wouldn't last long, and then we'd just put it all down to being a bit of a fright. We might even laugh about it at Frera next weekend, tell everyone the gory details and feel a bit like heroes.

Next weekend, next weekend. That was a lifetime away. I closed my eyes. A tear stuck in the corner near my nose. It would all be over tomorrow, I thought, willing myself out of that claustrophobic panic. It would be finished soon, for better or for worse. It could even end without a drop of blood being spilt, but somehow I wasn't convinced that I'd come out of this without a scratch.

At this point, Picci murmured something about taking a photo of these creeps for posterity, because he was sure he'd get a lot of money from some newspaper. How on earth could he think about taking pictures and making money at a time like this? He lowered an arm to wiggle up the window blind, cursing everyone outside as he looked at the empty tarmac and saw that all help had seemingly gone. Not even the fire engines were around any more. I told him to drop the blind, terrified of what would happen if he got caught.

'If only we could get hold of the camera,' he muttered again. His nonchalance scared me, as he seemed almost unaware of the danger I perceived.

The body of an American citizen who'd been shot through the head had been thrown out of the exit next to the cockpit door. Two or three hours after the start of the hijack, he'd been pulled out of his aisle seat and taken to the front. An hour later, he was dead. Mercifully, no passengers had heard the shot, so we were unaware of the episode, but some of the stewardesses had witnessed the killing and lived with the cruel scene going through their heads throughout that day. For what reason this man had been killed I do not know, but I imagine it was to show the various heads of governments involved that these hijackers meant business. They were also probably very angry, as the hijack had got off to a bad start. The two pilots of the jumbo had miraculously escaped before the hijackers had reached the cockpit, making it impossible to fly the plane. They now had the task not only of controlling the hostages but also of negotiating and waiting for a new crew, were one ever to arrive. Again, we passengers knew none of this at the time, and I only found out what had been going on some months later from newspaper reports.

Meanwhile, back in my seat, I was trapped with my thoughts and fear. Who were these people and why were they doing this to us? The questions continued to go round and round in my head. Why had they taken us hostage and what did they want? Were they thinking of flying us somewhere and, if so, why weren't we airborne yet? It seemed better to be grounded, though, as they might have wanted to blow us up in mid-air. Maybe they had decided to shoot us one by one in front of a global stage. If they took Picci, I was definitely going with him. If they shot him, they'd have to shoot me, too.

My head whirled on, unable to calm down, my imagination fixed in perpetual movement. A stewardess appeared. She had a large sports bag and was asking people for their passports. Finally – I lowered my arms in blissful relief as I heard her request for documents. Everyone was rummaging about, looking, and Picci fished ours out of his jacket pocket.

She came up to our row. We were among the last to hand them over. I watched her oval face and dark Indian eyes as she held out a slim hand. Her lovely features were impassive as she slipped the passports into a brimming bag. She made brief eye contact, but she didn't smile. Her lipstick was still in place, almost as if she'd recently applied it. She can't have been the nervous lip-licking type.

It didn't occur to either of us to say that our passports were in the overhead locker and unavailable. We just did as we were told. Her mind was obviously still functioning sharply, though, as, unbelievably, she had apparently had the courage to hide the American passports, either dropping them behind the seats or sliding them into her pocket. She must have had a lot of guts, as, had she been caught, I cannot imagine what the hijackers would have done to her. Her name was Liliana, and she looked only about 25 years old, but it was easy to see she had a poise and calm that defied her years. She saved the life of at least one American.

My mind, seeking release from the intense stress, digressed to the poor woman next to Picci. She irritated me with her sniffing and sneezing. We were bound to get her cold. Her nasal activities were driving me mad, so I found some tissues in the bottom of my pocket and gave them to her, hoping she'd take the hint. People who had colds should stay at home. I knew somewhere inside myself that my irritation was ludicrous in the circumstances, but I couldn't help such thoughts.

About three hours or so into the hijack, a woman's voice came across the intercom. It was the voice of the senior purser, Lita. 'Peter George, stand up and identify yourself. Please go to the front of the plane immediately.' The message was repeated and a new wave of anxiety washed over me. For sure he was an American. He had to be.

I immediately thought of the Achille Lauro incident of the previous year, where Islamic terrorists had hijacked an Italian cruise ship, picked out an American, shot him and thrown him into the sea. Then, in a seemingly unstoppable flood, I recalled the assaults made on Vienna and Rome airports in 1985, and terrorist attacks in Europe over the previous ten years. The Palestinian cause meant that Americans and Israelis in particular were vulnerable wherever they were. One US passport must have been found. Poor man, I wondered whether his life was going to be sacrificed as their example to the rest of the world.

Who would be the next on the hijacker's hate lists? As if I didn't know. I recalled the reaction to various terrorist attacks carried out in the early '80s and reflected that the British were not gentle in their approach to terrorists. The agreed line between Margaret Thatcher and Ronald Reagan was that there was to be no negotiation.

I looked about me, aware that there were very few Europeans on the flight in comparison to Indians and other nationalities. Perhaps I was the only British citizen on the plane and would be the next one to be chosen. It wasn't inconceivable that they would shoot a woman, and it might even be more effective in achieving their aims.

I didn't want to die. If I had to, I was worried about not being able to die with dignity. Absurd vanity. I thought about Picci and was sure that he would never be picked, as he was Italian and Italians had never taken a strong stand regarding terrorism.

Peter George was obviously as scared as I was, because he was lying low and not identifying himself. The voice came over again and again asking him to go to the front of the plane immediately. How sick he would be feeling, he must have been terrified.

I found out much later, when Peter came to visit me in hospital, that he was in fact British and had been identified because of his military bearing and blond crew-cut on his passport photo, and because there were seemingly no Americans on board the flight. Peter was actually a schoolteacher and he was greatly underweight because of the trip he had been on, so it was perhaps his skeletal appearance that saved him from immediate detection. He sat in his seat wondering whether they'd come and find him. His heart was racing as he weighed up the pros and cons of sitting out the situation. Did they really want him to go to the front of the plane or was this just a request that would eventually be forgotten?

I couldn't believe that we were involved in such a preposterous adventure. I kept thinking that it would be finished in the next hour, or few minutes, that we'd be rescued by some crack military team. I was convinced it had all been a huge mistake on the part of the terrorists and that perhaps they'd got onto the wrong plane. We weren't important enough for this to happen. They had the wrong people. Things like this didn't happen to people like me.

Eventually, I got up to use the toilet, after an excruciating wait of several hours. There was a queue of us lined up with one of the hijackers. He had his machine gun ready, controlling the entry and exit of passengers into the by-now messy WCs. I was free in there, but knew that the duration of that freedom was limited and timed. Any longer than the two minutes allotted and who knew what could happen.

I filed back to where Picci was sitting to find that he had been able to sneak our $3,000 out of the little yellow rucksack and strap the envelope under his shirt. By this point, the other hijackers had started talking to the hostages, establishing a strange relationship with them. At one point, one of the hijackers who spoke a little English, a good-looking boy with a military posture, well built with tight curly hair and dark eyes, actually confessed that he didn't like what he was doing and would have much preferred being out with friends or a pretty girl. He was doing all this for the love of his country, for he was Palestinian. In contrast, the youngest boy who had stood by patrolling the toilet queue seemed an adolescent but had the unreasonable zeal of a brainwashed psychopath. He guarded those of us seated at the back of the plane with a machine gun and hand grenade. I felt any excuse would have been good enough for him to shoot one of us, for he probably wanted to prove his courage before his comrades. I wouldn't have wanted him to be the leader in this ordeal.

Peter George had by now gone up to the front and was being questioned. He'd been unable to resist the insistent calls that he identify himself. He was waiting to be shot. The terrorist leader had asked him if he was a soldier, to which Peter replied that he was a teacher. Did he have a gun? Peter laughed, revealing a spirit few of us could have shown under the same circumstances. 'No, you're the only ones with guns round here.' He was told to kneel down by the cockpit door and not move.

Peter began to pray. He made promises about what he would do if he were to escape what appeared most likely to be his fate, and although he didn't believe in God, he made his pleas just in case God happened to be listening. He said goodbye to all his friends, and, having made his peace, prepared to die with courage. For that was something he felt he had to do. In dying he needed to show himself and the terrorists that he was a brave man.

Strangely enough, his fear then left him, perhaps because another hostess was pointing out a man on the ground outside the aircraft, who was trying to speak through a megaphone. The attention that had been focused on Peter was now diverted to the external world.

Communication wasn't easy because at that time the radio connection had not been made and the megaphone sounds were distorted. The terrorist, whose gun had moments earlier been aimed at Peter, spoke in his own language as he tried to make his demands clear. These were tense moments for Peter as exasperated threats were barked out to the stewardess: 'Now. You. Speak, you say this. Tell them we have the next body here to kill immediately if they don't pull their people away from the plane.'

'All people are to leave the area,' Jasmine called out in her lilting Indian accent. She obviously got through to their negotiator, a Pan Am employee stationed at Karachi Airport, as moments later instructions were given to everyone to evacuate the zone surrounding the jumbo. The person responding through the megaphone replied that if they were to call for a radio technician who was already on the plane, better communications could be set up.

Muffled conversation in Arabic took place as decisions were taken and once more the chief purser was called upon for help. 'Would Mr Kharam, the radio technician, come up to the cockpit, please. Mr Kharam to the cockpit, please.' With these summons, a new man with dread in his heart got up from his seat and made his way to the front, no doubt fearing for his life as he had no idea why he was being called. The cockpit door was closed after the man's arrival, and Peter was ordered to stay on the floor beside a pile of passports. Meanwhile, a younger terrorist came up from the lower deck to guard him and found Peter flicking through a passport he'd picked up.

'What you doing?'

'Nothing,' said Peter as he dropped it, unsure of what might happen next.

'Where you from?'

'London, and you?'

'Not your business.' The young man looked like an engineering student, with a neat short haircut and clean-shaven round face. He could have been a university friend.

'You like Thojjer?'

'Who?'

'You like Mogrit Thojjer?'

Peter thought it unwise to explain his political views regarding the British Prime Minister and simply said that he didn't, quite emphatically. In an attempt to change the subject, he then asked the lad if he was married. The conversation moved on and then stopped completely as this guard was called away to deal with some other situation.

Peter was convinced that he would be killed that day. All things considered, it was the only rational conclusion anyone might have come to, and so he tried to mentally tie up loose ends in his life. Attracting the attention of Lita, the senior purser, he conveyed to her his need to let his parents know that he loved them and that his mission in India had been completed. If she survived and he was dead, would she please contact his mother and father?

That summer, Peter had achieved one of his goals in life, which had been to say goodbye to his brother who had died on an expedition in the Himalayas in 1983 and was buried at the foot of a mountain there. What grieved Peter now was the thought that his parents could lose both sons, for he knew it would break their hearts to have to go through another funeral. This was such a burden to him that he was unable to fear for his own life in the way one would normally expect, and with this in mind he did what was probably the best thing under the circumstances, as it gave him the lucidity which fear tends to remove. He cleared his head of all thoughts and just waited.

Those of us in the tail of the plane dozed, never quite letting ourselves go, ready to jump into confused wakefulness, anticipating action of some kind. There was no hysteria, tears or stress-induced behaviour. Even the children and infants were quiet; almost as if they knew the danger we were in.

At about 9.30 p.m. on Friday, 5 September 1986, after 17 hours as a hostage, my world as I knew it exploded into a thousand pieces. It then became my arduous and desperate task to go and pick those pieces up and rearrange them so I could start my life all over again. The hijack was over, but the killing and terrible physical and mental destruction I saw around me, including the devastation wreaked on my own body, was terrifying.

Night was fast advancing and it was already dark outside. I wasn't hungry, only very stiff and yearning to be let off the plane. Without warning, the lights suddenly dimmed and began to go out. It was pitch black outside. The temperature soared in just a few seconds.

Something had failed, been switched off or had broken down, and all electrical power was cut off in the aircraft. Children sent up wails of discomfort in this suffocating heat, and frightened mothers sought to still their cries. Tension pricked our necks and ears, but despite all the signs that the situation was worsening, I was convinced that this was the beginning of the end of our nightmare and that we were going to be allowed off the plane safely. My feelings seemed to be confirmed when I saw row upon row of people resolutely standing up and moving into the aisles.

We were seated on the left-hand side of the aircraft in the last few rows from the back, practically within breathing space of the terrorist who was guarding us. Although I had seen he was standing with the hand grenade near his mouth ready to pull out the pin, and was taking aim with his machine gun, I was still sure that we were about to take our first steps towards freedom, and I too started to get to my feet, eager to be with those disembarking. I searched for Picci's hand but was yanked back down into my seat the moment I found it. Irritated, I hissed at him to move, as it was time to get off the plane. The temperature had reached the 50s by this time and the younger passengers were giving full vent to their misery and fear. Perhaps his lack of such an emotion during the entire hijack had armed him with a cool head and acute awareness, because Picci had taken in the scene and deduced the outcome.

'Get your head down, they're going to open fire!' he yelled in my ear. He bent over and pulled my face fiercely into his lap, squeezing both of us as closely as possible against the cabin wall away from the aisle. The only part of me that was unprotected was my back and bottom, which was sticking out towards the ceiling and aisle.

I'll never forget that bizarre shout in some Arab tongue. Even now a shouted word in Farsi, guttural and male, will bring on a dizzy sensation and my knees start to shake. It was their sign for the butchering to begin.

People dropped down under the automatic firing of machine guns and obliterating effect of hand grenades. The bullets found easy victims and a constellation of flashing lights lit up the smoke-filled cabin, accompanied by a staccato roar. One grenade ricocheted off the ceiling of the cabin, marking its path down onto me directly below in a flash of white light. One of my buttocks was blown off, and in the split second after the event, I wondered where it could now be lodged: on the back of a plane seat or on the ceiling?

There was an all-consuming pain, a crushingly heavy end-of-the-world sensation, and I felt the blood running out of me like a tap, fast and escaping. I was sure my entrails would spurt out of me like an afterbirth and was convinced I'd lose my soul, watch it disappear after my entrails. I couldn't take in what the hijackers had done. Incredulity floated around in my head as I chanted, 'Oh my God, Oh my God.'

My thoughts were crystal clear throughout, I never once benefited from loss of consciousness. Picci urged me up: 'Quick, let's go, come on,' for now it was time to escape. But in no state to respond, I merely whispered the same phrase as before, whilst all around me others did the same.

Peter heard the machine guns in stereo: the rounds in the front were deafening, and those in the back sounded as if they were in another country. Again the gunfire alternated, first the front, then the back, then there was a pause.

He looked across the corridor and made out the shape of the door, open by now and revealing the night sky. Grabbing the man sitting next to him, he spoke harshly, saying that it was time to get out before the firing started again. The man, overcome with shock, resisted and said that it was better to stay in their seats. Fear can be paralysing.

At our end of the plane, pandemonium had broken out, and I heard Picci shouting for the doors to be opened.

Firing continued sporadically, and I was being moved. My arms were pushed up and somehow my legs pulled out. Someone was helping Picci to carry me. Heaved over bodies, I could feel my blue and yellow T-shirt riding up until it was a gag around my mouth. Pitched headfirst down the rubber slide that had been activated on the opening of the emergency exits, I felt the cooler air, though it was still hot and muggy.

Picci threw himself after me. At the bottom he gathered me up under my arms and together we began the crippling drag in the direction of the tail of the plane. He pulled me in a wide sweep across the tarmac as far away as possible from our prison.

Peter tripped over a body, dead or alive he didn't know, and made for the doorway. His mountaineering boots stood him in good stead as he ran down the plane wing, unsure of how he should proceed but urged on by the sheer proximity of the terrorists. There was no chute down which to slide, and he wasn't going back into the plane. He tried to dangle himself off the wing, but there was nothing for him to hang onto, so he jumped, landing without harm on the runway below. Fit from his trip and much lighter than when he'd left for India, he was in excellent condition for such a drop.

Terror drove us hard, too, for we were sure that the aircraft would blow up, packed as it must have been with explosives. Unable to help in our escape, I pushed with my right leg as best as I could while the other leg lolled and bumped uselessly. Picci, with a strength lent to him by necessity, pulled me along determinedly, keeping an anxious eye out for help. But we were struggling on our own because there was no one around to help us – in all the time it took us to escape there were no police, ambulances, doctors, nurses, fire engines or army personnel anywhere near the plane exits. We had endured a hijack alone and were now fighting for our lives in the aftermath.

On reaching the perimeter of the airstrip, Picci discerned movement in some bushes. An old pick-up truck idled in the dark with a makeshift siren and light attached to the roof. We called for help, and two men came furtively towards us. 'Why no one come to help us?' I heard Picci gasp in exhausted broken English.

'We were afraid to come,' they replied, unabashed by their fear.

A large man picked me up like a broken doll and threw me over his shoulder. 'Oh dear God!' he murmured, flinging open the truck doors. Gently, he then placed me face down on the floor of the vehicle, and Picci scrambled in beside me, despite his fractured foot. The horn blared out into the dark as we started up, and the driver continued to sound his makeshift siren as we noisily rattled off to the local hospital, weaving our way in and out of the congested traffic of the city.

The journey can't have taken more than fifteen minutes, but to me it felt like two hours. Picci kept pinching me, asking me if I was 'still there'. I remember being irritated by the endearments he was murmuring, so completely out of character that I began to wonder if he thought I was dying. His tender words gave me little comfort, for I was past caring. My brain felt like uncooked dough. Sweat poured out of me and it seemed as if I were melting like a knob of butter all over the van floor, and for some reason I still remained conscious.

When we arrived at the hospital, I was put onto a trolley on my back and wheeled away fast by hospital personnel. Unable to see clearly due to my short sight and loss of glasses, I could only get the vaguest impression of what was happening around me. We ran the gauntlet of a corridor – I, horizontal, was aware of popping flashes going off from newspaper cameras and the fascinated gaze of a sea of faces watching the macabre events of the end of a hijack. I wondered about my lack of underwear, gone when the grenade had exploded, but it was a passing thought of little importance as we swished through doors into stretcher-lined rooms.

Peter picked himself up off the tarmac and saw scores of people fleeing the jumbo, jumping as he had done from the wings, falling down the chutes and running for their lives. He ran in the direction of some buildings where he met up with other passengers and another stewardess. He wondered where Lita was, having left her at the front of the airplane. The small group hid in a store cupboard in one of the offices they arrived at, fearing terrorist accomplices in the vicinity. They were discovered an hour later by Pakistani soldiers and escorted to the departure lounge that was full of dazed and traumatised people. An American journalist was circling, trying to get scoop stories from the passengers, and somewhere in the midst of such chaos the terrorists were trying to escape, having abandoned the aircraft and their weapons. They were caught, identified by their enraged hostages and taken away before justice could be meted out by the very people they had subjected to such terror.

Those seriously wounded had already been siphoned off and taken to hospitals around Karachi, or they were in a different place, out of sight of the majority of passengers. Mercifully, we hadn't had to fight for an ambulance because we'd been picked up from the airstrip and had arrived at one of the city hospitals before any of the others, so I was given priority treatment. My situation was serious, as, gasping for oxygen because of blood loss and at the same time extremely parched, I begged to have liquid. Tea was spooned into my mouth. There were so many people around me, hands touching me. Someone was cutting my T-shirt up the middle, another undid my blue plaited belt and one more tugged at my green plimsolls.

'Get more blood!'

'I can't find a vein!'

'She's going into shock!'

The doctors relayed those three short phrases in English, which even in my dire state seemed most odd. Why hadn't they spoken their own language?

In the seconds following, I went into another dimension, one that destroyed any preconceived religious notions held dear, when body and soul seemed one. I had been pretty sure up to this point that there was a God, or Absolute principle, waiting for me in a heavenly place. Instead, I boarded a ghost train and visited hell. Swooping and swerving down a blood-red tunnel, I watched horrified as devil-like faces mocked me in my terror and I felt surrounded by evil.

Laughter echoed round my brain. I had never felt so alone and neither had I felt such bitterness sour my being as on my last worldly journey I was left abandoned and without comfort. I felt profoundly let down and very angry. I was also terrified, because, contrary to my expectations, there was no one out there to hold my hand and lead me as if a child into the next world. That desolation and the physical ordeal I was going through brought a longing for the end, for oblivion and freedom.

I finally lost consciousness and fell into a void of the deepest blue with stars of the universe surrounding me. I was weightless where no pain existed, and hell and fear were mercifully left behind.

Lita was dying, shot as she tried to save others' lives, lying where she had fallen on the jumbo. She had opened a door and pushed children and other passengers out ahead of her, but was rapidly losing blood from her bullet wound. She was still conscious when her colleagues found her, but she died on her way to hospital in the ambulance. I think that hers must have been a lonely death with no loved one to comfort her or stand by as she passed on. I so hope I am mistaken.

Peter, amazed that he was still alive and unhurt, and feeling just about the happiest he had been in his whole life, partnered up with another passenger and together they decided to go to the Sheraton Hotel to recover and contact their families to let them know they were free. The next day, on Saturday, 6 September 1986, he spent his time speaking to the world press, explaining how 350 innocent people had been taken hostage and how those who were fortunate had escaped, those less so were injured and an ill-fated unknown number were dead, killed by young men in the flower of their youth, who felt they had a cause that justified mass murder.

2

KARACHI, 1986

IN THE INTENSIVE Care Unit of the Aga Khan Hospital in Karachi where I finally ended up, I awoke to a vision of green fuzziness. Blurred outlines glided about the place, and figures loomed back and forth over my bed. I was coming round, but only just. Hands pressed my body, and voices rose and fell. I was back, connected to my physical frame again, and overwhelmingly tired – conscious of the fact that I was still alive. I also somehow knew inside myself that I was back for good. Steven Shah, the doctor in charge of me, had equally strong convictions that I wouldn't make it past a couple of days given the state I was in.

Determined to focus on something, my eyes pushed up heavy lids while the voice of a doctor pulled me out of my dream world. 'You're awake now, Catherine.' There was silence as I waited for him to say something else. A long pause ensued. I then heard my own voice, strangely remote and slow, as if I had cotton wool stuck round my tongue. 'Yes, I know.' The man took my hand and held it between his two: gentle, paternal. 'Your father and mother are coming out from England to see you and should be here tomorrow. You're a brave girl, you know, and everything is going to be all right.'

Father and Patricia, coming out to see me in Pakistan? That was strange. Whatever had possessed them to travel such a long way just to see me? In the peculiar half-awareness of my drugged brain, my perspective was completely awry. Shocking revelations touched me as if I were underwater, gentle and unreal.

That was a day of slow awakening, but as I grew accustomed to consciousness, so the suffering intensified and I became increasingly aware of my physical plight. The distress brought on by the knowledge that life would be horizontal for a long time was a constant counterpoint to any other thought. I was being fed through my nose, but the green transparent tube was blocking my already myopic vision. Finally, after a laborious effort, I was able to draw attention to the nuisance and a nurse stuck it up out of the way with tape. Relieved, I lapsed into sleep only to reawaken with a raging thirst. I craved water and imagined jugs of the liquid lined up ready for me to drain. I was given a palliative – mean little ice cubes that burnt my mouth and were miserable compared to my mental brimming jugs.

Someone was constantly by my bedside ready to call for assistance at any moment should my condition deteriorate. A cold flannel was pressed to my face and a fan was placed nearby. I could feel a jerky breeze blowing over me, its motor whirring away in rhythm to the draught. The nurse asked me my nickname, and I mouthed 'Katy', although the effort was immense. She asked what I did for a living, and I silently begged her not to converse any more. The difficulty I had in thinking and coordinating my lips and tongue was similar to the energy expenditure of answering questions when you're very drunk.

At some point in the proceedings – what day, at what time I do not know – I was presented with a pen and piece of paper. I was told that it was a consent form that I had to sign for surgery. It must have been before my father arrived, otherwise the doctors would have asked him to sign any necessary paperwork. I seized the pen, which slipped from my grasp and was gently put back into my unresponsive hand. The nurse had to wrap her fingers around mine and then around the implement so that I could physically feel it. I concentrated as hard as I could and vigorously tried to scribble my signature, but I felt as if I was painting a wall and each stroke was an arm movement. That finally shocked me into the realisation that I was very ill. The heavy pen that seemed to weigh pounds represented my own weakness in direct proportion. It was a rapid and accurate deduction of my medical condition. My signature can only have come out as a cross, and it had taken such energy and concentration.

I was wheeled off on my mobile bed to theatre for yet another clean-up. The peppered and pulped gluteal muscles were unsalvageable and had long since been sliced away. What remained was a wound full of shrapnel pieces and fragments of blue denim skirt, so that once a day I had to be anaesthetised to have accessible bits of metal and cloth removed. After one of these sessions, I was awoken by someone who, speaking kindly, told me that if I wanted, I could see and keep the jar of shrapnel that they had collected. Through the haze that enveloped me, I perceived the jar. It was the embodiment of the hijack, and I actually managed a brusque movement. 'No, no, no,' I shouted in a whisper and knocked the container to the floor.

Telegrams were flooding in from all over the world. Friends from primary school, who I hadn't heard from in 20 years, sent words full of affection, as did my girlfriends from the School of Economic Science in London. Relatives and friends from Italy sent flowers and cards, and some of my clients from work wrote messages of encouragement. Despite my confusion and interminable fatigue, I felt borne up by the network of thought that was obviously spreading. I even got plants and gifts from people who didn't know me at all but had heard about the hijack. They were perhaps people who had spoken to my relatives and felt a desire to support them by doing something symbolic, thus helping to erase the wickedness of the hijack itself.

On about the fifth day, I began to get tense, worried telexes from Picci. He had been flown home on Tuesday, 9 September after being separated from me at the hospital where we had both been initially treated. I was whisked through a door off to the right to have my life saved while he was left on a bench at the entrance of the hospital to await medical attention from anyone who could be made available. There were so many people badly wounded and not enough staff to go round that he had had to wait a very long time. At midnight, the main entrance was full of people. Hospital staff in white coats ran in and out of doors that led off the vast entrance hall. People who had nothing to do with the hijack and nothing to contribute in terms of help hung around out of curiosity and got in the way of those trying to sort out the mess. Every so often, cries of exasperation rose up out of the confusion as doctors or nurses shouted at people to go away and stop holding everyone up. Every bed, mattress and blanket was used for the tide of injured passengers coming in. Even the bench where Picci had been parked was eventually taken from underneath him to be used for other purposes. Whether it was for a tired group of relatives, passengers or for a makeshift bed, he didn't know. He was just unceremoniously dumped on the floor with a yellow sheet to cover him.

In this lowly position, he sat for about two hours waiting, giving him ample time to take in his surroundings. The local hospital was a charitable organisation in Karachi and was clearly lacking in funds. Dim light bulbs hung from the ceilings. Ventilators twirled on wobbly light fittings and a filthy grey-tiled floor lent an overall squalor to the scene. You didn't need to be a genius to realise that if something was seriously wrong with you, this wasn't the place to get treated. Picci was exhausted and vaguely wondered how I was faring. He felt sure that I was not going to die and would never have tolerated my doing so, but he was well aware of the serious condition I was in.

He sat and watched and waited. Once in a while a doctor would come by and inject something into his arm. The doctor then initialled the injection site in biro. He began to gather quite a few signatures. Only at about the fourth injection did he refuse to be used as a pincushion any more and to this day he has no idea what drugs he was given and marvels at the fact that he didn't develop any fatal disease. In any normal situation, Picci would have been out of the hospital like a shot, with his hair standing on end, but he was in no position to follow his instinct.

His foot was swelling, as his right leg had been injured by shrapnel from the same grenade that had inflicted such devastation on my body. What had really caused a lot of the damage was the fact that he had had to drag me across the airstrip, despite his fractured foot, and so it was with growing pain and heaviness that he sat out this interminable stretch of time.

Only at about 2 a.m. did someone finally come to attend to him and that was the Italian ambassador. He was a tall, elegant and what proved to be practical man, who had come to find out the identity of this chap sitting on the floor. He'd been all round the hospital searching out the Italian citizens and had been told that there was a Picci Carati somewhere. Up until then, Picci's whereabouts had remained a mystery due to the fact that we had escaped in a completely different direction from the majority of passengers and so were not with any of those who'd arrived all together in a panic-stricken mass at the main terminal.

In Italy, across the national TV network it was reported that Picci was missing. Once he had been found there was great jubilation on the part of the ambassador, who, as soon as he could, hurried to inform the journalists that the missing guy had been found. But before doing so, he attended to the needs of his lost sheep, listening to the story Picci had to tell concerning me. Recounting the events, he explained how he wanted to get me out of this hospital at all costs and into one with a standard of medical care that was not going to kill me off. As he spoke, orderlies placed him on a trolley and he was pushed into the lift.

The ambassador kept pace with an efficient but harassed-looking woman and he scribbled down my name and details so that he could go and look for me. The lift doors slowly opened onto the first floor and the trolley was pushed into a small ward-like room. Things were no better there. The bare mattress stank of urine, and the numerous patients not caught up in the hijack gawked in fascination at their new ward companion. Minutes later, a table stacked high with suspicious-looking grey bandages and bowls of lurid-coloured disinfectant was heaved to the side of the bed. The ambassador went off to deal with the problem of locating me, while Picci was treated. Blood was wiped off his leg and disinfectant poured over the wounds. An orderly, on being given instructions from a vanishing doctor, trussed up his leg in bandages, after which another bowl magically appeared from somewhere else, and a plaster cast was slapped onto his foot and shin. The wincing and gasping from Picci did nothing to alter the determined movements of an overworked auxiliary.

No sooner had the operation been finished than journalists and a TV team appeared at the door with microphones and cameras. Introductions were done away with and one of the crew launched into complicated and detailed questions on the events of the hijack in English.

At the very best of times and in the most tranquil of circumstances Picci is not likely to speak this language. He understands nearly everything, but his everyday conversation needs brushing up. Needless to say, however, the moment was so surreal that he started to answer their interrogation and was doing quite well up to the point when a young and very scruffy-looking Pakistani boy popped up out of nowhere and, in the hubbub, started trying to take off Picci's left shoe. His all-leather walking boots were not the latest fashion, but they were solid and tough, and would last a lifetime. Clearly the young boy had come to the same conclusion and was deftly unlacing Picci's walking boot. The right one was balanced precariously on top of the table on top of the bandages. 'Yes, yes, please, I am making you comfortable. You are leaving please your foot,' he gasped, keeping his beady eye on the unguarded right boot.

Picci kicked weakly with his left leg in an effort to shake off his assailant. He also started to laugh at the whole crazy situation. He was trying to speak English to journalists about a hijack in which he'd just risked his life. An assistant past caring had fixed his leg so that in all probability he'd have to have the plaster drilled off the next day before gangrene commenced. He was in an almost medieval hospital and had been given up for lost. To cap it all, he was about to have his boots stolen by an impoverished child. His hysterical mirth was mercilessly recorded on film, and we have shots of him from that episode, apparently hugely enjoying himself on the bare mattress of a hospital in Pakistan. The crew eventually left and the child too, fortunately empty-handed.

The lights dimmed and Picci was expected to sleep for a while, but the all-night party was hardly over. The whispering and conversation that buzzed around the ward as the other patients talked of the exciting events that had occurred that night prevented him from sleeping. Two hours later, just when he was winding down and had finally started to doze, the Italian ambassador made his second appearance. Picci was woken up to be told that I had finally been located and had been given numerous blood transfusions. The doctors had stemmed the haemorrhaging and the ambassador, agreeing with Picci, said it was imperative, if my life was to be saved, that I be moved at once from this hospital to the Aga Khan Clinic, a modern structure which had been built by the Aga Khan and finished six months previously. All staff were European-trained and had access to the latest equipment, drugs and treatment. It was, of course, private.

Galvanised into action, Picci tried to jump off the bed to get me, but the ambassador was faster and checked his rush. The medical teams and surgeons had already been contacted in the new hospital and were expecting us, so there was no need to panic. An ambulance was waiting. The British Consulate, informed of the move necessary for my safety, were doing the paperwork and also trying to contact my family.

It was daybreak and the hijack drama was still unfolding. Those who were badly wounded were fighting for their lives; some only made it to see the dawn of that new day. My transfer happened much later due to a disagreement over letting me go. Seemingly the local hospital was reluctant for me to be taken away at such a critical moment, but the Italian and British consulates were adamant about removing me from those premises at once. That afternoon I was taken into the Intensive Care Unit of the new hospital, where I was examined and prepared for surgery. Both of us were now in the same place, because Picci had been taken there the previous day, but still he was not allowed to see me.

For a start he couldn't walk and there were no crutches available. He also had to have further medication as his foot was infected and the cast had to be taken off. This time his leg was washed thoroughly and an X-ray performed, which revealed that he had shrapnel lodged under his tendon and a fractured metatarsal. He was placed in a little ward with three beds, white, pristine and very modern. It was a long way from the turmoil and miserable surroundings of a few hours before. He drifted off to sleep as soon as they had finished treating his foot, which, for the time being, was put back into plaster.

Late in the afternoon of the same day he had another visit from the Italian ambassador, who asked Picci if he was willing to go home. It was not an easy decision to make, and he asked if I could be flown back to Italy, too. The ambassador was unsure if this was possible given the injuries I had sustained and the surgery I was perhaps undergoing at that very moment. It would be a little while before I was able to travel and no one could really give any definite answers as to schedules.

Picci was urged to make a rapid decision in favour of going back to Europe. The US forces would be escorting those able to travel to Frankfurt in a military plane, where anyone who needed medical attention would be treated at the special military hospital of Wiesbaden. Picci asked if he could see me first, but was told that I was probably still in the recovery room. Events took over from decisions and reluctantly he was wheeled down the corridor in his pyjamas, yellow and blue rucksack on his lap, to a waiting van. Just as he was being pushed through the main doors, he was handed a telephone with his cousin from England desperately shouting to him, 'Are you OK? Have you been badly hurt? Give me the phone number of your girlfriend's family in England. Is she all right? I have to ring the family with news of her.' The phone went dead as he felt tears of exhaustion and worry cloud his vision. He was taken through the exit onto the tarmac outside and helped with his fellow patient into the van. Concerned over practicalities, Picci opened the rucksack and pulled out my glasses and passport, asking that they be delivered to me, as I would need them as soon as I was awake.

His travelling companion was Swiss and as taciturn as himself. Both of them had been told that they were under strict instructions not to speak about their flight on the US plane to anyone and that on no account were they to answer questions asked of them by the press. No explanations were given and none asked. They were driven to the airport at high speed straight onto the runway, round to the back of a massive US military plane. Check-in procedures were superfluous and no one was the slightest bit interested in looking at passports. All that had been done via other channels. The van stayed parked for some 15 minutes or so with its two occupants gazing out of the window, transfixed by the spectre of the Pan Am jumbo still parked on the runway just as it had been during the hijack. Smoke slowly drifted up into the hot air, and a yellow slide, still partly inflated, hung out of the aircraft like the spilled guts of some enormous beast. At the level of the windows, bullet holes riddled the sides, a memorial to those who had died. The vision he had of the shredded buttock through which he saw a white hip bone and the memory of the smell of scorched flesh went through his mind continuously, and he turned his head away from the scene.

At long last, stretchers were pulled out of the bowels of the US plane and military personnel came down the ramps to fetch Picci and his companion. The two new passengers were carefully loaded onto their respective stretchers, told to lie down and were carried up the ramp into the aircraft. They were stashed away in special niches along with the other injured passengers, and the nurses moved silently and swiftly up and down the rows of passenger–patients, checking pulses and temperatures, drips and dressings. Picci and the Swiss boy were the last two to board, and take-off was imminent. Everything was a sombre military green, and the engines throbbed as they waited to be cleared. Picci took in the whole scene, fascinated by such a regimented and efficient finale to his 'visit' to Pakistan.

By the time they left, it was early afternoon. The passengers were quiet, many in pain and all of them numbed by the shock of recent events. Picci passed out once during the trip back home, on his way to the toilet. He hadn't eaten for two days but would not accept a bedpan, determined that he'd make it to the aircraft WC by himself. Apart from that episode, the journey went smoothly and they arrived at Frankfurt in the very early hours of the following morning. It was pitch black and drizzling, and presented rather a dismal welcome for them. Army vehicles were waiting for the new arrivals and one by one they whisked their cargo away to the specialised care of military doctors. The hospital, its patients not yet awake, opened up its doors to the latest arrivals, and Picci was placed in a small ward with an Indian gentleman who had a bullet in his chest.

They didn't have to wait long before the first of a team of surgeons came to inspect the two of them. At 5.30 a.m., the ward lights were switched on. A large man with a walrus moustache peered at Picci's leg, which was by now caked in old blood that had seeped through the plaster. The cast was very quickly cut off and after lengthy examination the surgeon announced that he was going to operate as soon as a theatre was ready. The anaesthetist was called and to Picci's total relief he turned out to be an Italian from Reggio Emilia. At long last, someone he could speak to in his own language. An epidural was suggested; this would enable Picci to make a much quicker recovery because he would be awake during the operation. The work to be done consisted of removing pieces of shrapnel and performing some plastic surgery on the sole of his foot, as a large lump of soft tissue was missing from the instep. The broken bone was an easy enough problem to resolve but not so simple was the removal of the shrapnel pieces, particularly those lodged beneath the tendons.

Picci was also agitated by another matter, one that, under the circumstances, made me laugh when he told me what had happened. Since the moment of our escape to the time of his operation, the $3,000 had never left Picci's body. The money belt was strapped to his bare tummy. Now that he was going down for surgery, he would have to give it into the care of personnel in the hospital for safekeeping. For him, the surgery and giving over the money symbolised losing control over his life, and this was a genuinely worrying prospect for someone as in control of himself as Picci. To alleviate his anxiety, he spent the whole time gabbling to the staff, even when he was given two numbing injections in his back and leg. Just after they gave him a tranquilliser he told them about his $3,000, his brain and tongue loosened by the drugs administered.

After he came round from the operation, Pan Am made its first appearance. They sent along a representative who was supposed to help out wherever she could with passengers' problems, but she wasn't prepared for the difficult job awaiting her. The Indian, a nationalised German in the bed next to Picci's, had lost his wife and son in the hijack. Both were shot dead. He himself was badly injured, as was his little girl who was in a different ward of the same hospital. In a situation such as this there are no words and no gestures that can give solace to a man so recently bereaved. The Pan Am employee arrived in a very business-like way. She had two bouquets of flowers. One, she gave to Picci and the other, she presented to his room companion. She was quite possibly uninformed of the tragedy that had overwhelmed this man's life. In his culture, presenting flowers may have infringed etiquette completely in such circumstances, for he took the bunch and, thrusting it under the woman's face, broke up the blooms, flinging broken stems and flower heads at her.

'I've lost my wife and I've lost my child and you bring me these? Get out! Get out!' The woman fled, frightened and appalled by her mistake and the wretchedness she perceived in the man's response.

Even Picci found communicating with her hard. It was just asking too much to have anything to do with an employee of the airline in a moment as delicate as this.

He ate for the first time that evening. He'd lost two or three kilos and looked extremely haggard. Having eaten, he went straight to sleep and awoke the following morning feeling considerably better. His foot was put into yet another plaster cast and it was when he was coming back from the cast room that he saw his brother waiting for him near the door of his ward. He was surprised because he'd expressly asked his family not to come. He was embarrassed by fuss and people putting themselves out for him, and would have preferred doing everything on his own. Even the journey back to Milan was something he had wanted to organise himself.

Filippo was quickly despatched to get a tracksuit or something suitable to wear for the journey home, as Picci couldn't very well board a routine international flight in Pakistani pyjamas, however comfortable or well made they were. All of the luggage that had been in the hold of the Pan Am plane was still in Karachi, waiting for the go-ahead to be loaded on to another flight, so everyone just had with them whatever they'd managed to carry when they escaped that Friday night.

He and his brother were booked on the 4.30 flight to Milan. Picci's already high cheekbones were even more prominent and his eyes hollow for all his jesting. At Milan Airport, his whole family was there to greet him, as well as the national TV network, all eager to hear the grisly details of his adventures. But Picci wanted to get home and rest, check up on his business and contact me as soon as he could. Television could come later. The full impact of the hijack and terrible experience still hadn't hit him. He was buoyed up by the incessant activity and being centre stage in events, and it wasn't until the following weekend that he fell into a deep depression and started to grieve for what had happened to himself, me and our dreams. The morning after he got back to Milan, he doggedly went into work by taxi on wooden crutches, determined he would be able to pick up the reins of his business efficiently and without a hitch. But once in his office, the pain and the knowledge that I was still in Pakistan began to fuel mounting panic, and desperate with worry he called Soraya, a close friend of mine, to ask for her help in contacting me, unable as he was to bear the burden and solitude of such an experience alone.

I had realised he'd gone home, because I had received a visit from the Italian ambassador who brought me one or two things Picci felt I'd need. I knew he was injured but not too seriously, because he'd been able to save my life. The fact that he'd gone back to Italy was if anything a relief, as it meant he was going back to normality. Unable to do anything to help me initially, he now frantically sought news about my condition.

3

DIAGNOSIS, PROGNOSIS

MY FATHER ARRIVED on the Tuesday of the following week with Patricia, my stepmother, and I was greeted by two strained faces peering down into my reduced world. The Foreign Office had phoned them at their home in England just after half past six the previous Saturday morning with the news that I had been hit by a hand grenade and was critically ill and paralysed. Father, a man who rarely showed emotion, was devastated, hardly knowing what to do, remaining in a state of dumb shock for the day. He gave out what little news he had to the rest of the family and explained that as soon as he could get himself organised he and my stepmother would be flying out to Pakistan to be with me. My young brother Cameron was given over to the care of Patricia's mother, who was to look after their house while they were away. Everyone in the family contributed, trying to help in some way or another.

Once in Pakistan, my father was better able to come to grips with the situation, although it must have been very difficult to take in the fact that his daughter had been involved in such a hideous experience. He suffered that feeling of impotence that hits anyone when they see a loved one in pain, and for the moment he could do nothing for me.

They were chaperoned through the visits and around the city by a charming Pakistani employee of Pan Am and stayed in a beautiful hotel in Karachi about a 20-minute taxi ride from the hospital. Every visit they made they were taken by kind drivers who, when they heard of my plight, expressed great sympathy and horror for what had happened. Father would later tell me how impressed he had been by the good people he met in Karachi.

The day after they arrived, my father explained, as gently and lovingly as he could, the extent of my injuries. Had it been possible, he would have physically held me in some way in an effort to shield me from so much distress. At least I was not paralysed, contrary to what the Foreign Office had told him. I had multiple fractures of the pelvis, and as a result could not move. The femur had a comminuted fracture at the neck, and the sciatic nerve had been rent and squashed by the explosion. I no longer had any gluteal muscles of the left buttock, I was also peppered with shrapnel up my back, in the genital area and in my legs, and I had massive bruising of the colon. The treatment was grim. If I could survive the shock and rampant infection coursing through my body, I would be in bed for about six months. Numerous surgical procedures would have to be performed as time passed. Optimistically speaking, there would then be about nine months of physiotherapy, and, needless to say, I would also be going through a lot of psychological problems.

The worst aspect of the whole matter, apart from the pain, was the frustration of knowing that I would not be able to conduct my own life for months. The idea, too, that I would be in bed for half a year was extremely depressing. There was even more bad news awaiting me, but it wasn't until I got back to London that I found out the rest of the story as far as my injuries were concerned.

This gradual and devastating awareness of just how terrible my physical situation was brought fragments of our previous holiday into my fractured consciousness, and along with images of the hijacking, a certain scene played through my mind. I was later to wonder whether I had received a warning in some hazy way, which I had chosen to ignore.

We had arrived in Lamayuru, a Ladakhi village high up in the Himalayan desert-like mountains, and were out walking early in the morning before moving on to Leh. We had come across piles of stones that constituted a pathway just outside the dwellings of the village. Picci, true to character, had joked about how the Tibetan monks managed to live in such stark and inhospitable surroundings. They could not possibly live on the beauty of their environment alone. How did they eat, sleep and control their sexual inclinations? What did they believe and how were they integrated in the life of the villagers and so on until I was fed up with all his questions. He could never let things go unless he had answers, whereas I didn't need to have answers immediately for me to grasp a reality. I needed to savour what was around me by looking, smelling, feeling and listening, and later I would ask my questions.

At a certain point in our meanderings, Picci picked up a stone and traced the lettering of Sanskrit on its flat surface. Looking around, he discovered that all the stones had beautifully written inscriptions carved into them, and the colours of the stones, grey-green, grey-yellow and white-grey, gently massaged our eyes as we pondered on their meanings. There were thousands of them in neat arrays leading to chortens, religious structures of about three metres high. The find had been rather perfect for the mood I was in, as I needed to be at peace with my surroundings. The wind had been icy, while the sun warmed our faces, and the blue sky promised scythe-like air would continue. I imagined the local people leaving their heavenly invocations behind after a morning pilgrimage and wondered what they had prayed for. I was just raising my head to ask Picci what he thought when I saw him slipping two fine examples of the stones into his yellow and blue knapsack. I was horrified and remonstrated hard, urging him to put the prayer stones back, as I felt their presence would bring us bad luck. He refused to heed my distress and instead teased me over my superstitious outburst. I knew, however, from my past that when I had as strong an instinct over something as I did on this occasion, it was best to listen to my heart. I was unable to change

Picci's mind, though, as he wanted those stones for posterity, and, rather than risk a row so early on in our relationship, I had bitten my tongue.

The stones had been a constant point of anxiety for me during that holiday, sitting ominously in the bottom of our bag waiting for the right moment to unleash their power. Now here I was, smashed up in a bed on the Indian continent, completely in the hands of destiny. Perhaps if we hadn't 'stolen' the stones, thus tempting fate, none of this would have happened. I vowed that I would get Picci to take them somewhere far away the moment I could, and eventually, in fact, asked a friend to give them to a university. These anxieties were mixed with terrible psychedelic hallucinations I experienced in and out of surgery and while on hospital drugs, increasing the power the stones held over me inordinately. The realm of the subconscious was in immediate and frightening proximity to my waking world.

At home, Picci was frantic to know everything about my injuries and his telegrams were getting desperate. Through the fog of semi-consciousness I realised that he needed to be informed of my condition if I didn't want him catching the next plane back out. I managed to tell Patricia what I needed to say in Italian and she sent off a telex informing Picci of my injuries. I made light of them, as I knew he'd send even more worried requests for news if I wrote the truth. As it was, he was asking me for superhuman efforts to impose my will over that of the surgeons and my father in asking that I be sent to Wiesbaden, the military hospital in Germany. He couldn't have realised how drugged up I was and hardly able to behave in a responsible and independent way. I could not have said anything to anyone, as I was using all the resources I had to fight the infections and fever before relapsing into unconsciousness after ten minutes of being awake. I was simply not in a fit state to make decisions.

Patricia and Father were being pursued by TV networks and did their best to fend off journalists hungry for tragedy and eager to divulge to the British public my near-fatal injuries. They refused to speak to anyone other than doctors and other members of our family, as they couldn't see how media coverage would help me.

On Friday, 12 September, the director of the hospital pronounced it safe for me to travel. There had been a long discussion about which hospital in the world I should be moved to. This decision had been hard given the fact that the best hospital was, in all probability, the one Picci wanted me to go to in Germany. The medical teams there were more than familiar with the types of injuries I had, and they had the means and expertise to deal with them. The catch, though, seemed to be that much of my recovery and improvement would depend on how hard I was prepared to fight for my health. And that would depend a great deal on my being first and foremost amongst people who cared for me. The great fear that the Karachi doctors had was that, now I was out of immediate danger, I would plunge into an all but inevitable depression, which I would have to face and overcome. Wiesbaden was a long way from home. Who would be able to visit, comfort and encourage me? My family would be far away and more than anything else I would need them. There was also a problem of finances. Who would pay for hospitalisation? The possibility of enlisting the help of Pan Am did not occur to anyone at the time, and, even if it had, it probably wouldn't have been something that my father would have been comfortable with. As far as he was concerned, they had already been very kind in flying him out to Pakistan and putting him and his wife up in a hotel, and, anyway, it wasn't the airline's fault that there had been a hijack, was it?

As a result of all these considerations, it was decided that I should be flown to London, where at least I could be visited often and, as a British citizen, be treated under the National Health Service. As far as treatment was concerned, it was felt that London was full of doctors and specialists able to resolve the most urgent problems. There was always time to think again once the most important things had been dealt with.

On Saturday, 13 September, therefore, a small Pakistani medical team, a stretcher with me on it, and my father and Patricia boarded a British Airways plane bound for Great Britain. The whole crew had signed a huge get well card and there must have been over 30 signatures inside. The captain came to see me before we took off and, under the disinhibiting effects of painkillers, I complimented him on his gorgeous green eyes. He returned the compliment by saying I had a very beautiful smile, and I clearly remember wondering why he hadn't told me I had gorgeous eyes too. Other than those few words, there was not a lot to converse about under the circumstances, and even in my wrecked state I was proud enough to wish he would disappear fast before he smelt the sweet gaggy odour of my buttock wound.

The seven-hour flight passed rapidly for me as I slept most of the time, only waking up twice to ask for injections. I remember how those shots became the only reasonable moments during my state of consciousness. Blissful pain-free minutes as the drug slipped into my system, cancelling bad memories and fears of the future.

That afternoon, we touched down at Heathrow, where I was delivered into the care of the National Health Service. On reflection, I confess to having mixed feelings about Pakistan. As far as I could see, it was a place of disorder and violence, but it was also where my life was saved, and one of the few places in the world where I have encountered people with a real sense of vocation in life. The medical teams of the hospitals in that city gave so much more than just their professional skills in terms of humanity and devotion to their work, and I believe that it was their dedication which pulled me through that first crisis.

4

BACK IN BRITAIN

WE WERE THE last to disembark from the plane. As I was lifted out of the back, a cloying blast of kerosene-laden air hit my face. It had been raining and the smell was particularly nauseating. My stretcher was gently loaded into a waiting ambulance, and my sister Francesca, a nurse by profession, was inside ready to take over the management of my situation from our harassed father. I looked at my sister's face, inexpressive at first, masking a storm of private thoughts about what had happened. Close-cropped ebony hair made her face pale in the darkened ambulance. She moved forward as if to embrace me, then checked herself, suddenly aware of the fact that it was impossible, and then she very badly held back her tears. I was so surprised to see her eyes fill that for a moment I thought something had happened to her. I had hardly ever seen her cry. Mercifully, the ambulance moved off from the runway to take us to hospital, distracting us all.

Traffic that evening was bad in London, partly because of it being Saturday and partly because it was raining. We also had a driver who was fairly insensitive towards the patient. Despite pleas and requests from my father and sister, he refused to put the siren on, so we had to lurch all the way from Heathrow to the city centre through one set of traffic lights to the next.

It was two hours since I'd had an injection for pain relief. A deep gnawing was slowly consuming my body as my pelvis was rocked and jarred every time the driver braked. As the effects of the pethidine wore off, my mind became a little clearer and I started to tell my family about the hijack. It was more an attempt to divert my attention than anything else, and it must have been a confused and incomplete tale. Neither of them asked me any questions, and their attentive faces and silence brought my storytelling to a muddled stop. When we finally reached the hospital, the porters pulled me out feet first and placed me, shouting, onto a trolley. My pain was distressingly acute in those moments, and I was unable to suffer in silence.

Saturday-afternoon arrivals, except for emergencies, were a little unusual. Though I was no longer in a life-threatening condition, I was still in acute need of attention, but nobody seemed in a hurry to deal with me. I was laid on a bed in the corner of the women's ward next to a little side room. My clinical notes were taken out from under my feet and placed on the side locker. The porters left and all became still and calm, but no nurse appeared. Francesca walked briskly off to the staff nurse's office. A young woman came out to acknowledge our presence and assure us that they had been instructed about what to do on my arrival. She told Fran that the ward sister was fully aware of the situation and she would be in on the Monday morning. It became apparent that on a Saturday evening no one was going to take X-rays or indeed hurry to my bedside to attend to my 101 needs on the spot. But Fran did expect some kind of activity and she continued to press for attention until the staff nurse commenced her routine blood pressure and temperature checks. She also had to insist that I was given more pain relief as soon as possible, as I couldn't hold out much longer and was beginning to whimper. As she went to get the pethidine, the nurse also saw how the intravenous gadget plugged into my wrist, used for inserting different drugs at the same time, was coming loose, and so she decided to change it. She seemed to take ages, fiddling about and grinding away at my arm trying to find a good vein, but given that I couldn't bear being touched in any way, two minutes could seem an insufferably long time for me. Once she'd finished, she took a wide roll of surgical sticking tape and proceeded to wrap my wrist to the elbow in this extremely resilient stuff. I knew it would be agony when they ripped off the tape the next time they decided to have a look at the site. It seemed such a small detail in comparison to the injuries I had, but the waxing I endured thereafter, as different shifts rushed through their duties and checks, was wearing.

Francesca stayed with me for three days. She had a little bed in a side room but hardly slept, kept awake by my moaning and cries. I had developed a strange form of cramp that was excruciating, affecting my legs and back. This provoked much yelling on my part and also the murmured prayers of a young Nigerian nurse who couldn't think how to further alleviate my distress. A vision of her joined hands over my bed that night was sufficiently spooky to shut me up extremely fast, giving her a short-term answer to her prayers.

Fran was lonely in her vigil and miserable as she wondered how I would ever get better in a cheerless, gloomy old place like this. She had been through her own kind of hell from the day in Longleat Safari Park with her family when she caught the radio headlines the day after the hijack. She and her husband and two-year-old son had been driving to the park when the news broke that finally the hijack was over. Then she heard that a British girl had been seriously hurt, and she caught my name. Although there must be hundreds of Catherine Hills in Great Britain, she was uneasy and as soon as she could find a phone, she called home. The phone was engaged for two hours before she could get through. My father would never normally have spent two hours on a call, so, by the time it was free, she knew it was me and was desperate for information. Father answered the ringing almost at once and confirmed her worst fears, although no one could say for sure what injuries I had. She was stunned and chilled to the bone. Her little boy, James, kept putting his arms around his mother trying to comfort her as she stayed wrapped in an appalled silence.

The following day, once she had gone down to the family home, she took charge of the situation, having seen how disabled with distress Father had become. Arranging the trip out to Pakistan had been a practical job, and she had felt easier because she was actually doing something, but she was also the person everyone phoned for news and she became almost hysterical with the incessant calls, where she had to repeat the same phrases and always be polite to people, never able to let go and cry herself. She had finally had to go to the doctor because she couldn't sleep any more, and was given something to help her calm down. Now, seeing her own sister in such agony was a ghastly experience, and those nights alone with me tested her strength sorely. She tried so hard to remember her professional training and remain detached, but it was impossible when dealing with one of her loved ones and she was relieved when the weekend was over.

The sister of the ward, whom I met on the Monday morning, was a brisk North Country woman of about 50 with short dark hair and pungent breath. Owlish glasses matched her round face and stocky figure. Over the following months I came to depend on her physically and a great deal psychologically, desperate as I became for some kind of affection in that sad and inhospitable ward. She could have been my mother in terms of age, and in that period I needed a maternal figure, but it was not long before I realised that to her I was just another patient.

The hospital environment certainly did nothing to lift my spirits. All paintwork was an uninspiring never-show-the-dirt grey that had become darker near the ceiling from the London dust over the years. To the right of my bed was a great old-fashioned sash window that was so filthy on the outside that I would not have been able to see much even if I had been able to get out of bed to look outside. I was in one of two beds behind a partition just at the entrance to the ward. On the other side were about ten beds that were mostly filled with old ladies who came in to get their spare parts fitted – hips and other joints. The ambulant patients used to come round to say hello and cheer me up, but, inevitably, they told me their stories of arthritis and broken bones. My mind sought happiness in an almost crazed desperation, and I wanted only good news and strong fit people around me so I shunned their presence. The bed next to mine remained thankfully unoccupied.

An airbed had been ordered because I couldn't endure the normal hospital ones with so many broken bones and a gaping wound. I had to be regularly 'turned' three inches to the right and then, 20 minutes later, three inches to the left to ease the pressure on my body and prevent sores forming. Four people were needed for the whole operation, as it had to be done with the utmost care and gentleness. In the grip of this terrible pain and using all my strength to withstand the spasms that contracted my body, I used the foulest language imaginable, which helped just a little to relieve the suffering. Unfortunately, I'd got used to the pethidine dose and needed a stronger one to have the same effect. And, of course, the dose wasn't increased.

During that first week, my future very much hung in the balance. I had been seen by Professor Jones, the orthopaedic surgeon assigned to my case, who told me that the laparotomy and removal of shrapnel carried out in Pakistan had been done well, but the orthopaedic operation had not been so successful. The screw fixing the neck of the femur to the head of the femur had worked loose. It would have to come out and be attached again, but the problem was when. Professor Jones didn't know if it was better to carry out the orthopaedic treatment I required first or if it was more urgent to carry out the plastic surgery. The buttock wound had to be covered in some way as soon as possible, as infection could easily be carried to the bones without an adequate skin graft, but if the surgeons waited until the new skin graft had become stable, then the head of the femur could well become necrotic. There would have to be some kind of a compromise.

It was at this early stage of hospitalisation that luck came my way and I was sent the one woman who was to provide me with any real moral support in that place. Shortly after Professor Jones's examination, his physiotherapist came by to see me and have a look at the damage. As she stood at the end of my bed, squeezing the toes of my left foot, she introduced herself as Teresa Phipps.

'Can you feel this? Can you feel that?' she said. I growled angrily and said that I couldn't feel anything and would she please go away. Unperturbed, she continued to scrutinise me with enormous, slightly protuberant blue eyes that looked as if they were continuously waiting for an answer to her questions. She was magnificent to look at, Junoesque from a Rubens painting. About 25 years old with red-gold hair pulled into a bun and a bouncy, saucy bosom, she exuded confidence and happiness. From that first meeting on, she came to my bedside twice a day. At first I hated her and grudgingly did the few things she told me to do. Her visits disturbed my sleep and dragged me into unwelcome consciousness. I couldn't deal with the reality of my situation at this stage and so I shrank into myself whenever she came by. She was later to tell me that I had been in so much distress that even she felt badly about working on me, but that it had had to be done otherwise my recovery would have been further restricted.

Teresa sailed in and out of the ward, her crisp clear voice ringing out from the doorway with a genuine interest in how I was that day. I grew to be very fond of her and was very grateful for her strength and dynamic personality. Once my pain had subsided to a manageable level she refused to accept my being depressed when we did physio. Before long she had her 'fledglings' coming to watch and then participate in my treatment. Her entourage were three pretty 18 year olds, giggly, helpful and eager to talk about doctors they fancied. In that first week I was not able to enjoy the marvellous qualities of Teresa and her girls, but, as the months passed, their visits became the highlight of my days. Their presence was refreshing and distracting, pulling me out of my own miserable world.

5

HORACE

MY AUNT CAME in to see me on the morning of the Wednesday after my admission to that hospital. Bibi was my father's sister and a very close member of the family. I had known her well since the age of eleven, when, three months or so after my mother died, she had come back to England from Canada after the break-up of her own marriage. She and her two children had come to live with us, making a large family even larger. As I had an older brother and two sisters, it must have been some task looking after six children in such tragic circumstances. As far as I remember, however, the two years she spent with us were very happy ones, although we never spoke of my mother. In order to deal with her death, we seemed to push her out of our lives. Once my father remarried, Bibi went to live next door, but the bonds had been forged and our beloved aunt was a focal point for all the family over the following years.

I was very relieved to see her salt-and-pepper short hair and warm but worried face when she arrived in the doorway of my room. In her wake there followed a lovely-looking woman called Sister Rose. It was the first time I had seen my aunt since I'd returned to Britain, and, murmuring assurances, she took my hand in hers, saying that Sister

Rose was the stoma care nurse and that she had come because she wanted to look at my stomach.

Stoma was not a word I was familiar with, and I just quietly accepted whatever it was that had to be done. She lifted my nightgown and began to mutter things about tape. Gradually she eased up the corner of the plaster and slowly began to tear away at a huge sticky strip that seemed to go on forever, right the way down my abdomen. I had to grit my teeth, for it hurt a great deal. She then snipped away at stitches, chatting as she did so and remarking on the skill and beauty of the cut and scar. I had been oblivious to the fact that my stomach had been operated on as well, and certainly did not know why I had been opened up, despite the fact that Professor Jones had already mentioned the word laparotomy.

Once she had finished her work with the scissors, she put her hand on my arm and, smiling briskly, started talking to me in a matter-of-fact way. 'Well, now, Katy, it looks good and clean and it's worked a little, but now it's time for you to learn how to deal with it yourself. After all, you'll have this for quite some time so let's see how quickly you can get used to it.' I hadn't a clue what she was talking about and asked her what it was that I had to get used to. Looking at me hard for a moment, she asked me if I really didn't know. I shook my head, watching her face in growing anxiety. With a long sigh and a momentary pause, she proceeded to inform me that I had a colostomy and would have to deal with its functioning perhaps once a day or more often.

I still did not know what a colostomy was. Evidently I was not making things very easy for the woman as she pursed her lips in worry. She took a deep breath and began to tell me as clearly and kindly as possible the ins and outs of the wretched thing, as I listened with increasing horror and revulsion. Negation, anger and disgust rushed at me as I tried to accept the bald and unsavoury truth. I wanted to take a knife and gouge out the offending area of my stomach. I couldn't bear this new disaster. 'Why?' I demanded. 'Why did they have to give me a colostomy, an anus coming out of my stomach wall? Wasn't the rest sufficiently horrible without this?' The nurse tried to calm me down, saying that it was temporary and at the most I'd have it for a year or two.

My aunt was as upset as I was and did her best to take away the fury and hatred that were fomenting my insides into sick rebellion. My eyes were bone dry and there were no tears for such outrage. I was filled with an awful sense of desolation and obviously needed time to assimilate the news.

Sister Rose's teaching of how to clean and care for the stoma went unheard that morning. She had shown me the various colostomy bags, both the see-through ones, useful for beginners so they could understand and watch the mechanisms of the stoma, and then the opaque ones that were much more aesthetically pleasing. She had talked about the foods one could eat and the foods it was better to avoid, and about the cleaning products and deodorants available. She gave me different tubes of cream and sprays of stoma perfume, lavender- or lemon-scented. She went on relentlessly, trying to hold my attention as she showed me the adhesive stoma applications that could be 'popped' over the offending gut. I was even told that I was lucky to have such a beautiful and small example, and that they were not always so perfect. In fact, she said she would mention it to the photography department, as it would apparently make a very nice illustration in a medical textbook. With this comforting thought, she took her leave in a waft of sexy perfume and glided out of the ward saying she'd be back soon. All the while I felt like a ticking bomb. After she had gone, my aunt tried to give me answers by saying that the colostomy was necessary as I couldn't move my body at all, for any reason, but her explanations were met with deep silence and she eventually went away telling me she'd be back the next day.

I felt cheated. I shouldn't have put up with the nurse's painful plaster removal but let rip with all the shouting I was doing inside. Why was I the only one to suffer? Why couldn't others go through what I was going through? Hospitalisation would have been so much easier to bear if I hadn't tried so hard to be an accommodating patient and hero. I was doomed from the start, in that a reserved English upbringing had well and truly gagged me. I never complained or lamented my situation. I endured much more than was necessary because I had this idea that it showed weakness of character to object or doubt. I now believe that the only person who noticed my 'bravery' was myself. It would have been better if I had thrown a few plates of disgusting National Health hospital food on the floor or put up a fight if I didn't like something that someone was trying to do. Instead, I was always mute and only allowed polite requests to fall from my lips followed by innumerable pleases and thank yous.

It was too much to expect that I accept the colostomy right from the beginning. I had been so proud of my young body before the blast, when it had been so much to my liking. Eventually I realised, however, that unless I learnt to accept these constant insults to my femininity, I would be unable to progress in health or in spirit. So it was with the stoma. I gradually learnt to deal with it. I was a slim, tall, attractive girl manhandling her own faeces. It didn't disappear down the toilet, unseen, with a bidet wash to restore scrupulous cleanliness. I had to remove the bag and clean the smelly mess on my stomach with tissues. The curtains around my bed were no barrier to the pervading odour around me. Humiliation heaped upon humiliation.

Tears spilled down my face those first few weeks in impotent rage. My mouth, tongue and jaw muscles would become numb with rigidity as I cleaned, washed and performed the stoma care, hating the hijackers and their barbarity with all my heart. Time passed, however, and even if I never truly accepted this inconvenience, at least it no longer weighed on my dignity as it had at the beginning. It was even christened by one of the nurses, who decided that Horace was an appropriate name for a colostomy. I used my sessions with Horace as moments when I could at least actively participate in my own care, for it was something to do in the long hours of those hospital days, and I'd console myself with the knowledge that at least it would one day be closed and I'd be able to function normally. I would remind myself that some folk had theirs for life, and one would need a great deal of forbearance to live well with such a thing on a permanent basis.

6

CONTACT

WHILE MY WORLD had changed, Picci was taking control of his once again, although he was still on crutches. At the same time, he was trying to keep abreast of news about me and my progress. He was in touch with my family every day but felt frustrated to some extent because everything was related second or third hand through my Italian aunt, and Picci never took anything at face value. He must have been very worried, not knowing the truth about what was going on, but short of coming over to England, something he was planning but didn't yet feel physically able to manage, there wasn't a lot he could do to improve communication. His English was not good enough over the phone to understand others in the family and mobile phones were still a long way off.

Aware of this distressing situation, one day my father came into the ward with a tape recorder and blank cassette for me to record a message to send to Picci. Very carefully, he placed the microphone near my mouth and, gathering my thoughts together, I spoke with what I thought was a strong, resilient voice. I said I was in good hands and that he was not to worry about me, that really everything was fine and I was going to get better as soon as possible. The message was brief, because any kind of concentration was exhausting for me.

Father carried off these few words that night, and my younger sister, Stephany, rang Picci and played the tape to him. It proved to be a dam buster, for as my slightly slurred words came to him, he felt the control he'd exerted over his feelings crumble. He told me that he put the phone down and wept bitterly. That episode was the first of many over the next few months where, whenever someone asked for news of me, he would feel a lump in his throat and have to excuse himself while he recovered his poise. Little things would set him off, and he always had to have a handkerchief at the ready.

Our first direct contact came some days later when Father discovered that down at the end of the hall there was a pay phone on wheels that could be moved to a patient's bed. He took it out of its niche and trundled it over to me, putting in as many 50 pence pieces as possible. He dialled Picci's home number and placed the receiver by my ear. My heart was banging all over the place as the ringing tone became the sole object of my total attention, assuming an importance I had never hitherto given it. Our separation had been drastic and cruel, and the phone was our first means of contact since the hijack. I heard him pick up the receiver and fell into his voice, as I would his arms. My eyes were brimming with tears as I asked him how he was, after which I didn't know what else to say. I waited for him to answer me, feeling the emotional energy building up inside. He paused and in the quietest of voices told me he was fine and how glad he was I had called. I didn't take much notice of his control or of this apparently quiet reception. He told me later that he'd had to sit down so that he could get out his tissues and that he, too, had lost his tongue. My need for his presence, his gentleness and solidness was great, and the yearning and passion and homesickness that torpedoed into me as I listened to his searching questions were absorbed within me to be dealt with later.

I couldn't find words to express what was going on inside. There was no time in this phone call. I had a few precious moments to tell this man everything and yet nothing, give comfort and take it by the ton, embrace him, kiss him and call his name. I had just a few moments to tell him I'd be coming home soon and that he was not to be sad. It all went unsaid, of course, because our commonplace questions were rather like boulders behind which we could hide. Exposure or loving words were just too risky and anyway the pips went.

As soon as I was alone, I replayed the phone call in my head, going over every comment, each question, remembering the tiny pauses, picking clean our conversation until there was nothing nutritious left, at least for the time being. Not wanting to return to the ward and my present situation, my mind wandered back to the first time we had met, in 1985, and I wondered why certain things happened and other things went nowhere.

Our relationship should never really have taken off, judging by how things started. He had been sitting opposite me at Maria's dinner table, rather fed up and dour looking. He definitely hadn't approved of me and shot numerous exasperated glances in my direction, as if I was trespassing on a family occasion. I couldn't have cared less. I'd just had my hair cut very short and was wearing a pair of tight grey trousers with a grey jacket and white shirt, and felt happy with the way I looked and how things were going at work. I was teaching English, freelance, in three different companies, ten hours a day, and was earning rather a lot of money for one so young. Maria had been my sister's student for the year she'd been in Italy and now that Stephany had returned to England she'd asked me to continue teaching her. Wanting to get to know me first, Maria had invited me to her house for an evening meal with her husband and his brother Picci, who was at that time without a girlfriend and, as far as I could make out, very pleased to be free of sentimental involvement. He could have been very good looking had he not glowered most of the time, although over the course of the meal he partly justified his irritability, as he talked of his company and the problems he was having with staff and trade union regulations. He was an engineer and managed a small manufacturing firm in Milan that he'd set up some years previously.

'How old are you?' I'd foolishly asked, taken by surprise that he'd evidently been working for quite some time. He looked as if he'd only just finished his degree at university. He had ignored my question and carried on with what he had been saying, and this apparent arrogance or incivility had annoyed me terribly. 'I asked you how old you were, or perhaps you didn't hear me?' I too could be bolshie.

'Forty-two,' Maria had answered while serving the rice, embarrassed by her brother-in-law's rudeness. Picci remarked scathingly that it was not polite to ask someone's age, so I proffered mine, 25, with all the cocky confidence young women can wield in certain situations. 'Old enough to know better,' was the barely audible off-hand reply as he continued talking to his brother.

He had succeeded in making me feel childish and insignificant. I certainly didn't like him after that treatment, despite the fact that I found his manner intriguing. It wasn't often I got the cold shoulder and it had long been a reaction I found intolerable. Who did he think he was?

He told me one day, months later when we talked about that first meeting, that he hadn't liked my hair, that he didn't like over-confident young ladies and that he'd had a ghastly day at work. He also told me that my tenacious love of my job, my youth and blue eyes had charmed him despite our brush over bad manners. He had asked me out because I was straightforward and didn't play games, and evidently had a strong character. He said that he was tired of coquettish Mediterranean girls, who knew how to play a man better than many of their Northern sisters did. Picci wanted to 'try' a foreigner and see if he didn't have better luck with one of us. He had had a long love affair with an Italian girl and after ten years he had finished the relationship, disillusioned and embittered.

Lying in my hospital bed, I remembered the first times we went out together, some months later after he had returned from a holiday in Peru, and after many phone calls. I had only been in Italy two years when we met, and my Italian was not very fluent. We were shy, both wary, yet at the same time fascinated by each other, and the first time we held hands had been for me as intimate as if he'd taken off all my clothes. He was rough but vulnerable, fun yet severe, and terribly, terribly curious. He had wanted to know why I had left my family to strike out on my own at such a young age, coming to Italy when I knew no one who could offer me the same security that a family could. It was hard trying to get him to understand another culture. I told him that I had wanted to leave everything I had known so that I could experience a new country and learn a different language, and that the thought of being in a responsible job in England had suffocated me. I hadn't even known what I wanted to do for a career and I had been very immature.

I'm not sure he understood me at all, but he loved to listen and so I told him everything there was to tell about my life, myself and my passions, my difficulties and fears. I basked in all the attention. But getting him to tell me of his life, on the other hand, was like shouting questions down a well. I never got answers unless I asked him about practical things. There were areas of his life that were closed off to me and, naturally enough, they were the places I most wanted to go.

I realised that with Picci I would be embarking on a journey that would consume me completely, and it was the first time that I was so totally hooked by a man. I had followed my head in this relationship and discovered a person who could be wickedly funny, generous, passionate, austere, hard working and a loner. He could also be ferociously hard. All these qualities attracted me and soon my heart followed my head, and from the sassy young woman I thought I was, I had gradually found myself handing over the keys to that sovereign state of psychological independence. I had fallen in love with Picci and was no longer in control of the situation.

Now the hijack had happened, and who knew how things would evolve. Strangely enough, it never crossed my mind at that point that Picci might want to leave me. The phone was to become a strong anchor in my hospital life, but it was what remained unsaid and what I could read between the lines that helped pull me through to recovery. That particular phone call warmed my world for some days to come and, although the reality of my depressing condition did not change, the mere fact that Picci was waiting patiently for me gave me renewed strength to will myself better and helped shield me from so much of the hopelessness that hovered around in my subconscious.

7

MOUNT VERNON

SOME DAYS LATER, Gregory arrived from Australia. He was my big brother and the news about what had happened to me had thrown him into turmoil. Fran had thought twice about contacting him to let him know of my ordeal and had waited a full week before phoning, afraid that he would have got the first plane over to Karachi, buying a pistol on the way, to then wreak his vengeance on the hijackers. She was wise to do so, as his first comment on hearing the news was that he would fly out to Pakistan and kill the bastards who'd hurt his sister. She managed to convince him that this was not a good idea, so he bought a ticket to London instead and flew out the following day. No one would let him see me until I was a little more coherent, as he would have been too upset and shown his feelings when it was better to stay calm around me.

One day that week I remember opening my eyes after hearing the beginnings of an angry conversation between my father and brother. They were talking about the hijackers. This was the first time that people had referred to the terrorist attack and I could sense their vehemence as they spoke. They were listing the different ways that they would kill the hijackers, and if I hadn't been so ill, I would have laughed at the incredibly gruesome things they were dreaming up. Hanging them upside down, cutting off their testicles and leaving them to die, cutting out their tongues, poking them in the eyeballs and cutting off their buttocks slice by slice: good Old Testament punishment, which at times, I confess, paled in comparison to what I felt like doing to them. Apart from that one time, no one asked me about the hijack directly and I certainly never mentioned what had happened after the explanation I'd given in the ambulance ride nor did I ask questions about whether the hijackers had been captured. My interest in them was negligible and I would only have been upset to hear news of them. For the time being my family tried to protect me as much as possible, and it became another taboo subject best forgotten.

Greg made it his habit to come in first thing in the morning, sit beside me, hold my hand and stay for the better part of the day. Most of the time I slept, unable to keep my attention on what he was saying due to a persistent temperature of 39 degrees. His own trials (his wife had left him) seemed far removed from my world, although he seemed to me rather lost when he visited.

Stephany, the baby of the family, came down from Newcastle where she was studying and stared at me wide eyed from the bottom of the bed, threatening to pass out. She couldn't really cope at all with the whole business and with a sigh of relief, having seen that I was alive and not likely to be passing on, disappeared back up north to her books.

The tubes hanging out of me were enough to give anyone with a delicate stomach a hard time. I wasn't eating, so a feeding hose was in place. The drip stand dangled various plastic squidgy sacks from its hooks, including the disgusting-coloured food bag, and to the right of the bed was the catheter tube and urine collector. Fortunately my colostomy was not on display, as I think that every member of my squeamish family would have keeled over had they seen it. Infection by this time was waging war and I was still being taken down to surgery every two days or so to have debris removed from my buttock.

In late September, I was transferred to a plastic surgery unit at Mount

Vernon Hospital, where my buttock was to be treated. My brother accompanied me to this new hospital in the ambulance. Autumn was proving to be a fabulous Indian summer, and I was relieved to leave the grim, grey ward of the hospital in London and be nearer home.

Mount Vernon was a strange building, with no stairs or lifts anywhere; warren-like, it spread out over a number of acres. The wards were housed in old army barracks and as such had a slightly more friendly aspect than the previous hospital. I had a small room all to myself at the end of one of the barracks, with French windows looking out onto a rose garden. They were open when we arrived and a magnificent huge airbed was waiting for me with its electric pumps huffing and puffing to keep the cushions inflated. I would have no more bedsores and my bones would hopefully no longer fill me with that grating pain.

The sister of the ward – chisel-chinned, very naturally blonde and of commanding character – reminded me of Fran in terms of her efficiency and kindness. Her mission that day was to restore some of my sabotaged dignity, and with the help of a nurse and two porters I was heaved gently onto the sighing bed, without changing the almost rigid foetal position I was by now locked into. Everyone was then dismissed, including my brother, and this gentle woman set to giving me a thorough bed bath, my first. It was a great relief, as no one had thought to wash me up to that point because of the pain I was in. My brother had also told her of the catheter incident where one of the young nurses had pulled out that snake-like intrusion by accident, and he'd seen how upset I'd been over it. I hated the catheter almost as much as the colostomy, and it was a source of anxiety all those months. She gracefully put out the fires of my indignation by telling me gently that the catheter would have had to come out anyway, as I needed to be completely and carefully washed. Fighting back an overwhelming desire to cry, I surrendered to the disinfectant bath, embarrassed by my horrid smell but grateful that I was finally being cleaned. She then dealt with the drip, vastly simplifying the appliance and giving my inflamed wrist a rest with a less cumbersome gadget plugged in through the other hand.

Perfumed and feeling calmer than I ever had in the previous hospital,

I waited for my father to visit, for now we were only a six-mile drive from home. This time he brought with him a small TV and switched it on immediately to see if it worked. We unfortunately caught the tail end of the lunchtime news. The Istanbul massacre in the synagogue of Neve Shalom had happened a week after the hijack and the September Paris bombings were also under investigation. A spate of terrorism had swept across Europe and there were others who were suffering tortures even worse than mine. I felt a wave of incomprehension and fear wash over me, and my father switched off the television as he saw my reaction to the sound of machine-gun fire. Looking slightly uncomfortable, he advised me to watch amusing programmes to keep my spirits up.

We did not refer to the actual hijacking further, as I couldn't face the memories and was too ill to converse. I could ask for one or two things that I needed, but then would feel too tired, or nauseous, or in too much pain to keep conversation going. The only things I thought of in that period were Picci, Frera, which was Picci's mountain retreat where we had spent weekends the autumn before, my house and freedom. All things of another world and a different place. I was already feeling a barrier between past and present. Life had so radically changed and I felt as if I had been torn from one existence and thrust into another. My head and cares, thoughts and attachments were of the old world; the contours of this new life would have to be accommodated, but I was not ready yet. I thought frequently of what had once been my bottom, and every moment that I imagined what the grenade had done was like stepping into a desert where there was apparently no life.

That afternoon I sank in and out of musing, too ill to exercise great regret or have any violent emotions one way or the other. My pain-killing injections cushioned me from too much analysis, and I looked forward to the afternoon dose so that I could sleep without dreaming.

The following morning there was an important doctors' round and they all appeared at my door. Like pills coming off the conveyor belt, white-overalled medical people dropped through the rather small corner door. There must have been about 15 people in the room by the time they'd all come in and there was hardly space to breathe let alone examine a patient. As usual, I was introduced as an interesting specimen and subject to questions and study. At the end of the visit, I overheard the surgeon who would be operating on me say to the staff nurse that I was to be completely taken off painkillers, which made me extremely nervous as I was due for an injection very soon. My buttock was to be dressed four times a day and my nasal tube taken out so that I could start eating properly again. Everyone shuffled out and silence settled as the doors closed.

I was left alone to contemplate the changes for about a quarter of an hour before Nina, aggressive sensible Nina from Malaysia, barged in towing a large trolley full of kidney basins, tweezers, scissors and gauze. Her accent was incredible and she bawled forth her greeting. 'Good mawning, Katrin, and haw are you today? Why this daw shut? Iss no good. We caan see you and we doon wan you doin' somethin' wrong.' She thought her joke uproariously funny as she propped open the door and began to work on me. I was told to lean over just 'leetlil beet', and she ripped off the adhesive tape and all the dressings. I desperately wanted a pain-killing injection and asked her if I could have one, dreading the answer. She refused, as I had known she would, and I started to tremble. She told me that they couldn't give me any more painkillers, as I was becoming too dependent on them. It was going to be horrible trying to get through the effects of withdrawal.

Nina took out a large wad of cotton and gauze, swamped it in chloroform and told me to sniff the fumes deeply. She said it would help dull the pain while she was cleaning me up. Usually they took me down to theatre for this operation, but now they were doing it 'live'. Nina was one of the best plastic surgery nurses who worked on me, highly skilled and extremely patient – if somewhat lacking in gentle bedside manners. I was slightly afraid of her, but then I feared a lot of people. My 'cold turkey' moaning and groaning, which lasted for several days, was greeted with irritated shouts of, 'You keep quiet now,' from the corridor as she tended to other patients.

Nina was quite ruthless in her descriptions of the wound as she cleaned it, and told me that there was a bit of bone sticking out here and smelly pus oozing out there from the brown bit. In her opinion it would be extremely difficult to cover such a huge wound, particularly one that was so infected, but the surgeons in Mount Vernon were very good. And on she'd chat regardless. However, her work over the following weeks of piecemeal laying of meshed skin over the offending area proved phenomenal.

The replacement skin had been harvested from my left leg with something marginally more sophisticated than a potato peeler. The top layer of skin had been stretched and meshed to make a little go a long way, and it looked like the latticework potato crisps you can sometimes get at the supermarket. Stored in what looked like a jam jar, it was kept in the fridge to be pulled out and used every morning by Nina. My left leg was incarcerated in something akin to green cling film, which had to stay on for at least two weeks while new skin struggled to grow back. Progress was slow, but it had started.

Nina always wore the same perfume, and I could smell when she was on duty. At the beginning, seeking reassurance and a morale boost, I would ask her if I was doing well and getting better, but she failed me miserably with her down-to-earth and factual answers, telling me I was an extremely sick girl and that it would be months before I was better. I soon stopped asking her for updates unless it was strictly related to how well my backside was filling in. She took some delight in answering my questions but had absolutely no interest whatsoever in her patient's emotional condition.

On one occasion when she was working on me, my brother arrived with an armload of post. He wasn't really supposed to come into the room, as the bed area was a sterile field when Nina was in the middle of her duties. But, although she was at times insensitive to others, she had grown fond of my brother and so let him stay provided that he was careful not to breathe all over me. This was the first time he saw the gruesome sight of the wound.

He had no funny quip to ease the situation. He was prepared

theoretically, but what he actually saw shocked him deeply. He simply came round to my bedside and sweetly kissed one of my hands, murmuring something about going out for a cup of coffee. Then he disappeared.

On 26 September, I had a procession of visitors bearing gifts. It was my 27th birthday, and I would have much preferred to be elsewhere. Life in the hospital continued with a succession of uninteresting events happening on my infinitely slow crawl to recovery. The feeding tube had been removed the same day that the painkillers had been stopped, and I had mentally looked forward to being able to chew once again. I didn't seem to have any appetite but imagined that once lunchtime came around I would eat something. A tray arrived bearing simply prepared food, but, to my surprise, I felt nausea rise up from deep within me and I started to retch. A nurse came by and saw me. She took away the food and asked me what was wrong. I had no idea except for the fact that the sight and smell of the food had made me feel terrible. The same thing happened the following day and the day after that. I just couldn't face the thought of solid food.

Perhaps it was my prone position, perhaps the constant fever, but food seemed to represent the hijack for some peculiar reason. Every time a meal arrived, I would be immersed in the events of Karachi and the butchering that had gone on. Meat, especially, made me think of the grenade blast and the machine guns spraying their bullets. I thought of blood when I saw meat, and my stomach went into spasm. Whatever food I was faced with, however, were it three peas or a piece of macaroni, within ten seconds I was sick. The slightest thing would put me off the terrible task of eating. A visitor who stayed over lunchtime meant that I wouldn't even try to eat. Meals went on for ages as I attempted to send down even a morsel, the battle usually lost before it had begun.

My only explanation for this self-destructive intolerance, apart from the obvious one being that I was also very ill, was that the only function I could refuse to perform was that of eating. Any other control of my bodily functions had been taken over by machines, doctors, nurses and orderlies. I couldn't even decide when to use the bathroom. I was immobile in a machine-controlled bed. I couldn't get up to get a book or paper, not that I had the energy at that time to read or write. I felt trapped by always having to ask for anything I needed and say thank you, even to those members of staff I couldn't stand. I feared that if I made a fuss about something and was a nuisance, I would more than likely be given a harder time than I was already going through. I was hardly in a position to query the doctors either or to ask for second opinions, and, even if I had been, such 'awkward' behaviour would have upset my family. Vomiting and refusing to eat were my own expressions of deep revolt and soon had the doctors stuffing large rubber feeding tubes back down my nose and throat, which I regularly tore out or threw up. I rapidly lost weight and my body began almost to consume itself, suffering under the irritated and cool gaze of the dispassionate professionals. Had they tried to understand that it was the trauma of the hijack that was tearing me apart inside, perhaps things might have improved, but no one seemed to understand what I was going through and at that time Post Traumatic Stress Syndrome (PTSS) was not widely recognised.

I was by now waiting to be taken back to the first hospital in London to have my femur operated on. In the meantime, I had to wait for the skin to 'take' and for the vast hole in my bottom to seal. As a resident of the ward, I had a set routine to follow. Every morning I had about 14 pills to swallow, which strangely enough presented no problem. I did not see them as nutritional, so had no spasms. Once awake, I waited for the doctors to do their rounds and admire my buttock, and then I'd wait eagerly for the nurse to come in with soap and water. Washing my hands and face was a one-hour project, as it was all done horizontally at first. However hard I brushed my teeth, I was unable to get rid of the constantly sour taste in my mouth. I was riddled with antibiotics, and the fact that I didn't eat meant that my tongue was an unhealthy white colour and my breath was far from sweet. The nurses were kind and gentle when they washed my lower body, realising how ashamed I felt, and they would usually try to distract me by chiding me for becoming thinner and thinner and not eating properly.

My bed was full of Froggy and Picci's letters. Froggy was my birthday present and the last in a series of silver frogs he had given me. He nicknamed me Frog right from the beginning of our relationship after I had told him a funny story, and the name had stuck. Froggy often sat on my chest near my heart, and I'd touch him to remind me of the love Picci felt for me.

It was towards the end of October that I decided that I would write back to him. We spoke by phone as often as was reasonable. But pay phones were ridiculously expensive if you were phoning Italy, and Picci couldn't call me in the hospital. I would keep him updated on the progress I was making, but it wasn't easy to maintain a normal conversation. My homesickness for Italy and nostalgia for the past were such that I knew I had to get better physically before I could feel comfortable on the phone. Picci would tell me his news and how his walking was doing. He still went to work using crutches, although he could now drive without difficulty. He was in the throes of looking for a large workshop so that he could expand his business, and he was extremely busy. His world was so much more interesting than mine, and I felt cheated by the gods. I hated saying goodbye to him at the end of our call as I was left to go back to my sad thoughts and the cold knowledge that my world had irrevocably changed.

On that particular day in October, my father helped me by setting up a clipboard to write my letter, and he held it for me as I wrote one or two things in a sloping scrawl. It felt as if I had forgotten how to write. The letters were wobbly and looked as if they were written by a child. From then on, however, writing became very important, as it was a new activity that engaged my mind and kept me busy until I was so tired that I would sleep.

My dreams were violent, though, and full of people dying, and I would wake up anxious and depressed. My daydreams, by way of compensation, were concentrated exclusively on Italy and my home in Milan, which now seemed a paradise on earth, and, of course, I visualised Frera. If the sun came into my room and lit up a corner with a vase of flowers, I would gaze at it until my mind wandered off in the direction of the Valtellina Mountains in Italy, and I would find myself thinking of Frera. I dreamed of the meadows in early summer with the full streams running through them and of the miniature spring frogs that jumped ahead of us as we headed up to the woods. The mauves, whites, blues and yellows of mountain flowers rippled through my imagination as I thought of our hideaway chalet. Diego, the innkeeper's little boy, sprang readily to mind as I remembered his cheeky face from the wild cherry tree outside the inn as he threw the fruit at us below, his red trousers full of holes and his face a smutty streak. I thought of his mother, Elizabetta, and the great family meals we had had in the old sooty kitchen at the inn, and wondered how they all were. Picci had known the family all his life and they were very fond of him. I was sure they would have been horrified to learn of his terrible experience. I had met them, liked them enormously and had been jealous to think of all the other girls they'd met who had been Picci's girlfriends. I had not wanted to be just another one in a long procession and had tried right at the beginning to be detached from too much emotional involvement. But Frera had wrapped itself round my heart and now would not let my imagination go. I'd listen in my dreams to the cowbells as the herd passed under our house on their way up to the higher pastures at five o'clock in the morning. I would picture the nutty-brown pine walls, the wood stove and the green shutters. I could hear the foghorn voice of Mrs P., who sojourned opposite us, and see the beautiful sun-drenched terrace where we had eaten many a Sunday breakfast.

Frera became an important sanctuary and gave my mind and body a break from the dreariness around me. This little valley had a power over me that was even stronger than my memories of my home in Italy, and I felt as if I'd known this place all my life. Early on in my recovery, I began to see this ancient iron-mining village as my regenerating force and hoped that as soon as I was able to travel I could convalesce there.

The most important thing was to get better physically, and in an attempt to trick myself into believing that I was recovering fast, I adopted a cheerful attitude. People were amazed at how I appeared to be putting a brave face on my misfortunes. Admittedly I was as brittle and superficial as glass, and perhaps to a discerning few I was just as transparent, but to some extent this hardening up of myself worked and helped me get through those supine days. I had been blessed with a sunny disposition and this helped considerably, although appearing serene was a strategic move, for I knew that if I seemed down and depressed a lot of the time, others might lose sympathy for me.

My stay in this hospital was coming to an end and so was Greg's visit. He came in with my father to say goodbye and stayed for an hour or so. For the first time since the hijack, a discussion arose about compensation. Up until then I had never even thought that I might be eligible for some kind of financial help and for a moment was interested in what they had to say. Both men were sure that I would get a considerable sum of money given the horrible crime that had been committed and the international circumstances involved; after all it was an incident of global interest and President Reagan himself had been called upon to intervene. They egged each other on, talking of money and bandying about six-figure amounts. In retrospect, I have to smile at the ease with which such sums were tossed back and forth as if it were the most logical and evident consequence of events. Neither my father nor brother was able to explain who would be paying out such a huge sum of money and they also seemed to forget that money is the most difficult thing to get people to part with.

At this time, I mentally handed over the responsibility of finding out about compensation to my father, which was an understandable thing to do but one that caused me difficulty later on. The subject finished there and was only raised by Picci many months later. Greg left for Australia and, as he promised, within a few days I had the first of his scores of letters, but my spirits were low as I had had to go back to the previous hospital and that horrible ward that was a far cry from the pretty pink room with its garden at Mount Vernon.

8

A STRAITJACKET

NOVEMBER, WITH ITS dismal drizzle, rough cold winds and leaden skies, does little for the spirits even for those who are well and mobile. Despite all my good intentions, my morale was about as bright as the dirty weather outside, and I was to struggle against mental and physical listlessness for weeks. My father came into the ward loaded up with paraphernalia from Mount Vernon. He was busy under the bed trying to find a socket for the TV when the sister came over, her suspicions roused. She crisply told us that televisions were not allowed in the ward as they created untidiness and were hazardous. Father remonstrated energetically but no amount of argument would deter her from sticking to her rules. Her power was total in this place and she could decide what was or was not allowed, so the TV was taken away. It was a cruel dictate for one who was bed-bound for six months, but it was an apt indication of the way this particular ward was run. I was the only long-term patient and rules were never bent in my favour. Life was extremely boring in bed and it would have been helpful for me to have had a distraction from my tendency to brood.

The three weeks I had to wait before Professor Jones operated on me crawled by. I'd been moved back prematurely to make room for a patient who needed a bed at Mount Vernon. It was by then a good eight weeks on from the hijack and a little late for bone repair surgery. However, everything possible had to be done to save the head of the femur, even if the odds were now stacked against a successful outcome. Doctors never gave me any predictions of success or failure with regard to their treatment and I rarely asked. I didn't want to know too much at that point. Everything was constantly in limbo, and I had no idea of what they expected the final results to be once I was out of hospital. The wound on my bottom was also full of weeping sinuses that refused to close over quickly, and so, rather than take risks, we had to continue the long wait.

In the meantime, my lovely physio had swept back into my life and proceeded to jump-start me into mental effort, even if the physical action was desperately doddery. When she was with me, the world seemed a lighter place, and I'd cling to her energy and physical presence even after she'd gone, in an attempt to steer clear of the mentally barren lands that lay before me. Sometimes I resisted the suffocating sense of hopelessness and sometimes I didn't. When I succumbed, I would lie perfectly still under my white hospital sheet, covering my head as well, and try to forget I even existed. Sometimes things became so bad that I was unable to physically move. It was as if all life had leaked out of my body and just the shell was left in the sordid half-light of a cloudy November day. This was the equivalent of purgatory. I wondered how long I could survive and when, if ever, I'd get back to Italy.

There were always plenty of visitors who brought things into the hospital for me, invariably food, which I subsequently gave away to nurses or other visitors. I was still not eating and ignored the scarecrow appearance I was acquiring. I tried not to look at my body, as it was now an unknown and extremely frightening landscape. Nightdresses and sheets were friends, as they hid the truths too harsh to face on a frequent basis.

On reasonable days, I read books and wrote to Picci about my thoughts and dreams or I'd just describe silly things that happened in the day that perhaps had made me laugh. When I received a letter from him, I'd have palpitations and my hands would shake. I'd quickly scan the page to see the way he'd greeted me and then taken his leave, holding dear his 'Hello, my love' and 'Goodbye, dearest'. They were nearly as good as a long embrace, and I'd call them back to my thoughts time and again during the day, until too often remembered they lost their intensity. His letters were full of news about my friends, my home, the people he'd met and his work. He went into great detail with his descriptions, so that I could participate in a life that I would be returning to. He often said that he would like to come back from work and lie in the bed next to mine, to be near me and hold my hand, so that we could talk about our days. I loved his words. He was such a reserved person that reading his thoughts and feeling his emotions was a great privilege.

Picci was making progress with his walking and had got as far as abandoning his crutches, although he told me that he was walking with a limp and his feet were very swollen by the end of the day. Then, finally, he announced over the phone one evening that he'd shortly be able to come over and see me. I was at once excited and worried. We prepared ourselves for the longed-for meeting. He was due to arrive on the following Saturday and I spent the remainder of the week thinking how I would woo him even in my ghastly pallor, but on the morning he was expected I was violently sick. The staff on duty contemplated barring his visit as I seemed so overexcited and stressed, but I managed to calm myself down in time so that such a drastic measure would not have to be taken. With eyes trained on the door, every part of me was ready for the greeting. He was typically late. As he came into the ward in his green Loden coat, I felt a familiar hammering in my chest and colour creep into my face. He had a noticeable limp and was thinner and drawn, his black hair now betrayed by one or two grey traces. Self-effacing as always, he took a chair from by my bed and apologised for being late as he sat down. He looked at me fleetingly and told me I was pretty and looked less stressed than when in Milan. He then took out his handkerchief and blew his nose noisily. His gaze never stayed on me for long, almost as if he couldn't trust himself, but he kept asking me questions about the next steps that were to be taken and what the doctors were going to do. I, for my part, was riveted to his form, the collar of his coat, the soft part of his neck where his hair met his skin, his large nose, face and hands, memorising every physical detail so they could be visualised in moments of need. Every so often he took my hand and stroked my fingers in gentle assurance as he talked to me of his life in the working world. He'd just bought the premises he'd been looking for in order to enlarge his business, but there were many problems about moving to the new site. He asked me for my opinion, which I gave knowing full well that I was hardly in a position to give coherent logical advice from such a different world. But our meeting was conducted very much on controlled civilised lines where open and emotional behaviour would only have upset that small point of balance we'd separately fought to achieve within. We didn't speak of the hijack or of the violent ending to the trip, as we had experienced those moments together and we didn't need to unsettle our apparent calm. Had either of us let our control go, I don't know how we could have gone on. There were too many awful things that we'd lived through and too many difficulties to overcome to allow us the relief of letting our defences down in front of each other. Once or twice his gaze held my own. That was all the reassurance I needed and I felt calmer knowing that despite all the damage wreaked to my body he was still in love with me.

Picci was staying in a little hotel nearby. When he left me on Saturday night to retire to his room, I felt I'd been set adrift to bob up and down on a sea of strange emotions. At the same time, his presence close by was deeply comforting and gave me so much hope. My Italian aunt and uncle were in London for the weekend and took Picci out to dinner that evening. They had helped him to understand my medical situation in the early days before we had made contact by phone. Together they went to a little Italian restaurant and exchanged news, my aunt and uncle filling Picci in on my extended family and about the relationships there were between the various members. Picci came to know even more of my family history than I did at that time and, with his insatiable curiosity, rooted out all sorts of nuggets that I would have loved to know about. It was a comfort to Picci to have met up with someone in the family who he could relate to and talk to from the same culture and background. Mimmi's naughty sense of fun and complete disregard for the Anglo-Saxon stiff upper lip gave Picci the necessary light relief he craved after an anxiety-riddled visit.

The weekend passed at the speed of light and soon my father and Patricia were at the ward door to pick Picci up and take him to the airport. They all sat around my bed, and I performed to the best of my ability. Smiling, laughing and chatting, I tried as hard as I could to make my guests feel it was worth visiting me. The effort itself tired me enormously, but I found that after everyone had gone I felt uplifted by the very fact that I had been able to hold my own. I was glad, however, that my man was living in another country and his visiting was restricted to a weekend every so often. I would have been hard pushed to put on such a show had he visited every day, and although I craved his nearness, I was afraid that my close proximity and my bad days might mean he'd come to reject me.

Once back in Italy, Picci wrote reams of advice about my eating and told me that I had to have steaks brought in specially. He thought it was all just a question of finances and wanted to give me vast quantities of money so that in some way a few wheels could be oiled. He suggested that I gave the nurses large tips so that they would treat me better and I had to explain to him that the biggest gift they might expect was a box of chocolates. This was a huge culture difference between Italy and Britain, for while in Italy any self-respecting patient had to tip the hospital staff in order to obtain the bare minimum of attention, paying off the nurses was unheard of in Britain. Picci just couldn't seem to grasp the different expectations and pushed this idea for a long time. He also had no idea of why I wasn't eating and thought it was due to my natural fussiness. I don't think he understood how food affected me and that I had in reality become anorexic, not because I thought I was fat but for so many other psychological and medical reasons. In fact, most of the hospital staff ignored my hunger strike just as they ignored the psychological aspect of the hijacking. It was as if they would only deal with the problems they could actually see. Though the other part of me, my personality, my emotions, my spirit, were suffering just as much as my body, it seemed that my psychological illness was strictly taboo. Had someone sat down and asked me a few basic questions about how I was getting on inside my head, it would perhaps have eased the burden of so much internal conflict.

I remember one doctors' round near the time of surgery with particular pain. Professor Jones usually had about six students who followed him around on his visits, learning about patients and their various problems. On this particular occasion, however, he arrived with a group of eight. They gathered at the foot of the bed while the professor gave the same introductory spiel he used whenever he came to see me. He reeled off who I was and what I'd been through, always with the same dry intonation that managed to relegate me to the pages of a textbook. This time, instead of closing my eyes to block out the images before me, I chose to look at the faces surrounding me, trying in vain to make some connection with these young people, for they were all about my age. They were young, attractive and looking forward to promising futures, a mixture of men and women in their 20s embarking on their careers.

It was the turn of a young man to inspect me, make his comments and ask relevant questions. Without asking my permission or even addressing me, and hardly looking at me, the student medic pulled back the sheets and exposed me in a short nightdress in complete disarray. I was mortified as the gaze of all these students raked over my thin body, taking in the catheter, the colostomy bag, the wasted hairy legs and ghastly wound. I had not been able to shave my legs and being dark-haired they were hardly a pretty sight. My curled-over position was more or less rigid, and there was no way I could rearrange myself to cover up some of the sad display. Young men who three months previously might have turned their heads to get a better look at me now scribbled notes about this weird and ugly specimen. I stared horrified at the faces. There was definitely no connection now they'd uncovered me. Not one of them gave me a reassuring smile, not one of them even attempted to acknowledge that I was human. I might as well have been a pickled embryo in a laboratory test tube. What I think unnerved me totally was when I saw a young and very lovely girl at the back of the class blow a bubble with her gum as she looked in total disinterest out of the window. I became very angry and, struggling, pulled the sheet from the hand of the student and covered myself up to the best of my ability, mortified and isolated in my misery. I reached into my innermost self and closed the door on the world. This would never ever happen again. No one would abuse me in this way.

The minute the troop had disappeared out of the door, I asked one of the nurses if I could speak to the sister and told her that I refused to be used as a star model for any future student tours. She merely shrugged, saying that they had to learn somehow. Without patients, how else were they to get to know case histories, she asked me. Unfortunately, she'd missed the point. Hands-on learning is, of course, often a good thing, but my condition was hardly as straightforward a condition as a hip replacement. I was more determined than ever not to be an obliging doormat.

It was shortly after this episode that my aunt went to speak to the sister about contacting a psychologist. I hadn't spoken to her of the unfortunate episode, as it was just one of the difficulties I was facing every day, and my way of coping was not to speak about the negative things that happened. Up till this point, no one had considered getting help from the psychiatric department. It was a step that inevitably required a great deal of reflection, and perhaps those looking after me had not got that far in considering what I needed to help me recover faster. The sister came to me the following morning saying, 'Your aunt thinks you should see a psychologist. You don't look as if you need one to me, but if you want one, I'll get someone in.' I felt the sting of embarrassment. Had I been showing signs of mental derangement? Was I unhinged? I replied that I was absolutely fine and, of course, there was no need to see anyone.

That was the end of that and no one did come in to see me apart from a rather ineffectual chaplain who made me want to throw things at him. I didn't believe in anything any more since that frightening experience after the hijack where I'd seen all those devils' faces, so his request that I pray with him was met with a baleful and scornful glare as I deliberately picked up a book to read. The poor man left me very quickly and shot past my bed every time he came into the ward, scared that I might tell him exactly what he might do with his supplicating and worship should he linger for an instant.

There was now nothing left of the old religious teaching that I'd firmly believed in for the first 26 years of my life. As a young girl, I had followed in the wake of my parents, becoming a member of the School of Economic Science. This institution was based in London and run by a Scotsman with a certain amount of severity in his manner and in the way he managed his school. He had initially started courses in economics before the Second World War, but he had come to believe, as time went by, that there was also a need in people for some kind of spiritual guidance that was not being properly addressed by the established Church. Courses were set up in the evenings where spiritual texts from different sources were examined. Students were asked to see how they could be integrated into their lives so that their everyday actions might become more meaningful. No single religion was seen as the only answer to helping a soul through life, as each one, it was thought, promoted more or less the same principles as another. Buddhism as well as Christianity received a lot of attention, and the Sanskrit language was studied within the specialist groups of the school so that ancient works might be studied in the original.

Gradually the school had grown and spread to different countries throughout the world. In the '80s, it also opened up day schools in

London that followed the national curriculum and even sent students on to Oxford and Cambridge. I went to a very ordinary convent school for girls in Rickmansworth but spent 11 years of my life following the evening courses once a week in the centre of London and was involved in the early youth groups that spent two weekends every month on a retreat at Waterperry House in Oxford. There, we were monitored, taught and guided through a Saturday and Sunday of studying not only our ordinary school homework but also Vedic Maths, Sanskrit and music. We also learned how to do housework, bake bread, hoe the fields, gather in the onion and potato crops, even when it rained. The general emphasis was on leading disciplined, hard-working lives. We were also instructed in meditation, which I disliked intensely. We had to be up at 4.30 in the morning, with duties to perform for the rest of the house, so when meditation came round I would slumber in the chair I was sitting on, quite relieved to catch up on sleep. I did not know what meditation was about in the mystical sense, never experiencing any enlightenment or feelings of peace, probably because I didn't really apply myself to the activity.

My youth was bizarre by most standards, but it served as a preparation for the life I would encounter as I moved to university and then on to Italy. I attended a Church of England school and then a Catholic school for girls. I was familiar with the rituals of both denominations but was involved with neither, never attending church on a Sunday. Spiritually, I believed in God as a huge power that could mete out punishment when and where necessary. I felt I knew at that time that everything given to us in life was the fruit of past lives, and that we could invite good or bad to come our way. We could also become saints or sinners as we wished. Our emotions were to be kept at arm's length, as they would more often than not corrupt our clear thinking and muddle up the path of right and wrong. Things were pretty well defined for me in those days, even though I was not the happiest of souls during my teenage years.

There was a very subtle sense of rebellion that accompanied me throughout this period of my youth and perhaps reflected my freedom-seeking personality. I never liked being told what to do, especially by men. We females were supposed to hold them in the highest esteem and obey them regardless of what we might feel. No doubt I misinterpreted what was said at the time, but I felt uncomfortable with the feminine role I was expected to play and chafed against all the petty rules and regulations in the school that were promulgated by the men. Unfortunately for me, God was also a man, and my relationship with him was propitiatory and ingratiating. I was always afraid that he disapproved of my behaviour and felt that whatever befell me was largely my fault.

Given such an education, it was hardly surprising that after the hijack I wanted to spit at religion in general and servants of religious practice in particular. How could I ever accept that I had deserved to be involved in as hideous an experience as a hijack by doing something wrong in a past life or the one I was living now? So I gave no more thought to religion, nor did I hold inner discussions on God, and woe betide anyone wanting to appeal to my presumed need to search him out.

9

STANDING AGAIN

AT THE END of that dreadful month, Professor Jones operated on the head of the femur. The pelvic pain that had gradually abated over the weeks as the fractures mended came back, and I was left with agonising lesions in my genital area. In order for the surgeons to manipulate my bones, I had had to be anchored to a central pole in the middle of the operating table. The pole acted as a resistance to the pulling and pushing necessary to get at the hip and I came out of the theatre with mashed soft tissue due to shrapnel that was still embedded in the flesh being ground against the pole. The horrible catheter tube was back in place and emerged from a battleground of cuts and bruises. I hated the tube more than ever and, although a minor problem compared to the rest of my missing parts, it was a considerable irritation. The skin graft had also received rough treatment and some of the delicate tissue had rubbed off. Though these may have seemed minor setbacks, they were terribly significant to me as they had been gauges by which I measured my progress.

Teresa kept up her visits twice a day to prepare me for standing. She made me work as hard as she could within the confines of an airbed until even I could see that there was improvement and began to feel encouraged. A week after surgery, Professor Jones announced that he wanted to see me upright. Teresa beamed as she called for extra hands to help with this mammoth procedure. In contrast, I was terrified, thinking of all my appendages and wondering what life would be like from a vertical position. She ordered me to eat something, so that I could find a little extra strength, and told me that a team of helpers would be back in half an hour. With that, she glided out into the corridor, and I was plunged into uncertainty. My imagination ran riot as I thought of the effects of gravity on all my tubes, terrified that things would leak and smells escape. I searched frantically for my bowl and was sick yet again. I still clung to memories of a pretty, healthy body, refusing to acknowledge the grotesque thing it had become. I was desperately thin, gaunt and grey, and my bones showed through, continually reminding me of my own mortality. Thank God I didn't know then just how long recovery would actually take. I could not have wittingly undergone the long journey.

One of the nurses brought me a basin of warm water in which to wash my face and hands. I took a brush and gently gathered my hair into a ponytail, going through a ritual of physical and mental preparation. I looked at my face in the hand-mirror, diving into my own eyes and trying to plumb their depths for answers, yet the sad countenance I saw seemed to be that of a stranger. My eyes were cool, without expression. How could so much be going on in my head and there not be a trace written in those eyes? Where was I to find a helping hand of courage in the blank depths? Ashen and so unclean looking, I relaxed my furrowed brow, trying and failing to see what I had once liked. I brushed my heavy brows with a finger and tried to smile, but my lips fell immediately back into an expressionless line. I put the mirror on the little table beside me, no longer curious, and glanced at the white sheets littered with my long dark hair that was falling out by the handful, lustreless and dull, just as my eyes had been. I dug around for Froggy and enclosed him tightly in the palm of my hand. He calmed my fluttering stomach as I waited for Teresa, Kate, Emma and Sal.

Another female nurse had been recruited for the occasion and there was a male nurse ready to catch me in the event of my passing out. Apparently this was the norm for people who had not stood up for months. Teresa, holding me under my arms, pulled me up from my prone position. I felt uncomfortable about her proximity, as I knew I was sweaty and was afraid of my bad odour. I turned my face away from hers, careful not to breathe on her. Sal and Emma pulled my legs to the side of the bed, and the others took care of the drip and catheter. Teresa then held me in a bear hug and tipped me vertical. She gently released the tightness of her hold and placed a walking frame in front of me to use as a support. Everyone was concentrating on my face. Seemingly my lips turned blue as blood struggled to make its way round my body, but I did not faint. My delight at this success broke across my face, and all my supporters clapped as they saw me smiling. I looked out over the dreary rooftops towards the Telecom Tower and then down at my luminescent feet. I felt extremely long; the floor seemed miles away. I was an elongated sapling deprived of light, swaying with weakness in the still air. I could feel my right leg, although it shook all the time, but the left leg was numb. I had no feeling except for a tremendous heaviness on that side of my body.

Perhaps this was the turning point as far as food was concerned. To walk I'd have to use energy, and energy could only come from eating. That much was clear and, although I was not likely to start demolishing plates of NHS food, there was a logical direction that had to be taken. My nutrition had actually improved a little in that I was able to eat crackers with, of all things, sandwich spread. I was only able to feed myself during the night when the lights were out and the other patients were sleeping. For some reason I found it easier when I could be private and there was nobody forcing me to do something I didn't want to do. At about three o'clock I'd wake up, call the night nurse, ask her to draw curtains around me and switch on the little reading light. She'd help me find the crackers, and while I prepared this frugal meal, we chatted about all sorts of different things. This nocturnal feeding was the only moment in 24 hours when I would eat, and it was also the only moment when I became free of the whole hijack story and felt as I used to feel. The side effect of this habit was that I had to have most of my teeth filled on getting out of hospital.

It was around this time that I became aware of a new and rather peculiar sensation. As I rolled from horizontal to vertical off the bed before standing up, I noticed a grating sensation in my bladder. I felt as if I had a duck egg inside me. When I was lying down, I felt nothing, but the movement forward was uncomfortable and stung my bladder. I told the staff about this, but they insisted it was the effect of gravity on my body. However, blockages of my catheter became more and more frequent, and the urine became cloudier and evil smelling. I was told to drink more and the problem would clear up, but I was afraid that if I drank more I'd become a huge balloon whilst waiting for a nurse who could afford the time to come and fiddle with the valves to siphon off the urine. The day came when no one heeded my pleas for relief from yet another blockage. My stomach had been getting harder and harder, and I could stand the pain and indignity of this retched piece of apparatus no longer. It had been inside me for over three months and I can only recall it having been changed once. Even I managed to work out that it must have been full of bugs. A dream of going home for the day around Christmas, coupled with an intense loathing for that instrument of torture, gave me the necessary guts to seize it and rip it out, regardless of the consequences. As I did so, I bellowed to obliterate any pain there might have been. I wet the bed copiously and, delighted by the relief I felt, vowed that they would never be allowed to put another catheter up me ever again. A nurse came rushing over with an orderly, and I triumphantly thrust the horrible thing under her nose and told her it had come out. She was annoyed, particularly about the bed wetting as the rubber cushions would need a disinfecting clean. She took the catheter from me and peered at the end. It was indeed encrusted, and it was small wonder that it had become blocked. An orderly changed the bed and settled me back after considerable fussing about. She even brought me a bedpan, and I rejoiced as I tried to get on it. My happiness was short-lived, however, as the nurse came back armed with another of those awful tubes, and, unwrapping it from its plastic sterile encasement, she moved towards me in determined intent. Whether it was due to my doggedness or a physical blockage in my urethra, I don't know; but, try as she might, she was unable to insert the catheter. The more she pushed, the more I resisted, amidst fuming on both sides.

She certainly had no respect for me as a patient. I would have liked to make her swallow food tubes and force feed her, insert catheters up her urethra as roughly as she was trying to shove it up me, make her deal with her own colostomy, humiliate her and exasperate her as I had been over the months and give her a taste of her own medicine. Her insensitivity was insulting. In the end she walked away from the bed, taking her cross face and miserable intentions with her. I grinned from ear to ear as I thought of my new-found freedom. At last, I had now regained some independence. Disasters occurred due to the cystitis I had as a consequence of infection, but I could deal with all that, as I knew I was gradually getting better and had eliminated one of those hospital horrors that unnerved me every hour of my admittance.

During the same period, I was seen by a surgeon called Mr Lax, who would eventually close the colostomy. He examined me and thought that I might be incontinent if I didn't practise squeezing my sphincter muscles once I had been reconnected to the colon. So, together with my physio workout I also had to do sphincter training.

I was now able to get up and wash in the basin of the little side room opposite my bed. On the inside of the door, there was a long mirror. I looked like Mahatma Gandhi after his hunger strikes with my bandaged bottom. It was still being dressed with creams every day but I hadn't seen the wound with a mirror. I hadn't been ready to look at it before, but now that I was up and had even washed my hair in the sink, I felt that perhaps the time had come to see it. As Giselle was cleaning the area, I casually remarked that I hadn't seen the damage yet. She laughingly said that it wasn't a pretty sight, and carried on with her sterile swabbing job. I pulled out a mirror from my locker, and, twisting slightly, I asked her if she would place it so that I could see for myself. I expected to be shocked and was vaguely disconcerted because I wasn't. In fact, I reacted very little to the vision of what had once been my backside. It was now a huge hole, red and liver coloured, and I wept without additional grief or pain, but simply because to do so was part of the ritual. The anguish connected to that part of me had eaten away at the inside of my head for months, and I'd been well aware from the first that my backside was horrible to look at. There had been a long preparation for the worst, and the sharp impact had been absorbed. This was now merely the final acknowledgement of a new state of affairs that, certainly, I did not accept, but one that I had to temporarily put mentally aside as I concentrated on the problems I was having to deal with on a daily basis.

10

ROHO AND HOME

RATHER THAN STANDING up, I was much more worried about being able to sit down, believing, as most people do, that one sits on one's bottom. Teresa had already thought of these problems in her efficient way and had contacted a special company that could help with the difficulty. She arrived with a huge box one morning, announcing that I was about to have a well-earned treat. As she undid the parcel, which must have weighed about six kilos, she kept breaking out into laughter. She pulled out a large-barrelled blue bicycle pump and slapped it on the bed in satisfaction. That, she informed me, was to keep it inflated. Then, after a bit of a struggle, she hauled a huge cellophane bag containing a gelatinous wobbly black thing from its tight confines. Teresa applied all her strength to the business of tearing the resistant plastic apart to get at the Roho cushion, for that was apparently the animal's name. Eventually, the creature plopped out onto the wheelchair by my bed, and I looked on in amazement at this extraordinary piece of apparatus. It was a special cushion for those who'd suffered first-degree burns, who had deep bed sores or indeed had parts blown off in that area of their body, meaning that they couldn't sit down.

The cushion, just out of its wrapping, was deflated, but it already had the appearance of the most extraordinary sex aid I could ever have imagined. It consisted of a square of black synthetic rubber into which were moulded about 50 phallic-shaped inflatable and life-sized protuberances. What did I think of that, she asked. Teresa, searching for the little valve on the cushion, then explained the laborious red tape she'd had to work her way through in order to obtain this contraption. They were, she said, extremely expensive and as difficult to obtain as gold nuggets given the financial plight of the NHS. I dutifully thanked her, wondering how on earth I was supposed to use such a monstrosity.

'The best bit's to come,' she joked, asking Sal to help me out of bed. I was glued to the procedure as she manfully screwed in the pump and started working on filling the cushion up with air. Her face took on the colour of an apricot with her gold blonde hair falling in stray wisps as she pumped away. All of a sudden the phallic shapes began to pop up in rude salute and I stared at it aghast, half laughing and half staring in disbelief at the audacity of the thing. 'I can't sit on that, Teresa,' I gasped.

'Well, you'd better after all it's taken for me to get hold of it. Pity it doesn't work.' She threw the double entendre at me naughtily, while she gently helped me to sit down. I was reluctant, as I didn't want to sit on the wound even if it was covered in thick wads of dressing, so Teresa gave me a brief anatomy lesson, pointing out that no one actually sits on their buttocks. One sits on one's thighs, she informed me. My thighs were perfectly intact, and so, with panic removed, I tried out my new 'chair'.

It was the first time in months that I was going to actually sit down, and I felt awkward and extremely stiff. The cushion helped to evenly distribute my weight so that I didn't squash the injured side. There was no discomfort due to the missing buttock, but there was a strange new sensation I would have to get used to. Although the lack of muscle didn't directly affect my ability to sit, I was definitely aware of the loss and experienced a peculiar lopsidedness. Furthermore, I suffered unbearable pain in my hip joint. This pain did not augur well, and I asked myself if the head of the femur was in fact bonding onto the neck. It was early days, but the sharp and deep discomfort took away the refreshing fun we'd had over the cushion. I was helped off the chair after two minutes of pain. This was not the relief it was supposed to be, simply because the unpleasant sensation came from another source. Despite this discomfort, I was instructed to use the chair and cushion as often as possible, staying out of bed whenever I could.

The sister then told me that I would enjoy eating my meals out of bed, sitting up in a chair. This suggestion/decree led to further misery. Eating was still pretty much a subject I didn't care to talk about, and although I ferreted about in the night with my crackers, daytime feeding was as arduous as ever. The association of eating with the chair and the chair with eating proved to be a disastrous partnership. The acute physical pain in my hip distracted me from my meals, which needed a high degree of concentration. The idea of almost ritualising my meals by putting me into the chair put paid to progress as far as both sitting and eating were concerned.

Christmas was around the corner and I continually pestered all staff, doctors, physios and nurses about going home for a day visit. The only answer anyone could give me was 'it depends'. My bladder control was a little better, but I had constant cystitis and a light temperature much of the time. I kept on about this 'thing' inside me rolling around, but everyone maintained it was an infection or some gynaecological problem of little importance.

I made my own way to the bathroom on endlessly slow trips across the ward, during which the greetings of fellow patients were almost sufficient to cause my literal downfall. I was still so weak. Indeed, there was one particular evening when I was feeling most unwell and just a little down. Coming back from a painful time in the toilet, I was walking bit by bit towards my wheelchair when I lost my balance. All the old ladies cried out from their beds in alarm as I spreadeagled out backwards onto the floor. I fell as if in slow motion and landed softly. A nurse came hurrying over and picked me up. I was so far from being well that I began thinking that it would take a lifetime to get better. This fall triggered off a heavy depression that lasted several days. I think it had something to do with my uncertainty about going home, too. I was desperate to get out of the hospital and could hardly bear the ward, nurses and smell of sickness, my own and others, any longer.

As a result I withdrew from the world. It was one of the few occasions in hospital where I dwelt for so many days inside a part of myself that was devoid of life and where I thought dying would have been a better alternative to this intolerable suffering. During that period, there was no hope, no light and no energy. I saw nothing except for darkness and could hold onto nothing that I might remotely believe in. My love for Italy and my boyfriend were forgotten, and I experienced that terrible feeling of being alone in the world. On Sunday morning, I could stand the situation no more and asked a nurse to help me into the chapel. I threw down the proverbial gauntlet at God. If he/she gave me a sign that he/she was around, then I would come out of the depression. I stood at the door, looking intently at the altar, waiting for some supernatural light to spread from the cross, or at least for some light to come into my being, but I had to withdraw after some minutes because nothing was happening and my leg hurt. I was helped back to the ward where lunch was waiting, congealed on a plate on the wheelchair table: packet mashed potatoes, macaroni in white sauce and boiled broad beans. The very sight of it made me want to take the plate of food and either screw it into someone's face or throw it with all the fury I was capable of mustering at a wall whilst screaming my head off.

I didn't do this, of course, terrified as I always was of the repercussions that would have inevitably occurred. I longed for loving people to take care of me and thoughtfulness to be the order of the day. Fuelled by an anger that shook my voice as I spoke, I told the sister I was going home. I informed everyone that I felt much better and pushed myself to walk more with my crutches, trying to appear in control of things. I even made a show of eating.

This all paid off, as on 16 December I went home for the day, equipped with a very large nappy, and the drip was finally taken down. Teresa came in to dress me and gave me lots of advice as she wheeled me down to my father's car. It was an extraordinary sensation to be outside in normal daylight. The morning was glorious and there was a cold winter nip in the air. I was bundled up in a large brown rug from the car and lifted into the front seat. I didn't even notice Teresa leaving me.

Frosty and sparkly and fizzy were the words that seemed to echo through my mind as the car headed out of London. I revelled in my freedom, speechless with joy. My eyes drank in the London sights as we swung in and out of traffic. I watched people walk their dogs. I read pub signs, noticed the clothes people wore and realised that I, too, was part of the hurly burly of life. We drove past fields, the rich dark earth promising life; we overtook cyclists hell-bent on developing their calf muscles, and I felt the dormant but incredible power of nature in all I saw. I was also poignantly aware of the continuity of the world, the city, life – regardless of the fact that I had not been there. The car drive alone gave me a spurt of energy stimulating me to get back on form, and I silently thanked everything around me for showing me that there was a way out.

Familiar in its prettiness, the house stood indifferent to the human drama unfolding. My father opened the car door and with great gentleness, first pulling my feet and then hooking me round the waist, he levered me out. He handed me my crutches, and I wobbled to the door in subdued triumph. Everyone was there to greet me, including my youngest brother Cameron, son of my father and Patricia, whose huge eyes took in the wheelchair that was bringing up the rear. Pot plants and flowers filled the porch and the age-old smell of my family home brought back strange sensations. I felt I had been away for 20 years.

Greetings and smiles of welcome followed me into the sitting room, where the sofa had been placed near the fire. I was helped to lie down with lots of cushions. The old black cat was brought in to keep me warm and all the letters people had kindly sent that week were laid on the coffee table next to me. Cameron was banished to do his homework because he had to be taken back to school that same evening and also because he was far too agog with questions. Patricia was in the kitchen preparing lunch with her mother, and I was slightly tense about the problem of eating, not knowing what my reaction might be to a plate of food.

I was utterly spoiled, though, and, unable to concentrate on letter reading, felt I was in heaven. There was a wonderful view of the garden, beautifully looked after, with its statues and steps, trees and bushes. With the sunlight beaming down, the world seemed benign, and I was overwhelmed with gratitude, seeing things with fresh but starved eyes. I had no words to offer anyone.

Lunchtime arrived, and Cameron importantly sounded the gong. He pushed me into the dining room, attempting to run at the same time. He was sharply rebuked, but, naturally, at ten years old, he was fascinated by the wheelchair. Everyone sat down, chatting and laughing while I observed their expressions and their faces. I listened to their voices as if for the first time.

Patricia's lunch was the turning point away from anorexia. I sat down at the table weighing 46 kilos, having lost nearly 20. But from that moment on I stopped losing weight. She had prepared everything in miniature. The vegetables were finely cut and steamed. Tiny slivers of plaice fillets in breadcrumbs with lemon were served golden brown on a central platter. There were small rolls of home-made warm bread and small dishes of butter. All was without seasoning, apart from a little salt, and it was all boiling hot. The best dishes were used and cut glass set out. I felt honoured and touched by so much thoughtfulness.

Then something miraculous happened. The usual spasms I would get during the daytime in front of food gave way to mouth-watering hunger pangs. I ate my fill, savouring the wonderful food. I even went back for another helping. Despite the fierce pain in my hip joint, I couldn't stop smiling. I was as surprised as everyone else about my appetite, never having expected such a remarkable turnaround as this. While the conversation flowed on, I cast my mind back to the previous two weeks, of how I had reached rock bottom as far as my morale was concerned. I felt as if this meal might really mean that the only way on was up.

The day passed, and I was taken back to the hospital glowing with happiness. It was harder than I expected to have to return to the ward, but I needed to attend to my various problems. I was also exhausted from having sat up for so long and been without the airbed. I was put straight onto it and left to mull over the events of the day. I had reached a milestone. If I was able to stay at home for one day, then surely I could stay overnight. Then and there I decided that I would be going home for Christmas and that I would come back the following day, regardless of what anyone else might have to say.

11

STANMORE

CHRISTMAS PASSED WITH only a few hitches, one being that I went over my time limit, sleeping for two nights instead of the one, and getting back to hospital proved to be torture. I was unable to bend my leg at the hip without electric-like shocks shooting up into my pelvis. We got round that problem by calling our family GP, who gave me a shot of pethidine, and in no time at all my father and the doctor tucked my legs back into the car. I was dry mouthed and glassy eyed for the entire journey, and, as a happy side effect, I was even detached from the distress of having to re-enter hospital. On arrival, I was thoroughly told off by the staff nurse for having taken such a strong drug. She said that I should have rung for an ambulance and warned me that going home would not be quite so easy the next time. 'Stuff her,' I thought as I got into bed, thinking of the two days I'd spent at home. How dare she treat me as if I was a naughty boarding-school pupil?

Good news, however, was round the corner. Just after New Year, I was told that I would soon be changing hospitals to move to the rehabilitation centre in Stanmore. Perhaps even Professor Jones had come to realise that the ward up on the eighth floor was a sad and dreary place for someone trying to get better. I was deemed sufficiently recovered to be able to abandon the airbed to sleep in a normal one that I could get in and out of by myself. 'By myself' or 'on my own' were crucial words. They acquired a special status in my mind and meant freedom and health.

Soon after this news I received a visit from the hospital gynaecologist. Throughout the previous months I had contemplated at length my new physique and the implications involved. The change that would inevitably take place in the physical relationship between Picci and myself caused me a lot of worry. Up until this point there had been no one in whom I could confide my fears, and all I really needed at that time was someone to listen to my concerns. The poor man was obviously finding his visit difficult, unused to women needing guidance of a less straightforward nature, and, rather than just extend a warm hand and humane smile, he tried valiantly to answer my questions. He was also under the misconception that I would have a colostomy for the rest of my life, and once he was in full spate, I felt inhibited about setting him right.

He gave me an unrealistic and idealistic explanation of the way Picci would have to behave if we were to rehabilitate a love life. As a lover, Picci had not been anxious to please but took it as a matter of course that I would direct him in my pleasure. His urgency was more than an aphrodisiac, allowing me to be equally ardent and demanding. Admittedly, we were at the beginning of our relationship and things tend to be animated at the start. It had been intoxicating having someone who wanted to savour and 'have' me. I had been very confident about my body, being slim, muscular and young, and had often taken the lead. Now things were not likely to be the same, and the possibility of finding compatibility at such a level was anyone's guess. I certainly couldn't imagine a repeat of previous scenarios of frenzied passion as we tore each other's clothes off, neither could I imagine him languorously and gently whispering sweet nothings in my ear. He wasn't the sort.

The doctor waxed lyrical about the understanding and complete selflessness that Picci would have to manifest. Horrified over the descriptions of getting used to making love with a third party, that of the colostomy, for ever and ever, and imagining Picci's flight from anything quite so disgusting, my face must have registered miserable shock, for the doctor's useful advice dried up and he quite abruptly vanished. Alone and unable to tease out the awful strands of ifs and buts, I did the only thing I could on such unbearable occasions: I picked up a book and switched off the mental spotlight.

Tests came back from the laboratories showing that I had all manner of vague infections, and everyone rejoiced that all my moaning about something rolling around in my bladder was nothing more than slight candida, no doubt caused by the long stay of the catheter. I was completely unconvinced, knowing full well that something was wrong. But, until I'd followed a course in antibiotics, I had no choice but to put up with my discomfort and growing incontinence. I was incubating an intense dislike of certain members of the hospital staff. There is nothing worse than not being taken seriously, especially regarding one's health.

Picci came to see me a couple of weekends later at my family home, and we spent time together. He was looking much better, had put on a little weight and was limping only very slightly. He was also a lot more energetic than he had been the last time I saw him. He saw me walking for the first time unaided on my crutches, and I wasn't on good form. Strength was slow to come back to me, and a walk to the kitchen was extremely torpid. He was worried by my evident lack of improvement from his last visit and began to question me as to why my recovery was taking so long. He kept on until the implication was blatant that I was feeling sorry for myself and not struggling back with the verve and vigour he expected of me. I felt cut to the quick, unable to accept negative judgements and wanted him to leave and fly back to Italy if he was not able to understand that I *was* getting better but at *my* pace. It wasn't as if I could choose the speed. I was, under the circumstances, going as fast as nature would allow.

We parted on strained terms, which did absolutely nothing for my morale, and I felt depressed for some days. I realised that Picci felt it was time to move on to a new scene in this particular saga. He had introduced the subject of finding lawyers who could represent us in a case to obtain compensation. The thought of having to find a lawyer was a nuisance. I felt irritated and put upon that he should have brought up yet another problem that seemed insurmountable. With all the time in the world to reflect, he maintained, I might do well to come up with ideas on how to investigate the legal aspect of our situation. The inference was that I was letting myself and our objectives go. He was impatient for me to return to Italy so that we could pick up our lives again, and he wanted us to be together. However, pursuing aims and goals requires serenity and drive. I was already struggling with my physical recovery, and it was more than enough to cope with. I responded to encouragement and I was upset by his disapproval.

A few days later, I received a letter from him, which helped realign us. 'Dearest,' he began:

> As I said in my very first letter, I am here waiting for you to come back home to me, and if I seem to be hard on you, it is certainly not because I have thoughts about finishing our relationship. Our relationship is living very much in its own right. It is unique and very unusual, for not everyone has such a strange 'love story'. In some ways it's the stuff of books and films, but we cannot even compare it to them. After two hours or three hundred pages, the stories always finish. Our story isn't ending, although we don't know how it will turn out. Every one of our moments is alive and unpredictable. It's you and I who are writing our own love story and our own book, so take heart and don't get upset if I seem to ask a lot of you and expect better progress. Push yourself to your limits. I know it is all so very hard for you . . .

Just one small note of recognition was sufficient to encourage me, and I began to think about the question of lawyers, talking to my father to see if he could come up with any ideas. It was a useful diversion and made the time pass a little quicker. Indeed, the second half of January proved to be considerably faster moving than the previous slow months.

My periods came back on 20 January, as if to remind me that I was still a normal functioning woman, and I took heart from the auspicious occasion. The gynaecologist had assured me that I would be able to have children, although carrying a pregnancy would mean that I would have to be in bed for the better part of nine months. He had also said that there would probably be repercussions on the rest of my body that would have to be evaluated if I was thinking of becoming pregnant. I didn't pay much attention to the note of caution, simply because I didn't feel that anyone could really predict my medical future. I was convinced that with my absolute need to return to the physical condition I had been in before the hijack, the problems I had would resolve themselves as time went on. There was never any doubt in my mind.

My enthusiasm for getting better doubled, and I was told that on 22 January a bed would be available for me at the new hospital. The infections had by now cleared up but not so the rolling sensation, and I brought the problem to the sister's attention again before I left. I felt she thought I was inventing things, however, when she said that I could bring the matter up when I got to the new hospital.

In comparison to the first hospital in London, the Royal National Orthopaedic Hospital of Stanmore on Brockley Hill looked like a wonderful primary school in the middle of a large, beautifully kept park. I moved into Ward 106 with my own small normal bed. I had my cushion, wheelchair and holdall. There was a small kitchen where patients could eat and even cook if they wanted. The ward was carpeted and the patients were for the most part not bed-bound.

Right at the end of the ward was a little sitting room with a TV, and we could go and sit there for a chat or to relax at any time of the day. Everyone was fitter than me, and I was delighted to be amongst healthier people. For the most part they had chronic medical conditions and needed tests or daily treatment for a period of time. There was a lovely woman, bent almost double, who was suffering from osteoporosis at the age of 45, and she was having treatment via a drip for a certain period each day. Lolly, a girl of my age, had had a viral infection that had damaged the nerves in one of her feet. She walked with crutches because her ankle continued to turn in on itself, and she had so much pain that she couldn't put her foot on the ground. The doctors had never seen anything like it and were examining the possibility of amputating her foot. Despite the obvious suffering which each of the women on the ward was enduring, they seemed on the whole a cheerful group, ready to help and support each other when the need arose.

The ward sister was a very large woman who moved swiftly, her clothes chafing her large form and a lovely smile illuminating her face. As soon as I arrived, I informed her of my bladder problem and begged her to do something about it. I asked her the following day if anyone was coming in to see me, and she told me that she wanted to read all my hospital notes to sort out who I was and what problems I had had before making any decisions. By this time I was wearing huge incontinence towels, as I could no longer control myself, and I was also in constant pain. The sister looked as if she would not be reading my notes anytime soon, given the work there was to get through that week with new intakes and a shortage of staff, and I began to despair. I decided to phone Professor Jones and ask him to intervene. I went to the pay phone and dialled his office number. Fortune would have it that he was there and I explained in no uncertain terms that it was time something was done. He agreed with me and said he would organise an X-ray of my abdomen to be taken immediately.

I was examined the following day. From this X-ray it emerged that I had a bladder stone the size of a small egg, which was made up of the minerals and salts that had accumulated over the months because of the catheter. It was a great relief to know what was wrong and it seemed there was someone who would do something about it. A Mr Hanson was called from Edgware General Hospital to see me. Never has an operation been so quick, simple and effective. I was on a short course of antibiotics and within a week the incontinence had disappeared. I felt very angry with the nursing staff and others who had dismissed this problem way back in December when the solution was really very simple. The sister was also up in arms, for she had overheard my conversation with Professor Jones on the phone and asked why I hadn't waited for her to decide what to do. Understandably she was upset as I had undermined her authority, but I felt that my situation had called for drastic measures. The sister was not an unpleasant person and did her job well, but this time I had had enough of being submissive and accepting.

12

MEN

I WAS IN Stanmore for about six weeks as an in-patient but allowed home at weekends. My strength was coming back, and I made efforts to wear make-up despite the rash of spots and allergies I was getting. I was dressing by myself, although pants, tracksuit bottoms and socks thwarted me, as I couldn't bend over. I spent ages in the shower room in the mornings, sitting on a stool under a stream of water, scrubbing away as if there was six months' worth of dirt to eliminate. I was now in charge of the dressings on my buttock and was glad to be attending to myself, getting acquainted with the new me. I pestered the new physio, who was nowhere near the calibre of Teresa Phipps, to find out ways for me to be more independent, exercising day in and day out to strengthen non-existent muscles and encourage the slow re-growth of the sciatic nerve. I had a permanent brace to keep my dropped foot flexed at 90 degrees. It was ugly but necessary if I didn't want to find myself flat on my face having tripped over, or with a permanently pointed foot frozen downwards.

In spite of these visible improvements, for which I should have been dancing with joy, I seemed to be emotionally unpredictable. The normal framework to which I had attached my world had been torn away from me, and, jelly-like, my old emotional responses to events and news no longer held firm. I remember my father telling me that Cameron, my little brother, was going through a phase of striking matches and was fascinated by fire. My reaction had been exaggeratedly alarmed and I had insisted that Father and Patricia take him to a plastic surgery ward to see what happened to people with third-degree burns. I was terrified of him suffering as I had done were he to inadvertently start a fire.

I would at times feel elated for no reason at all and then, after a few hours, feel a lethargic depression creep up on me. It was as if the thermostat that had regulated my emotional responses was broken, and I had no idea how I might react in any given situation.

It was obvious that I had been deeply disturbed psychologically by the hijacking. This came out not only in these fluctuating highs and lows but also when I was coming round from anaesthesia. Twice in one week I was taken off to surgery to have lumps of emerging shrapnel removed from my feet and back, and, seemingly, I had to be sedated as I became agitated and called out for people to stop hurting me and to keep me away from the hijackers.

Now that I was making better progress with my physical health, however, and time was moving on, finding a solicitor was becoming increasingly important. Although we had no idea where we would eventually sue or who we would sue, we were aware that some time limit, within which such action could be taken, would apply. Therefore, the sooner we got going the better. Nor could we wait to find out information until I was completely recovered and back home, as investigating the possibilities of using a British lawyer would have proved more difficult once I had returned to Italy.

I was not in touch with any other passengers who had been on the plane, apart from Peter, because, as far as I was aware, I was the only British national who had been severely hurt. Finding out what other British passengers were doing as far as seeking compensation was concerned was something that at that time neither Picci nor I had considered.

Father got in touch with one of his friends who worked on the Stock Exchange, who in turn contacted a lawyer friend of his who agreed to see us. The meeting was arranged for the following weekend. During the intervening week, my father received a letter from the Foreign Office with a note attached from a Mr Manning of Birmingham who wished to get in touch with me. In the note, this lawyer claimed that he was an expert in the international conventions that governed air traffic laws and expressed a desire to see justice done in a case like mine. He said that he'd read about my serious injuries in the newspapers but had not been able to get in touch with me directly. He had therefore written to the Foreign Office, etc., etc. My father was heartened by such a 'kind letter' and suggested we get in touch with this man. So, we arranged a meeting with Mr Manning for the following Monday. He assured us that he already had business in London and that it would be no trouble to fit me in after the two appointments.

These two interviews with the lawyers were indicative of the difficulties that were to come and left us all with jangled nerves for different reasons. Picci arrived on the early flight from Milan on the Saturday, and, after picking him up, we headed straight back into London. On the way, he pulled out the two tickets we'd used for our Pan Am flights. He turned to the back of one of them and read out loud the contract agreement into which we had entered by buying the seats on Pan Am. I glanced at it, thinking to myself that he was being the usual stickler for detail. I quite honestly thought that my case was so incredible and terrible that the agreement rules would not pertain to me and that I would be considered differently – after all I'd nearly died. In fact, however, the ticket contract was actually very clear. Under the terms of the Warsaw Convention, the maximum sum of money I could expect the airline company to pay was 20,000 US dollars, based on an assessment of the injuries I had sustained. This money could be claimed immediately without even having to go through a lawyer.

Despite the contractual clarity, the meaning refused to sink in, and I dismissed the issue as we drew up outside an elegant house in a sweeping white crescent which corresponded to the address of the lawyer we had found through my father's friend. We rang the bell. A tall and large-boned man answered the door. His casual dress struck me, for he was wearing a green cardigan, polo-neck sweater, tracksuit trousers and bedroom slippers. He welcomed us in a great booming voice and ushered us into the breakfast room.

Forty minutes into the interview, Picci, who'd been very quiet, watching what was going on between the lawyer, my father and myself, muttered under his breath that the lawyer hadn't a clue what he was talking about. I was scared that his Italian could be understood and heartily wished he would keep his thoughts to himself for the time being.

Picci was right, however. Mr Burnes in his carpet slippers was not analysing the problem from a legal point of view. He was, of course, extremely interested in the story, as everyone always was, but he had not identified the point of departure from where we could take legal action. It was Picci who pulled the old airline coupons out of his pocket and, placing them on the table, told me to get the gentleman to read the ticket agreements. Mr Burnes gave them a cursory glance and dismissed the Warsaw Convention that was so simply stated on the back. The lawyer instead focused our attention on America, saying that as Pan Am was a US airline, we could sue them in the States, where it was well known that high awards were offered. On what grounds we could sue, this lawyer didn't explain, but heaven only knew what I might be worth.

Picci was fuming, talking to me in Italian about how this chap was just a lot of hot air and could we find a way of getting out. Father was jovial and satisfied, convinced that we could hand the whole problem over to this man who would make sure my future was financially secure. Picci wanted to know, in detail, the precise legal steps by which this man could win compensation for us. Pinning him down, however, was impossible, and an hour and a half later we were outside the house with tension between my father and Picci. The latter was angry that nothing had been seriously examined and we had received only vague promises of excellent law firms who worked in America, and my father was angry because neither of us was terribly impressed and his comments about this man being charming, hospitable and so helpful fell on stony ground.

The ride home was a silent one. I was torn between the two very strong male figures in my life, not knowing who was right. But I was conscious of the fact that I had to follow one of them, for I was in no fit state to strike out on my own. Picci and I read and re-read the ticket. It was clear that there was very little we could do and that we were eligible only for the sum of $20,000 or less, unless we could prove that there had been negligence or wilful misconduct on the part of the airline.

The meeting with Mr Manning followed much the same course. He arrived on our doorstep on the Monday afternoon, after I had been given permission to stay at home from the hospital. He was another tall, charming man, who greeted my father and me very warmly. Sherry and peanuts were served in the drawing room, and we were all on our best behaviour. He launched into his sales pitch, telling us in the most convincing tones that he had engaged the services of his great lawyer friend in America, where he assured us there was a 95 per cent possibility of success in pursuing Pan Am and winning our case. Mr Manning was very smart, well aware of the emotional weakness I was experiencing, and he played the part of the sympathetic and understanding lawyer well, but I saw his sharp eyes taking in the kind of middle-class conservative family we were, and perhaps he was imagining that I would accept him as my lawyer with little resistance. Picci, however, had urged me to pay great attention to what practical suggestions he might make and to ask for explanations. Whatever I didn't understand should be clarified. If the clarification did not make sense, then I was to ask again. Nothing is inexplicable, Picci said. If the explanation continued to be woolly, then the explainer himself didn't know what he was talking about.

Picci was a wise person, but it took a long time for this message to get through to me. He was not at the meeting, having returned to Italy, but he would be ringing that evening.

Mr Manning, encouraged by my father's enthusiastic noises, relaxed and then warned us against other lawyers who, when they heard my story, would find the case, and, more to the point, what I was worth, very interesting. They might try to get me to sign a retainer form, meaning that I would agree to their acting on my behalf as my lawyer. He told us that in his profession there were lawyers who actually followed victims of terrible accidents to hospital so that they were on hand to persuade overwrought relatives to retain their services. 'Ambulance chasers, they're called,' he said with the full weight of his professional disapproval. Before I could stop myself, I asked him if that wasn't precisely what he had done through the Foreign Office. Conversation jarred momentarily, but, full of resources, Mr Manning smoothed his way through the awkward moment. My father threw me a look of irritation and the meeting rapidly drew to a close. I shut the door on Mr Manning, saying I'd let him know as soon as I could what I'd decided to do. My father then proceeded to give me a piece of his mind, saying that I was showing absolutely no enthusiasm whatsoever despite all his efforts.

Upset, although I said nothing, I recognised from the two meetings we'd had with these lawyers that my father was not able to coldly dissect and assess what people were saying. At the same time, I recognised that he was genuinely concerned that I should be in good hands, but, like me, his lack of experience in legal matters made him very trusting of others' so-called expertise. That evening I spoke to Picci, who demanded to know what Mr Manning was going to do for us in concrete terms. In which country was it possible to take legal action? Italy, America or Great Britain? I was at a loss as to how to answer except to explain Mr Manning's idea of consigning the whole case into the hands of an American colleague. What questions had I asked Mr Manning? I couldn't tell Picci that I hadn't known what to ask. That conversation didn't go well either.

Time was passing and we were both worried that the statute of limitations, the time within which we could sue, would soon expire unless we made a move. Picci decided that we should make enquiries in Italy about suing the airline company, on the grounds that they had abandoned the plane with all the passengers on board. In escaping via the hatch behind the cockpit door on an ingenious pulley system, the captain and co-pilot had been speedily lowered down onto the tarmac under the nose of the aircraft, but they had also left the passengers and cabin crew to an unknown fate. At the same time, my father told me that he felt I would be better off following Picci's advice in the legal battle for the practical reason that I would be going back to Italy. He added that, although Picci wasn't my husband, it was very apparent that he had taken over responsibility for me as if I were his wife. I was relieved not to have had to make that choice between following Picci or my father.

We never saw Mr Manning again after that meeting and, apart from a few letters he sent, only heard of him some months later when I was contacted by the airline company in connection with a letter he had written on my behalf and which I knew nothing about. Over the following months we narrowly missed falling prey to all manner of unscrupulous lawyers looking for a quick buck. Picci, a little older and a little wiser than me, was aware of the sometimes duplicitous nature of this professional category. Every time I'd get enthusiastic about some new possibility, he'd step in to find out if the carrot was worth running after.

13

A HICCOUGH IN PROCEEDINGS

MARCH 1987 OPENED her doors on what promised to be a beautiful and prematurely warm spring, and I was sent home for a week before going in for the operation to close the colostomy. Plans had by now been made for my return to Italy, although Father felt these hopes to be optimistic as I was starkly thin and still very weak. Looking after myself would be a problem, but Picci was adamant that I return to Italy after this operation, because, morale-wise, he knew I would be better off in my own home. I couldn't wait to get back, and my heart was lighter than it had been since the beginning of this dreadful story.

Mr Lax, the surgeon, had told me that I couldn't eat for a week after surgery, and that frightened me as I was worried about falling into the trap of refusing food again. I desperately wanted my old life to pull back round me, and I imagined driving my car, symbol of an independence dear to me, and the rush of going from one company to another to teach. Work had been busy from 1985 to 1986, and I'd established some excellent contracts. I hoped that in the ensuing year I'd be able to start work again. Of course, I would have to wait until

I could walk properly, but little by little I was sure I would get there.

The day came for me to be re-admitted into hospital, and, clutching a packet of biscuits and my overnight bag, I walked into the general surgery ward. The biscuits had assumed an importance way beyond their due. They represented my re-established eating habits, and I always had one ready to nibble. I didn't undress until the evening and stayed by the lifts perched on a chair, loath to adopt the role of patient. At midnight I was told that I couldn't eat or drink any more and that I had to turn in for the night. I finally changed into my nightdress, mentally resisting the whole NHS and thus making sleep wait before it stole over me at about two o'clock.

I woke up the following morning with a sore throat and, a little concerned, asked the nurse, making light of the problem, if I could still go ahead with the operation. She assured me that there was no reason why I should not be allowed to proceed, even though in my heart of hearts I felt that I wasn't well enough to undergo any surgery. I'd built my hopes up so much, however, that I couldn't possibly have pulled out at the last minute. I went down to theatre with vague misgivings.

Things at first went well after the operation, except that my sore throat developed into a full-blown bronchial cough and I rasped up green catarrh and felt awful. A week passed, and I became progressively worse, for not only had the cold become flu but I was also getting bigger and bigger. My guts seemed to be fermenting. I frequently complained of discomfort and bloating but was told that it was all normal. I began to feel alarmed that I'd have to stay in hospital longer than I had imagined and had a feeling that something was very wrong.

Emergency staff were finally called in the day I was picked up off the floor having vomited and collapsed in the bathroom, and Mr Lax ordered immediate surgery. I was in agony and curled over myself, scarcely breathing as the pain was so bad. My urine was full of blood, and, terrified, I asked the sister of the ward if I was dying. She didn't answer but took a large syringe full of painkiller and hastily injected it into my thigh. Convinced that this might be a real emergency, I asked a nurse to bring me the phone and called Picci to say I was being taken down to theatre and that there was something wrong. I didn't know if I was going to make it this time and wanted to say something about us, about what he meant to me, but at the same time I didn't want to frighten him. He was already terribly alarmed, though, merely by the three or four words I managed to utter as I breathed out goodbye.

The operation was carried out, but I came round haemorrhaging badly and had to be taken down again for re-suturing. I was very ill once more and in the hands of people whom I felt I couldn't trust. The colostomy was back in place, and I was much worse off than I had been before I went into hospital. Over the following nights, I was full of cold fury and refused to speak to anyone, turning my face away from any contact. I had suffered a twisted colon that had perforated because of faecal matter lodged in the lower intestine, and this had provoked a nasty dose of peritonitis that was then further complicated by a probable embolism in the lung. Excruciating pain seared through my chest and my right lung filled up with liquid. I breathed with the utmost difficulty and felt as if my life was hanging by a thread. My temperature peaked at 40 and I lay propped up on cushions, consumed by the pain. A week in this place had set me back two months, and it was as if I was being punished for ever having dared challenge fate by thinking I could return to Italy and happiness. I thought of my mother who had lain dying in hospital with her bloated cancerous stomach and felt shivers of fear go through me. Two old women had already passed away in the night, and in the morning I saw the unmade beds where they had removed the dead occupants across the way from where I was lying. I was strung up to a drip pole where litres of antibiotics were draining into me. If only I could have inflicted the same cruel fate I was enduring on the hijackers. A worse punishment I couldn't think of.

My plans had been completely destroyed as far as Italy was concerned. Why was I having such bad luck? The moment I was conscious enough to use a phone, I rang Picci and managed to keep him from coming over immediately. The thought of him seeing me in so pitiful a state was too much, and I didn't want him to witness the grey blob I'd become. Three days later, however, the disappointment and despair were too much to bear alone, and on the phone in tears I told him for the first time that I couldn't take any more. For the remaining two days no one could say anything to me without me hurling accusations at them, particularly the doctors. I seethed, telling them that there was somebody somewhere who'd made a mess of me and that more care should have been taken with the surgery and treatment. I asked them why they hadn't woken up earlier to the fact that I was ill. I'd told them I had felt huge and that there had never been any peristaltic movement in my gut. They should have realised that something was wrong. I asked them why they hadn't thought to use an anti-coagulating drug to prevent an all-too-predictable embolism, for I had picked the brains of one very young doctor, asking him how he thought an embolism could have been prevented and he unwittingly furnished me with my ammunition. The answers I received to my requests did not placate me, and only the student medics stood around long enough for me to throw my shots of white anger at them. I asked the hospital staff every morning and every afternoon to let me go home. I was told that only when my temperature had subsided would they consider discharging me. I demanded to know how long they expected me to stay and was told that maybe three or four weeks would see me through the disaster. I felt that this was long enough for me to be consigned to the mortuary and vowed I'd be out of there as soon as I could make it to the lifts.

Picci in the meantime, and unbeknown to me, had sent a telex to the hospital director, accusing the doctors of having been negligent. He refused to believe that all this agony couldn't have been prevented. Whoever read his letter never replied, and he arrived on the Saturday morning, striding down the ward with the sort of look that meant he would call the police should it be necessary. I shrank into my pillows, pleased to see him but not pleased that he should see me and smell me. There was a distasteful odour of old cabbages floating round my bed due to the resurrected and leaking colostomy, and I felt terribly embarrassed that he might notice this. Perfume would never hide that kind of smell, and I resigned myself to the fact that he would see me down as he'd never seen me before. In fact, I cried from the time he came to the time he left.

He sat by my bed, having given me his presents of a pretty silver ring and bracelet, telling me that as soon as I could go home he would book my ticket for Italy. With or without the colostomy he wanted me with him and said that at least he'd be able to keep an eye on me there and look after me better than they were apparently doing in England. He tried to divert my attention by asking me a lot of technicalities about what had happened in an effort to calm me down. My stomach hurt constantly and my right lung felt as if it had been hole-punched. He promised me that the colostomy would be removed in a private clinic so that I'd never have to experience a similar environment again, and then he left, telling me he expected a call the following day and that I was to try to get some sense out of the doctors about times and future plans.

As usual, Picci gave me strength, and I immediately started pestering the doctors again about going home. I must have exasperated them with this refrain, for at the end of the following week they said that if I really wanted to, I could discharge myself. I also think that Picci's angry letter might have had something to do with my being humoured in this way and allowed home despite a high temperature. Within minutes of them giving me this go-ahead, I rang my father, who came up to the hospital and gathered up me and my belongings. The colostomy could be dealt with after a few months when I had completely recovered from this ordeal.

The new colostomy was not as cooperative or as easy to deal with as the first and I treated it with the intense contempt I really wanted to mete out to the doctors who I believed had made a mistake during the operation. I also knew, however, that orthopaedic problems such as mine could easily cause embolisms due to prolonged bed rest and, although it had not occurred during the time I was first in hospital, it was not surprising that it had happened this time. It was possible that our anger was misplaced on this occasion, but it was very difficult not to be emotional and blame others when things went wrong, especially after what we had been through.

Picci now told me to get in contact with Pan Am in London. I had vaguely been in touch with some of the employees who had come to visit me in hospital right at the beginning of October of the previous year. They had been kind and were horrified by the state I was in. One of the guys who had been in to see me was called Tom, and he worked in the ticketing department. Once out of hospital I called him and asked if he would find out about Pan Am paying for my flight to go back to Italy. He rang back almost immediately to authorise a seat on British Airways that Pan Am would finance. I was extremely grateful, as the money I had in my bank would be needed for when I was convalescing. I flew across the Channel at the beginning of May armed with colostomy bags, medicines and great joy. Before leaving, I was booked into the King Edward VII Hospital near Marylebone to have the colostomy closed on 8 June. Someone somewhere had spoken to an organisation connected to the hospital about my plight, and I learned that this anonymous benefactor was going to pay for the theatre and ward fees. Such generosity was strange yet comforting, and I decided that if I had the means later on in life, I would try to pass on such kindness.

I boarded the BA flight with some trepidation, as this was the first time I had flown after the hijack ordeal, but given that I wanted to continue living in Italy I'd have to get used to travelling by plane. The choice not to make a big thing out of flying was mine, and I made it there and then. Life was going to be hard enough, and the less I gave in to possible phobias, the better I would cope and the more I would be able to do. Explained in two short phrases, the effort required to be 'tough' might seem easy, but avoiding falling prey to anxieties and fear was a gruelling and lonely process. It was one of my better survival techniques but had its price.

Picci met me at the airport in his bouncy red Citroën 2CV. We were subdued in our greetings, as I felt wrecked after the flight. Accompanied by the tinny purr of the car, we slowly drew away from the airport in the direction of home; slowly, so that I could look at the surroundings and take in the fact that I was actually back. Picci accompanied me to my flat and handed over the keys. While opening the door I thought of the times I'd lain in hospital and dreamt of this moment. Somehow, however, the plane journey had already spent the internal fireworks of joy I'd so long anticipated, and I felt quite calm as I walked into my hall. I inspected my bathroom, bedroom, kitchen and sitting room. Everything was clean and tidy, including the windows and floors. There was food in the fridge and a little vase of flowers on the table.

Eight months is not such a great length of time, but moving from one life scenario to another was totally disorientating. Everything was at once familiar, but I felt like a serpent looking at its old shed skin. There was no substitute skin at that moment, and the feeling of vulnerability and nakedness unnerved me. It was a sensation that was to accompany me for a very long time.

14

FRERA: BACK TO REALITY

OVER THE FOLLOWING few days, I was able to move round the house more easily, but I was unable to carry anything, both hands being occupied with my crutches. Every evening, Picci came round to cook for me, bring mail and chat about his work, how I was coping and my impressions of life. This was quite an effort for him, as he lived in the centre of Milan while I was on the outskirts, and it took about 35 minutes to drive to my house. He was also very busy during the day and put in long hours at work.

From a practical point of view, it would have been easier if we lived together, but Picci had never even got as far as staying the night with me in my flat. We went away at weekends together, but he felt awkward about sleeping over during the week. Our relationship had only just got off the ground when the hijack happened, and we hadn't had time to think about living together or getting married. Now was hardly the right point to start thinking about such things, and, to be honest, I didn't feel ready to take such a step. I'm sure that Picci felt the same. There were so many problems distracting us, not least the quest for compensation.

After a brief search, I found a lady who came in to do the washing, cleaning and cook lunch for me each day. She occupied my mind to some extent in that I had to give her instructions, send her out to do the shopping and listen to stories of her family. She was company for me so I couldn't brood, and I also spent hours on the phone drawing vigour and comfort from my friends, catching up on their news.

During my absence, Picci had taken my car to the garage and had a special device put into the gear stick that made the clutch automatically depress without me having to fumble around with a numb foot and dead leg. The idea of being able to drive gave me confidence. I could be independent and begin seeing friends and students I knew from my old companies, many of whom had corresponded with my family and me over the previous months. I spent a day or so whirring round San Felice, the residential area where I lived, which was relatively free of traffic. As I was stiff from lying in hospital and still very bony, sitting in a car proved to be painful, so I put cushions under my left leg and missing buttock to serve as props and give me a bit of suspension. Soon I was off for brief jaunts, and the welcome I received from those who knew me was overwhelming. People came up to hug me with tears in their eyes, pressing my hands between theirs. Stories were told of how they had heard about the hijack, and I was asked constantly if I would be coming back to teach them. I felt wonderful after my visits and basked in their affectionate goodwill.

The second weekend I was in Italy, Picci decided to take me up to the mountains to a town called Cervinia on the Italian side of the Matterhorn, where his family had a little flat. He thought that the sun would help heal my skin and bring colour back to my cheeks, in addition to the trip giving us two days together. I must admit that I was slightly agitated about the thought of going away for the weekend, as it meant that I would have to deal with Horace in the flat. I needed to take all of the paraphernalia with me and would require lots of clean running water. Even though Picci was full of discretion and pretended that nothing was difficult, I felt strained.

This would be the first time we had slept under the same roof for nearly nine months and things were very different.

When we arrived, I couldn't help recalling our last weekend together in Cervinia before the hijack. Picci had equipped me with a pair of skis and sealskins, and we had undertaken a gruelling three-hour climb up the mountain. He was teaching me to ski the hard way, convinced that it was the quickest. I remembered the sensation of looking down onto Zermatt from the dividing crest between Italy and Switzerland, just below the pyramidal mountain, and had felt elated by the arduous climb and brisk mountain air. On our way back down, we'd slithered together for a few hundred metres while Picci had tried to get me to do the snowplough. All of a sudden I'd got the hang of it and was off on an agonisingly slow descent that seemed to last a lifetime and cost a week's worth of stiff muscles. I also remembered getting a scarlet bottom as I sunbathed naked on top of a large rock. It was sheer devilry on my part, as I knew Picci was a little strait-laced and fearful of trained binoculars, but my provocation loosened him up and I had felt full of youthful confidence. I could almost feel our sun-warmed bodies hugging together, a painful recollection.

I was straying into a difficult area and so looked out of the window to stop the thoughts. As I lay on the bed, I gazed out at the Matterhorn, a canine tooth surging up out of the wall of rock towards the sky. A plume of cloud like a volcanic wisp of smoke touched its peak. It was magnificently beautiful and momentarily halted the video clip in my mind.

The light was fading and Picci came into the bedroom carrying a glass of wine for me. We toasted each other and our reunion. Normally restrained in any demonstrations of love, or deep confession, for some reason we now held each other's gaze. His eyes locked into my private world. The pain he saw, I saw, was profound. It was a moment of frightening self-abandon that could have alienated us from one another in its intensity. I felt like a soldier looking into the eyes of my enemy, fearful of a negative reaction. No warm embrace buffeted our immense solitude. It was the moment when we faced the knowledge of what we had both lost, of what we had both been through, of the unpredictable and frightening future and the infinitely painful past. He took my hand and his eyes filled with tears. I was shocked by the sheer depth of whatever it was we'd experienced and was consequently speechless. Then, suddenly, the moment was over, and, abruptly, he stood up and went to prepare supper in the kitchen. No words had been spoken and neither of us could have said anything to make things better. We were together in the aftermath of the hijack, yet at the same time terribly alone. Only time could heal all our troubles and in what way we could not even begin to guess. That made us afraid.

After our return to Milan, the weather, which had for the most part been chilly and rainy throughout May, at last began to improve, and I asked to go to Frera. After the weekend in Cervinia, which had gone reasonably well apart from a problem with Horace who didn't like changes in altitudes and was inordinately sensitive to cold temperatures, Picci had promised me that the moment the weather got better he would drive me to the place of my dreams.

It was a glorious Saturday. Bright clean air with a gentle breeze invited the whole of Milan to the countryside, so, of course, we weren't the only ones on the road. Spring was pushing forth in a single momentum of beautiful new green leaves, flowers, branches and emerald grass. Lake Como was a calm mirror with fleecy clouds and mountain peaks reflecting off its surface. We wound our way into the Valtellina valley following the curling lakeside road, which made for an enchanting trip but caused me considerable pain in my hip joint. I tucked my hand under my thigh, trying to ease the pressure there and the heavy nerve-racking pain. I was unable to sit in any position where I didn't feel that penetrating ache.

At this point, no one had really talked to me about my future and nothing had been said as yet about the possibilities of my never walking again without crutches. Professor Jones had warned me that the fracture might not heal, but he had said that there were alternative treatments available. Despite the pain I was in, I really believed it was all just a question of time.

As we approached the S-bend into Aprica, we dipped off to the right down a little slipway that ducked down into a fairy-tale glen full of horse chestnut trees and lush grassy banks. We were diverging into Val Belviso, valley of the lovely face, a narrow cleft off the Aprican Pass. This was the beginning of my dream. I loved this prelude and feasted on all that surrounded me. The car groaned slowly up the mountain road, enabling me to take in the vibrant spring colours. We crossed the little bridge. Ah, how good life could be and how full of joy. The sun had come out for me and was chasing away the sadness that had been my shadowy companion for so long. I was literally touched by the sun as we opened up the car roof, and I could smell the sparkling air and sweetly perfumed ferns. The sky was very blue, and we moved into the open valley where fields full of mountain flowers gave off their delicate perfume.

Mrs Bianchi, the owner of a hostelry in the first little village, was busy that day preparing *pizzoccheri* for her customers. Pizzoccheri was the regional dish of pasta made from their local wholewheat flour, with chopped greens and mountain cheese mixed all together and then drowned in fried garlic butter.

We drove past the little church and finally arrived at the small frescoed sanctuary where the outstretched arms of the Madonna welcomed all who turned left into the parking space in front of the 'Rifugio Caterina'. They had heard us arrive, and out of the kitchen came Elizabetta, Caterina's daughter-in-law. She was half-smiling, but her eyes were large and questioning. I got out of the car and walked towards her, beaming and overcome with happiness at being back in my other world. She was overcome with shock at the change in my appearance but quickly recovered herself and with great warmth and motherliness guided me into the kitchen for it was lunchtime.

Nonna Caterina was trapped at the end of the huge kitchen table cutting up a mountain of vegetables. The moment I appeared, her hands flew up in angry joy. She was 76 and very much an Italian mamma: broad and stocky, with only a couple of front teeth left and her hair pulled back into a neat bun. She squeezed her large stomach round the edge of the table and, taking my hands in hers, kissed me twice. She too searched my face and tutted at the pale apparition before her. With her half index finger – legend has it that she'd amputated it herself after a viper's bite – she admonished Picci: 'I've always said you should stay here in Frera for the summer instead of gadding about the world. I don't know why you young people have to go catching aeroplanes. Frera's lovely. What's wrong with having your holidays here with us?' I had problems understanding her as she could only speak the local dialect and instead of listening I watched her spraying as she expostulated. Her vast blue pinny stretched and heaved as she talked, orchestrating her speech with waving arms.

Massimo, thin and a little stooped, came through the doorway. Shy and softly spoken, he put his arm round Picci's shoulders and shook his hand, saying, 'Well, you've finally brought her back.' He bade me welcome and opened a bottle of Inferno, the local sharp red wine. This was Caterina's son, and Elizabetta's husband. His children adored him and he them. Greta, his daughter, at 15 was already mature with lovely eyes and a vivacious bright face. Her long dark hair was swept back so that she could serve at table in the evenings and at weekends. She was plump and had dimples when she smiled, and her hands were adorned with gold and silver rings, her wrists with bangles and she wore large hoop earrings. She was a mountain gypsy with her adornments, long skirts and proud carriage. She ran back and forth to the kitchen on busy weekends, from one group of tables to another serving customers, a strong country wench who gave as good as she got.

Diego, Elizabetta's little boy and Greta's younger brother, was four years old when I first met him and possessed of a wild, free, woodland spirit. His lively black eyes were as quick as his intelligent curiosity. Until the age of nine, his black hair was cut in a long bob with a fringe that nearly covered his face. He was short and stocky, with a strong neck and shoulders, taking after his mother. He was healthy and vibrant, and always rather grubby, as he lived more in the woods behind the kitchen than in his own house. For four months of the year with no school to confine him, he roamed Val Belviso, fishing, going up the mountains with the gamekeepers, or on hunting trips early in the morning in autumn. His was a charmed life and one I gently envied. That summer, we became friends, and a strange but enchanting relationship developed as he became my little guard and companion.

At the weekends, Diego used to get up very late, having spent the previous evening in the company of regulars, usually 'the fishermen' who came to eat at the inn. He slept in his parents' large bed in one of the stone outhouses. The toilet was up by the pigsties near the tumultuous stream behind the kitchen and there was no bathroom. Washing was done outside in a sink with gallons of gushing icy water. Hot water was used for washing hair only, because it had to be heated on the range and took ages to boil. That magical Saturday morning, Diego came in through the door, looked at me without registering who I was and nudged past everyone to get to his seat ready for lunch. I was just one of many who came into the kitchen to eat. Greta was due back any minute and the water was boiling ready for the pasta 'to be thrown'. She arrived, dumping her colossal schoolbag on the kitchen floor, and greeted me warmly as her mother served up lunch. As conversation flowed, I noticed that it dawned on Diego who I actually was. From that moment on his eyes were two shiny black pebbles trained on every aspect of my person. He didn't say a word throughout lunch, but I could feel him studying me and wanting to 'have a go' on my crutches, just like all the children I was to meet.

The lunch was sumptuous: pasta mixed with mountains of parmesan cheese, followed by roast pheasant, a present from a gamekeeper, salad from their orchard and the inevitable bowls of sharp cherries from the tree in front of the inn. Lunch with the family was held in the outhouse kitchen, a smoky and very rustic building with pots and pans that hung in a clattering metallic assortment from the beams. The cooking range was prehistoric, but in good working order, with a vast black surface that gave off blasts of heat. There was a log fire at one end of the room and the kitchen sink at the other, and it could sit 15 happily enough. This meal was a living dream for me as I listened to cowbells floating in on the breeze from faraway pastures. Diego's tractor noises lulled me to sleep later, and I was infinitely happy and grasped every second of physical well-being that I was offered.

While I was outside, Picci and Elizabetta talked and agreed that I was to spend the summer months, July, August and September, with the family at Frera, so that I could completely convalesce away from Milan. As soon as the colostomy had been closed, I was to come directly to their inn. Picci took me up to see the chalet before we left and I felt a sense of peace flowing through me. Except for the sound of the stream running below and the birds, the silence surrounding the house was soothing to my heart, and I was quiet as we drove back to Milan, calmer than I had been for many months, for this was how I'd envisaged my return to normal life.

While in Italy during this first stay, I went to see the orthopaedic surgeon in Milan who had looked after Picci on his return from Karachi. After looking at the X-rays, he was brusque and blunt. To begin with, he told me that, as far as he could see, the bones were not uniting and that this was due to the interruption of the blood supply. Many of the veins had been damaged in the grenade blast. The second piece of bad news was that he considered a hip replacement to be foolhardy given the fact that I had no gluteal muscles to hold the joint in place, and therefore in all likelihood it would dislocate. He was sure that at this stage the hip area was full of bacterial pockets around the shrapnel and that, although things were quietening down, an operation could well cause a new outbreak of infection. His advice was to do nothing except remove the dead head of the femur. I was to follow a programme of intense physiotherapy and accept, at least for a few years, the situation of walking with crutches.

I was stunned. This was the first time someone had actually come clean about the future, and I found it shocking. My vision veiled over with tears as I struggled for control, not wanting to accept that what he said might be true. Both Picci and I had imagined different news, and the surgeon was surprised by such a strong reaction on my part, as he was quite convinced that I had already been apprised of my medical condition, including the prognosis. I realised, however, that I had ignored subtle hints over the last few medical visits regarding my walking possibilities, as they had not been what I wanted to hear. Undeniably, his 'cruelty' was kindness in the long run, as, unable to escape from such a clear prediction, I started to review my prospects in a different way, assimilating the idea that I might always need crutches to walk in the future.

15

COLOSTOMY CLOSED

PICCI WAS TENSE one morning at the end of my stay as he prepared himself for an interview with lawyers. He'd been given their names from a friend of ours who worked in the shipping industry in Genoa. I couldn't wait for this meeting to be over so that we could get out into the sunshine and have lunch somewhere by the sea. I wanted laughter, light and to be with Picci without worries, not cooped up with stuffy people to whom we'd have to pose agonising questions in order to ascertain their interest in our case and their ability to resolve our problems.

The meeting took place at the firm's offices, and the two lawyers who came into the library were of middle age, subdued and professionally leagues ahead of those in Britain we had contacted. What documents we had – newspaper cuttings and copies of the tickets – had been sent to them a few days previously so that they would have time to think about the problem before we arrived. The crux of the matter seemed to be whether there were any grounds on which we could sue the airline company for negligence. From newspaper articles and our memory of what we had seen as we escaped from the plane, various issues arose – among them the fact that the cockpit crew had completely abandoned the aircraft and that the security measures in place had clearly been insufficient.

The actual juridical problem of suing in the States proved to be something that needed a great deal of consideration. An American colleague with whom they often worked had pointed out that a judge in the US, depending on the state, might well refuse even to try the case, claiming that jurisdiction depended on where we'd bought the ticket. Of course, the right to sue would inevitably also be aggressively contested by Pan Am.

They swiftly moved on to the question of fees. If the case went to court in America, led by their American counterpart, there would be a contingency fee contract. If we lost the case, there would be no fees to pay and I wouldn't owe anyone a penny. Their part in all this would obviously come out of the contingency percentage agreed upon with the American lawyer. The slow measured behaviour of these professionals, who weren't immediately selling dreams and who were themselves not entirely sure they had a good case, was the most convincing aspect of the entire interview and we left feeling a little more knowledgeable. Unfortunately, however, this firm would later refuse to take us on as they felt there was insufficient evidence to prove that Pan Am had acted negligently.

We closed the lift doors behind us and the whole of the morning was wiped clear from my mind as we set off to a restaurant. I should have realised that our problems had hardly begun and that the road was going to be long and torturous. Enjoying a Ligurian seafood lunch was hardly going to sort out my financial future, although I would feel better for an hour or so. I would not always want to count on Picci's generosity, however much he loved me. I would have to try to think about my long-term future, instead of short-term immediate happiness, even if doing this was going to prove very heavy going.

Slipping back into an existence was not easy. Nights were difficult. I was alone in my flat, happy to be back in Italy but frightened by nightmares that were often of total destruction of places I knew, and

I was dismayed at the insomnia that kept me awake until the small hours. Solitude brought out the spectres of my chaotic inner state, so often suffocated and ignored during the day. All memories of the hijack and initial hospitalisation came out to torture me during the night and tears would flow for long periods. I would fall asleep in exhaustion at about four o'clock in the morning without feeling relief. There seemed to be no end to my distress.

Daylight came and the ghosts withdrew, letting in fragile contentment and life. I neither spoke about my nightly afflictions nor dwelt on them during the day. Picci gave me great moral support, and I instinctively felt it dangerous to expect him to listen to me in my attempts to process what had happened to me. I could not speak about the hijack and the fears for our future that I had. More than anything else, I wanted our relationship to survive, and I needed to believe in something that was without messy complication. I kept my secrets close to my chest and wore a different face during the day.

When I arrived back at my father's house in England, everyone agreed that Italy had done me a lot of good. The fact that I felt refreshed and looked much healthier with a tan somehow made the imminent closure of the colostomy seem less of a trial than I expected it to be and, in fact, the operation went very well indeed and was performed by the same surgeon as before but in the private King Edward VII Hospital. I returned to Milan with a clean tummy, and from then on forgot that I'd actually ever had a colostomy.

16

CONVALESCENCE

THE EVENING I returned home for good, Picci kissed me. It was brief and passionate, and very much an unspoken declaration that we might pick up where we'd left off. I felt overwhelmed, for it had been almost a year since we'd had physical contact. Nothing further developed, but I imagined the kiss to be a sign that things would progress, and I went to bed dizzy with happiness. Perhaps there were to be none of the problems that I had imagined.

Within a week, Picci had driven me up to Frera with my suitcase full of summer clothes, books, paper and paints. He had provided me with money, as I still hadn't started any form of work, and I had my car, which would give me freedom to go to Aprica once I was stronger. Picci's flat was one out of nine in the large chalet-style building that was situated in the shade of the vast dam his father had engineered in the late 1950s. The building was square with yellow ochre walls and green shutters, about a kilometre up the mountain track that twisted and curved away from 'Rifugio Caterina'. It had been the workers' canteen and a dormitory for those visiting the dam site but had been converted into flats and sold off in piecemeal fashion to those families who had been particularly involved with the construction of the dam. They were considered holiday homes and could only be used in the summer, as in winter the water pipes leading from the dam inevitably froze over.

The chalet stood on a plateau and was a regular foraging area for foxes, badgers and deer during the small hours. Cars crept into the parking area in the pre-dawn gloom, unloading mountain walkers in the summer looking for a quiet day out, and noisy local mushroom pickers who swarmed into the valley in the autumn. The holiday homes were full of ageing widows who had the complete run of the place in July and August. Gossip was rife and in the years to come we were always tempted to do something scandalous just to give them something to talk about. That summer there was no need, for what had happened to me was more than enough to keep them going for the next few years, let alone a couple of months. Unfortunately, their chat floated directly up from the 'parlour', a communal terrace under our third-floor window. It was a suntrap with a tree conveniently placed, providing shade where Mrs P., the alpha widow, had first refusal. The parlour could easily accommodate about seven or eight people on deckchairs, chaise longues or the garden bench. Six small grandchildren could play happily at the end of the parlour, spilling over, if they needed space, behind the back of the house. A couple of dogs could lie down on the green slope of garden further on down and the whole place usually became extremely animated in the late afternoon when the ladies descended from their abodes with much calling and door banging to arrange themselves in a circle with their knitting and needlework.

Once they started up, they sounded like a flock of crows. The rise and fall of their comments, punctuated by often repeated 'really?', 'well I never' and 'is that so?' drove me crazy, especially when I was trying to read a good book with the windows open. They took it in turns to make espresso coffee, and discussions on grandchildren, so and so's wife, the quantity of mushrooms that year, the humidity or terrible cold would weave back and forth to the strain of some music that an irate occupant of the chalet had put on in an effort to drown out the noise. Afternoons were always like that at Frera, and Picci and I usually caught the tail end as we came back from our wanderings. Inevitably we would be cross-examined about where we'd been and what we'd collected in our rucksacks. Blueberries or wild strawberries, or even the Porcino mushroom? All was scrutinised, picked up and judged, including us.

Despite Picci's abhorrence of others' curiosity and talk, he felt it would be good for me to have a little company. He wanted me to use the chalet flat during the day, where I could wash and do anything I needed away from Diego's family, and during the evening and night he wanted me to be down at the inn so that there was always someone immediately nearby should I need help. With this in mind and in agreement with Elizabetta, he took me round his chalet, and gave me instructions on how to light the cooker, use the stereo and lock up, all simple things which suddenly needed explaining, despite the fact that I knew the place quite well. I wasn't to use the bath unless Diego was outside the door, ready to run down the road for help should I slip or fall, and he was given the responsible task of being my little helpmate during the day.

Down at the inn, Greta and I slept in the bedroom next to Nonna Caterina, and I had to get used to her stertorous snoring that almost made the bed vibrate. Greta no longer noticed it and fell into profound slumber the moment her head touched the pillow. I didn't always sleep soundly during that period, but the sadness that tried to linger in my head didn't get much of a look in next to the snoring.

Picci slept in the chalet when he came up at the weekends but initially insisted that I stay down with the family, and I felt a little forlorn far away from him that first weekend. I felt even sadder as he waved goodbye to me on his return journey to Milan, where he had to get back to work. All I had to do was rest, sleep and eat meat, fruit, pasta and cheese until I could eat no more, for he had given strict instructions to Elizabetta that I was to be well fed.

Down at the inn, everyone was obsessed with weight. Along with the pigs, I was weighed regularly to see how much I was gaining. I'm not sure which of us ate more, the pigs or me. I was given gargantuan quantities of dairy produce, namely the rich mountain butter that Mario, one of the local farmers, brought down on his piebald pony. Meat was fried in panfuls of the stuff and it was lavished on rolls with home-made jam from the orchard fruits. Heaps of pasta with fistfuls of Parmesan cheese were passed down the kitchen table to me, all eyes quietly on my mouth and plate, and I was questioned as to why I hadn't eaten if anything was left. I must have packed about 4,000 calories away each meal, and I felt energy coming back to me daily. My hair, which I'd cut short to get rid of the dryness and lack of shine, grew back in glossy dark curls. My eyes, too, became brighter and colour was back in my skin. I watched this progress in the mirror each day while Greta rubbed cellulite-diminishing creams into her legs.

Friday was weighing day, when Greta and I would go to Aprica, hazarding the journey down the narrow and busy mountain road. It was rather scary because there was really only room for one car and the descending traffic had to make way for the ascending vehicles. The car was not particularly responsive to commands on such an incline and before the season was through I'd mashed the clutch as I jerked and shuddered into the grassy lay-bys, dutifully respecting the mountain code of conduct. I spent most of the downward journey leaning on the horn, hoping that whoever was round the corner would think fast and pull into a lay-by so that I didn't have to back up the mountain, risking our lives and a total breakdown.

Once down in the little village, we stopped off at the chemist's and ceremoniously weighed ourselves: Greta aching for the arrow to go backwards after great dietary sacrifice while I urged it forwards after a week of stuffing my face. For consolation, we then went and bought ourselves large ice creams to make up for the disappointment, as for the first month or so Greta lost not one ounce and I didn't put on any weight. Halfway through my convalescence, I suddenly tilted the scales and over the following weeks proceeded to fatten up by a kilo a week. Greta struggled to lose her excess body fluids, for she was convinced that it was all water retention, but she was a large-boned girl and fond of her food. I loved our jaunts together, revelling in the fact that I drove and was the one 'in charge'. She was fine company, telling me stories about awful teachers, her friends and the boys she had fallen in love with. In many ways she was a lot older than her years and knew how to treat me, even when I cried for no reason at all other than because I was happy to have come out of the dark tunnel.

I walked with difficulty but set myself goals every day, stretching my limit in some small way. I had to improve even if the improvement was scarcely noticeable. Down in the town of Aprica, many of the people there knew who I was and what had happened to me. Most of Greta's extended family lived there, and aunts and uncles, relatives and friends were well aware of their guest up in Frera. People greeted us and asked after my well-being, pleased to see me getting better. I became particularly attached to Zio Ernesto, Nonna Caterina's brother, whose daytime hangout was the bench outside the post office. He used to be the gamekeeper up in the valley and was one of nature's guardian angels. Slightly younger than his sister, he had a walnut-coloured face from years of sun, with twinkly creased-up eyes. He was always smiling. He was broad and rather stout, always impeccably dressed in his green jerkin, flannel checked shirt and tweed jacket even in the height of a hot summer. He looked very much the retired countryman with his brown woollen tie. His felt hat rarely left his shiny pate unless he was doing an imitation of a male woodcock beating its wings in a courtship dance. Then the hat was removed and with rapid concertina-like movements between both hands he made a flapping noise that sounded just like the beating of wings. This sound, he maintained, could attract a female woodcock and had once caught a poacher, who, thinking that he had tracked down a male bird, found himself pointing the barrel of a rifle at a man banging his hat. Ernesto nabbed his poacher but had risked a pellet spray in his face all the same. Marvellous stories such as this one filled Saturday and Sunday evenings at the inn.

On my first Wednesday evening in Frera, I heard the deep throb of a motorbike at about 8 p.m. but thought nothing of it, as I was not expecting anyone in particular. When Picci rounded the corner carrying his crash helmet, I was delighted. He pretended that coming to see me was a run-of-the-mill occurrence, and to show me that it was nothing special, he talked to Elizabetta for most of the time, no doubt to ask her how I was getting on. He then went to bed early that night, as Milan was three hours away and he had to be up at dawn to get to work before his employees arrived. His gesture of coming to see me midweek meant a lot to me, however, as I knew how tired he was at the end of the day. From then on he arrived every Wednesday.

Over time, he noted my physical improvement and watched with not a little envy how Diego accompanied me everywhere like some personal little bodyguard. Up until then, Picci had been his favourite, but I was news and had the special attraction of crutches. When I went for my morning wash, he accompanied me up the hill in the car. We spent afternoons painting and drawing together with his friends. He was inordinately proud of his position in my life and never stopped telling guests that he was looking after me.

The first time I walked up the hill to the flat with Diego, I got to the top of the kilometre stretch after a two-hour hike, shaking and wet with perspiration. I stood in the middle of the plateau, triumphant that I'd made it. Diego, bored by the time it had taken me to get there, had rushed off to see who was in the house. I leant on my crutches catching my breath. My hip hurt, beating out its discomfort, and my fingers had gone numb in both hands because of the pressure on my median nerve from leaning on the handles. My shoulders and pectoral muscles felt as if they'd dragged an elephant up the hill, and the sciatic nerve sent electric shock tremors that made my leg twitch, but I was still very pleased with myself. I was glad to have made that climb even though it made me realise how long the recovery process was going to take and how it was going to depend solely on my own efforts. No one could strengthen my muscles or rebuild my body except myself and it was going to take a lot of energy and determination, particularly in the face of my own feelings about my physical appearance.

July sped by and the blue skies turned white and weary, loaded by a mugginess that took your breath away. Picci struggled through sticky city days that were particularly exhausting as orders flooded in. It was his busy month, and he had to meet the summer deadlines.

That August I went through much mental anguish. Our first embrace on my return had not brought about further intimacy, and, shaky as I was about the way my body looked, I found this lack of closeness almost unbearable given that my appreciation of Picci had grown enormously and I was physically much more expressive than he was. I lived in hope and told myself to be patient, as I was already very lucky to have someone like him by my side. So I resisted, lying awake at night blinking away my tears. When I could hold back no more, I tiptoed out of the flat and sat on the balcony looking up at the sky, seeking oblivion in the darkness around me. Breathing deeply helped, and the natural surroundings cushioned my bruised ego and frustrated desire.

Picci was my staunch supporter, but we trod lightly around the consequences of the hijack. The future, too, was a question mark and, as such, increased a growing sense of insecurity in me. There were so many practical problems to address in order for me to reclaim life that Picci and I as a couple were left little time to become true loves once again.

We often discussed the need to get a court case started before it was too late, but were still unsure of which direction to go in. We were in touch with the firm of lawyers who were dealing with the Townsend-Thoresen disaster and the King's Cross fire, who had successfully taken aviation cases to court. They had at first been interested in our claim, but as they began to investigate the American possibilities and British verdicts in similar situations, they realised that in neither country were we likely to win our case.

At the end of that July, a Mr Richards from the company wrote a full and clear letter explaining why they were unable to take us on as their clients, suggesting at the same time that we try suing in Italy. He wrote that our chances could be quite good given the fact that Italy, if he remembered rightly, had not been a signatory to the Warsaw Convention, meaning that the blurb on the back of the tickets meant nothing at the time of purchase. This was news indeed and was worth pursuing. We also felt grateful that this legal firm had behaved properly in refusing to deal with our case, giving us detailed reasons why.

Mr Manning had sent a couple of letters that I left unanswered. Then, at the end of July, he wrote two letters in quick succession, underlining the fact that in certain states in the US the statute of limitations was only one year and we were running out of time. At that point, exasperated by his ungrammatical letters urging me to speak to his American colleague, I wrote to him asking him to get in touch with Mr Richards, so that they could put him in the picture with regard to suing in the States.

He did so and then promptly sent off another flurry of correspondence that invited me to speak to his colleague who would be citing the airline in California, where it was much more likely that a judge would hear our case. Confused by contradictory advice, I suggested to Picci that we try to phone Mr Manning from Aprica one afternoon so that we could sort out once and for all the question of America. The following morning, therefore, we phoned from a call box and were unable to get through. After three or four tries, we gave up, feeling that there was something not quite right going on. Fate had played its part and Mr Manning dropped out of our existence once again. Picci was suspicious of anyone going to so much trouble to hook us onto their line.

We thought about the lawyers from Genoa once again, but they had already been quite firm in their refusal to take on our case. We could have returned to them with this new approach regarding the Warsaw Convention, but Genoa was a long way from Milan and we felt that we had to find someone who was truly expert in the field of aviation law.

At that stage we began seriously to consider whether we actually needed any lawyers, at least for the first contact with Pan Am. It was fairly apparent that I would be needing further surgery of some description – my buttock was missing soft tissue, my sciatic nerve was half working and, of course, there was the orthopaedic problem that was still undefined as far as future treatment was concerned – and Picci wanted to make sure that I got the best medical care available. I didn't want to automatically go back to the surgeons who had hitherto operated on me because I didn't know whether I was in the best hands. Perhaps I could find someone better or a team of specialists who might consider my injuries in their totality. Each surgeon had previously operated on his bit without a round-table consultation with everyone involved. It would be great to discuss all the treatment I needed simultaneously to work out a cohesive plan.

Picci began to think about approaching Pan Am directly to see what kind of response we could get. The idea grew. Why not ask the airline company to find a specialist team and assist me in whatever needed to be done for as total a recovery as possible? It would be in their best interests to help me walk again. We felt that by involving Pan Am, whose reputation was at stake, my chances of recovery were greatly increased. Going it alone, I could easily fall into the hands of someone who might not be up to the difficulties my case presented. I was not as convinced as Picci that a large corporate company would respond favourably to a request that was not solely financial. But it was a first step. So we wrote a firm letter to the legal adviser of Pan Am, asking for their help in finding specialists in firearms injuries. I was not necessarily abandoning the expertise of those who had treated me plastically and orthopaedically so far, but our letter would at least bring my state of health to the attention of the airline. We posted the letter from Aprica and hoped for the best.

How strange it was that it hadn't occurred to either of us to write directly to Pan Am first. Why had we immediately thought of putting things into the hands of lawyers when it was so simple to write a letter? But our new line of approach by no means meant that we shelved other projects. Indeed, our next step was to find an Italian lawyer who over the following year would file suit in the Italian courts. We were both much relieved at the prospect of dealing with someone on home ground: Picci, because he could get on the phone and talk without an interpreter, and me, because I wouldn't have to be the interpreter.

At the end of August, there were terrible floods and landslides down the whole of the Valtellina, and for three days the valley of Frera was cut off until the bulldozers came up the mountain to remove the sludge and earth and fallen trees. The day of 4 September dawned and I felt a strange lethargy grow within me. I didn't consciously think of it as being the day before the anniversary of the hijack but somewhere in my psyche I must have been aware, as I was reluctant for the next day to dawn. I remember waking up on the morning of the 5th with a strangely detached feeling and the sensation of everything moving in slow motion. It was only in the evening that I realised what date we had passed through and, turning to Picci, asked him how his day had been. His reply was a slow smile, and he simply said, 'At least we're here to tell the tale.'

At the end of the holiday, I had gained ten kilos and was nearly back to an acceptable weight. I decided to stay on at Frera for another month, however, and Picci came to collect me at the beginning of October. I was a great deal better and a lot happier, itching to get back to my working life. But before I could do that I had to fly back to England to see my orthopaedic surgeon.

17

POLITICIANS

ONCE AGAIN I contacted the Pan Am offices in London and in particular Tom in the ticketing department, who had booked my flight with British Airways. This time I put in a formal request to Pan Am asking them to pay my fares to and from England when I had to see surgeons and specialists, and after some hesitation it was granted. I was deeply thankful not to have to ask Picci to subsidise me any more. I was still waiting for a reply to the letter I had written to Pan Am that summer, requesting their help in finding a team of medical specialists who could help me walk again.

Professor Jones was his usual quiet self, giving me only a minimal understanding of my future prospects. This time he did indicate that the hip didn't seem to be mending, although he couldn't write off the situation there and then. He mentioned bone grafting from the other hip should the fractured femur need some help, but we had to wait and see otherwise we'd never be sure that the situation had been investigated as far as possible. He asked me to come back in March of the following year so that he could reassess the situation and make a definite decision about what to do, but he, too, warned me that I might have to start trying to accept my condition as something I could do little about. I didn't tell him of my visit to the orthopaedic surgeon in Milan, nor did I tell him I was looking for second opinions via Pan Am, as I thought it could possibly alienate him from me and offend him.

I enjoyed my stay in England, but could feel a certain tension within me. My family, happy with my progress, found that I was not as serene as they would have liked me to be. I had explained nothing of the legal non-progress we were making and the frustration it was causing, and they tried to infuse me with their own brand of optimism concerning my life in general, repeatedly assuring me that once I had turned the corner of 1987 I would be able to put the hijack and its miserable consequences – physical, financial and emotional – behind me. I was unable to determine on what basis they could be so confident that life would get better and could only conclude that blanket positivism was easier for them. But it depressed me when people spoke in this way, as I felt effectively silenced by their understandable wish for me to be cheerful and 'all better'.

The exception to all of this was Bibi, and I visited her the moment I was free from appointments. Bibi, or Biba as she is variously known to her nieces and nephews, was on a permanent voyage of self-discovery, lending her sympathetic ear to those who wanted to relieve their burdened lives by talking. Her quest for self-enlightenment meant that she was always involved in some kind of group, whether it be connected with the church – Catholic or Church of England, to her it didn't matter – or a Jungian reading circle. She had dozens of books written by psychologists and religious personalities in her house and was interested in anything that gave her a better handle on human nature. She was positive in the face of adversity, giving support and, most important of all, practical help wherever she could, and she was tolerant and understanding of many different kinds of people, aware that none of us is perfect. It was she who came up with the idea of writing to politicians for some kind of help and compensation. I had kept only her up to date on the difficulties of finding a lawyer who knew what he was talking about and she, protective and scandalised by the fact that I wouldn't automatically be paid an adequate compensation, began thinking of ways she could help. I found her non-judgemental support extremely useful, and it gave me the chance to speak about things that I would normally have kept to myself.

She explained how some weeks previously she had ordered the whole family to write to their local Members of Parliament regarding the hijacking. They were to ask about organisations offering assistance to someone in my situation and whether they knew of a trust fund for victims of terrorism or had suggestions about how I might obtain compensation. Her questions were practical and required simple answers. The replies had started to come in, but many of them proved to be utterly useless. The most humane, helpful and sincere was that written by David Owen. He actually wrote to Pan Am to ask them what they were doing concerning my health and compensation. Most of the MPs approached turned to the Foreign Secretary for advice, and he passed on the letters to Lord Brabazon of Tara, the Minister of Aviation and Shipping, who must have had an avalanche of mail from my family, too. He gave a diplomatic response, probably sick and tired of being in the centre of a tornado, citing the Warsaw Convention and the limitations it imposed. We were, of course, already very familiar with its stipulations and seemed to be getting nowhere. He put the blame for such a low limit of compensation fairly and squarely on the US Senate and, while he was right to a certain extent, that didn't help me. As to the suggestion put forward by my aunt to set up a fund for victims of terrorism, he felt that this was a problem for the Home Secretary.

Nigel Lawson, Jack Ashley, Norman Tebbit, Sir Geoffrey Howe, John Patten and many lesser-known names were among those included on the political correspondence rounds. Their letters expressed great sympathy for my situation but failed to provide any practical advice. My case highlighted many ethical problems. Problems such as adequate compensation for victims of terrorism abroad – who so often become political pawns – cried out for government participation and interest. It also transpired that I was not eligible for compensation from the Criminal Injuries Compensation scheme either. A letter from the Right Honourable John Morris QC MP indicated that I would have been given compensation had the injuries been sustained as a result of a criminal act on home soil, or on a British vessel abroad, but not on a US plane. Norman Tebbit felt that it was unrealistic to expect the British Government to take responsibility for matters quite outside its control or jurisdiction. He suggested I pursue the case with American lawyers in the courts of the US, but we had already tried that avenue. Mr Roger Sims, the MP for Bromley, wrote to my uncle saying that there was no international fund I could turn to for compensation and in the circumstances there were no further steps that he could suggest.

My aunt posted off another volley of letters following up on some of the suggestions she'd received, and she was sent a letter from the US Senate. They explained that the Montreal Protocols, which among other things included agreements pertaining to levels of financial liability, were in the process of being submitted for ratification, which meant that the limit of airline liability would be raised. Even if they had been passed at that time, however, it would have been too late for me to benefit. I am also sure that the limit of liability would never have even remotely reached the level of compensation I felt proportionate to the injuries I'd received. It was all one great frustrating maze with seemingly no exit.

Before I left for Italy again, Bibi asked me if she could take my story to the media, as she felt that I might get a reply from Pan Am if the TV or radio got hold of the injustices that were going on. At that time, though, I was reluctant and wanted to write to the airline company again before going public. I didn't want to cause friction or hear them refuse my request because I'd talked about the problems on air.

I arrived home to a fermenting Picci, keen on action, for in my absence he had opened a letter that we'd finally been sent from Pan

Am's insurance company. They asked me for clarification, as they were perplexed about who was representing me. Apparently a Mr Manning from England had written a rather confusing letter to them saying that he represented Miss Catherine Hill. Was this true and would I please inform them what the situation was. I couldn't believe the audacity of this man, who had offered us no practical advice and never been encouraged to act as our lawyer. The next day I sent off a terse letter to Mr Manning requesting that he desist from further correspondence on my behalf and stating clearly that I did not want him to provide legal representation. Over the following week I dispatched another letter clearing up the confusion with the insurers of Pan Am and repeating the same request I'd made concerning my medical treatment. They had probably already received the same letter, forwarded on from Pan Am, but I had to address them on the matter and be sure they didn't ignore my request.

I waited a month or so for a reply, which finally arrived in the form of a standard letter in the middle of September.

> An examination of your airline coupon discloses international travel and as such, the provisions of an international treaty known as the Hague Protocol are applicable . . . Pan Am's responsibility is limited to $20,000 based on provable damages . . . After having carefully reviewed all the information and documentation which has been provided to us in connection with the injuries you sustained as a result of this most unfortunate incident, we are prepared to recommend a settlement for the limit of liability under the Hague Protocol, to wit $20,000. Should you find this offer acceptable . . .

From the moment I received this missive, the green light flashed for an all-out telltale story on Pan Am. I ran off a sharp reply to the tune that I had not asked for financial compensation but for help in physically getting better and walking again without the use of crutches. Months passed and I received no reply. I sent a telex to Pan

Am to remind them that I'd written. Finally, in December of 1987, I got a response, which stated that US Aviation (the insurance company) were acting on behalf of Pan Am, so Pan Am's position regarding my request was the same as that of the insurance company. They wished me all the best and signed off.

It was depressing to receive such a dismissive and cool letter when the request had been of a humanitarian nature. Indeed, I couldn't understand why I hadn't been taken seriously. During my hospitalisation, Pan Am employees had visited me from their London offices and knew how long I'd been bedridden. Following the various phases of my recovery, they were pleased when I had at last flown back to Italy. There were some lovely people in the company, and I remained perplexed by the decisions taken at the top. What could we do to make Pan Am listen? How could we get their attention? Although drastic, the media now seemed to be the only option open. There was potential for an embarrassing exposé and I trembled at the thought of humiliating a company as big as Pan Am. The problem was who to get in touch with, how to tell the story and where – in Britain or Italy? Picci felt that the timing might just be too early. He asked me to wait a little longer so that we could get the case filed in court.

It was now spring of 1988. Finding the right lawyer was an undertaking of no small proportions, as behind the smart suits and pensive expressions were all levels of expertise and a variety of hidden agendas. There were also very few aviation experts, although nearly all the men – for we encountered few women in our trawl of the legal profession – were willing to act on our behalf and 'have a go', regardless of their particular speciality. Picci was convinced that we had to get an expert on aviation law, but neither of us had any professional connections whatsoever. Lawyers are not allowed to advertise in Italy, so there was no information available regarding their fields of interest.

Finally, after many dead ends, Picci managed to organise a meeting with the president of the Law Society. He had had to make countless phone calls to the secretary until someone must have realised how desperate we actually were. From that interview, an appointment was set up for us to speak to the president of the Airport Association, who would without doubt know an expert. He duly introduced us to this expert, a lawyer called Mr Napolitani, and we were to meet up in May on my return from Stanmore Hospital, when he would come up from Rome to talk to us about the case.

I went down into the operating theatre in Stanmore Hospital in London not knowing exactly what they were going to do to me. Neither for that matter did Professor Jones. He told me that the head of the femur was in a bad way and that he needed to go in to see if it was salvageable with bone grafting. He also explained that giving me a hip replacement might be possible, but he would have to take samples of tissue for laboratory tests to see if there was any low-grade infection still there. So I was examined and decisions taken whilst I was under general anaesthetic. At the conclusion of the surgery there was sadly absolutely nothing that could be done to save the hip joint, as the bone had completely disintegrated and crumbled on touch. Professor Jones removed it, and with it much of the pain I'd had for so many months, but there was no prosthesis on the horizon either. The pathology results were such that no hip replacement operation could be considered, as an infection would have flared up just as soon as the prosthesis had been implanted. This infection would have caused rejection of the hip replacement, if not worse, so it was wise just to leave the situation as stable as possible.

I returned to Italy, my enthusiasm dampened by the operation, though my hip stopped aching and I abandoned one crutch around the house. My legs looked as if they had gone through a sausage-making machine. Lack of movement meant that the muscles were slack and the left leg had become steadily more purple and waxy. I went for massages to ease the situation, and when I was horizontal, my legs regained a normal colour. Their appearance disgusted me and

I only ever wore long skirts, refusing to touch my left leg, particularly below the knee. To me it was diseased and unhealthy, and I was to spend a lot of energy insisting that loving friends inspect my wounds. I searched their faces for their reactions, hoping for what, I have no idea.

This phase lasted for about two years, probably until such time as I began to accept my body with its new form. At the time it was an obsession with me. My tummy bulged with keloid scars and was numb because many of the nerves had been severed. It occurred to me, rather ironically, that it was precisely those physical points I had been so proud of that were the areas worst hit. My face was constantly aflame with acne-like spots that I couldn't eliminate, however much I tried. I thought perhaps they would go once a sufficient period of time had passed since the last anaesthetic, but they persisted for months on end. For the time being I was not how I wanted to be and pined for what I had been. It was no easy matter searching for serenity and equilibrium when so much had changed, and I could have done with another me with whom I could laugh and make light of those heavier moments.

In that period I think I actually missed my mother more than anything else, as I'm sure that I would have been able to draw strength from her sagacity and sense of fun. My mother's absence had been a threatening and occult pain during my adolescence, and now, as an adult, I could acknowledge that I missed her as a person and figurehead, often feeling an overwhelming need for her presence after the hijack, someone who could ease the emotional pressure I sometimes felt so unable to deal with.

I was deeply disappointed with the disinterest shown by Pan Am, and it also led Picci to change his mind about telling the story to the media, so I wrote to my aunt allowing her to contact the press, just as she had been encouraging me to do for months.

The media ball began to roll just before we were due to meet the lawyer from Rome. It was extraordinary how it had all come about, almost as if fate had been waiting for the go-ahead from me, for no sooner had one of my aunts received my letter telling them to make a move when a golden opportunity presented itself and, with trembling voice, Bibi seized her chance.

She was in her dressing gown early one morning in April 1988 when she heard a phone-in on the Nick Ross programme on the radio. It was, apparently, fascinating, all about hijacks and the effects they had on hostages. Listeners were invited to call in and contribute if they had ideas or views on the subject, and, naturally, anyone with first-hand experience was very welcome to tell their story. Also joining in the debate was a psychologist from the first hospital I'd been in, a specialist in handling trauma caused by torture, terrorism and violence, who spoke eloquently on the sort of problems that would arise with victims of such crime. Nervously, my aunt phoned in and was immediately pushed to the top of the queue once her story had been briefed. Within 30 seconds she was on the air, the only person who had been directly affected by a hijack. She briefly described my injuries, accused Pan Am of turning their back on me and asked the psychologist why, if he was a specialist in treating victims of violence and employed by the same hospital where I had been a patient, he had not been informed that for many months there was a hijack victim on the eighth floor, suffering terribly as a result of what had happened and in need of therapy.

She was a star on the programme and the rest of my family heard her speaking as they were ironing, doing the washing up or taking the children to school. They were all silently cheering her initiative. The psychologist asked if he could set up an appointment to see me. As soon as my aunt put the phone down it rang and the first of the newspapers were on to the story. Tabloids and daily papers wanted first pickings, and my aunt had to choose which one she would give the story to.

I was surprised to receive a phone call from the *Daily Telegraph* wanting to interview me. My aunt must have been very busy. It was the end of April and a journalist and I agreed to meet up in Milan at

Picci's offices near the station. Before I really knew what was happening, there was a photograph of us both in the newspaper with the whole story of the hijacking and Pan Am's conduct down in black and white. I anxiously waited to see what the effects would be of the Hill–Carati thorn in the Pan Am side.

On the swell of the wave of curiosity and sympathy the story had created, I was asked to speak about the hijacking on a TV programme called *London Plus*. A young team researched cases in an attempt to expose situations of injustice, divulging both sides of the story. A legal representative for Pan Am, Mr Elsie, was contacted and asked to give his version of what was happening. He was filmed in New York and had to account for the fact that they had ignored my letters and pleas for help. He was embarrassed and uncomfortable, and I immediately identified him as enemy number one. He said that they had offered me compensation ($20,000), though he did not specify how much, and that they had offered to pay all my medical bills (I received this in a rushed DHL letter a few days before the programme) and that the company agreed that the compensation levels were too low, but they were reluctant to pay more because that would mean they would be setting a precedent. He said that they had been in constant contact with me ever since the event but had had trouble finding me. I had been in hospital for the better part of a year and had been sending letters to them regularly, so I couldn't imagine how they'd managed to lose me.

A lot of these answers needed clarification and the truth was partial, but at least Pan Am was beginning to have a face. They had also been forced to commit themselves to making sure I received the best medical attention available and for this I was overjoyed. On TV, Mr Elsie had looked hot and upset under the lights although I have to admit that he did not have a sinister leer nor did he seem to be adept at deceiving others. He looked harassed and vulnerable. I was a bit disappointed, as I had rather wanted a surrogate villain on whom I could vent my frustration.

At the end of May, in reply to a letter she had sent, my aunt received a missive from the president of Pan Am explaining that the hijacking really was nothing to do with them. It was blamed on the airport security force in Karachi. Pan Am felt that it had not been negligent in any way and that the terrorists had gained access to the aircraft by breaching airport perimeter security, rushing past an armed guard on the steps of the aircraft. Those aspects of security were the sole responsibility of Karachi Airport, he said. Indeed, Pan Am was not allowed to have its own armed personnel at the aircraft.

I puzzled over the content of the letter. Since the hijacking, I had taken more of an interest in the political issues concerning the PLO and had realised that there were countries believed to be sympathetic to their cause. Pakistan was one of these. Why, in a period of numerous terrorist attacks, particularly on aircraft, had more attention not been paid to the possibility of a hijacking taking place? Why had Pan Am risked landing in Karachi when the right to guard her own aircraft with her own people had been denied? Why, indeed, had Pan Am used this airport given the political situation? I was slowly beginning to realise that I had to research the attack and the reasons why it had ended so terribly. My case might hinge on a number of discoveries. I had to find out much, much more so that I could realistically ascertain what had happened and defend my right to compensation. It would help me channel the anger I had deep within me, and I had an inkling that this could be a mission to correct an injustice and prevent me from remaining merely a victim of circumstances that were beyond my control, in an incident for which everyone was attempting to avoid blame.

18

MEETING NAPOLITANI

AS I ENTERED the room in the offices of the Italian Law Society ahead of Picci, a small man with inky black eyes got up from his seat and extended a plump hand, the fingernails of which were bitten to the quick. He whipped out his business card and presented it to us. I tried to concentrate on this while feeling distracted by a desire to study this man calmly. He was a member of all sorts of committees and councils and taught at university. His qualifications sounded perfect.

We seated ourselves around an oval table to discuss the possibilities of suing Pan Am in Italy, and began to size each other up. Clearly Mr Napolitani was the first on trial in this meeting, and he had to start off by selling his ability, something he did convincingly. Contrary to many of our previous experiences, we were actually able to get straight answers from someone and they appeared to be very accurate and in keeping with our thoughts and expectations. This lawyer showed us that he knew exactly what he was talking about, practically blinding us with his thorough comprehension of the laws and regulations of international civil aviation and the Italian juridical interpretation of them.

He told us that as our hijack had occurred in 1986, it had fallen within a period where the limit of liability pertaining to the Warsaw Convention had been ruled as inapplicable in a lawsuit in Italy. Therefore, there was no specific figure attached to the limit of liability. Put extremely simply, it would seem that all we had to do was ask for a suitable sum for compensation because the $20,000 stipulated on our ticket contract was no longer valid.

We were less confident that we would win solely as a result of this ruling and were convinced that we should find out to what degree Pan Am was actually responsible for what had happened. Only by combining the two things did we feel we would have a possible case. I explained this to Mr Napolitani and found the lawyer receptive to our strategy. The meeting drew to an end and we said goodbye. He was heading back down to Rome, his place of work and one of the most beautiful capitals in the world, and I slightly envied him for where he made his living and had his residence. We turned to our host and thanked him for his kindness in having organised the meeting with this lawyer. He bowed in acknowledgement, wishing us all the very best for the future.

At that point we were very relieved to have spoken to someone so knowledgeable, and now we just had to decide whether or not we wanted him to act on our behalf. We had to decide quickly as we had to file suit before the end of July and it was now the end of May. Albeit with some hesitation, as he was the only aviation lawyer we had spoken to, we came to the conclusion that Napolitani was probably our best bet, and so we phoned him to ask him to prepare a Power of Attorney so that he could act on our behalf immediately.

In the meantime, we received a letter confirming the promise that Pan Am would try to assist in my physical recovery, and they asked if I would please choose a date so that the representative of legal matters for Pan Am could come over to Italy and meet me. Our court case started on 23 July 1988 in Milan and a new phase began in September when Picci and I went to our meeting with the Pan Am representative.

19

MEETING PAN AM

I CHOSE MY clothes carefully for the interview with Pan Am, not wanting Mr Elsie to think that I was some insignificant individual who could be dealt with in three minutes. Images of sophisticated wealthy women shot into my head as I tried to find matching pieces of underwear in my knicker drawer. Underwear always brought out the worst in me, as I was forced to reflect on what had to be covered up. Picci was OK, I grumbled to myself, as all he had was the slightest of limps and his defect would go away. Nothing would remove my horrible scars or give me back what had been so violently taken away. Plastic surgery might help with the mechanics of keeping a prosthesis in place but it was madness to think that my body would ever be without massive scarring.

I angrily slammed the drawer shut, turning my attention to the outer layers, for there was never any answer or salve to the fact that I was unable to accept my new body. I rifled through my clothes and picked out a dark-blue suit to wear with my better jewellery. I hoped that Mr Elsie would think I came from a well-to-do family used to dealing with pots of money, someone to be taken extremely seriously and to whom adequate compensation was a figure containing lots of zeros. I polished my shoes and tried to find a decent bag, which wasn't easy. It was one of the things I'd stopped using since the hijack, as they were so awkward to carry. Money belts, however, don't look good on elegant blue suits and neither do mini rucksacks, so I eventually folded a 50,000 lira note and put it into my pocket, and went to the toilet for the third time that morning.

We were to gather in the offices of Mr Napolitani's procurator, a Mr Botti, in Milan at 2.30 p.m. Pan Am's representative was due to arrive half an hour later and we had to prepare what exactly we were going to say. Given that it was hugely premature to try and negotiate a financial settlement, especially when we didn't know the final extent of my or Picci's injuries, we saw this first meeting as an opportunity to start putting forward requests and to test the waters. Mr Napolitani listened to a condensed version of how we had finally gained Pan Am's and poor Mr Elsie's attention. We hadn't spoken to him about our media gambit in our first meeting, and I think he was somewhat alarmed by our dealings with the press and television, and surprised that we had asked for medical help, but throughout this briefing he said not a word, only pressing the tips of his fingers together in concentrated thought. We stressed the importance of Pan Am's involvement with my physical recovery, to which he agreed, and we recommended to him that we also ask for an advance in funds so that I could live without having to ask Picci for financial support. My independence mattered, and I wanted to be answerable only to myself, whatever my relationship might be with him.

The procurator was watching everyone. Once every so often his eyes flickered over in my direction and I wondered what he was thinking. Then the doorbell rang and I looked at Picci nervously. He winked at me in conspiratorial sympathy as we listened to the shuffling about outside the door while bags were put on chairs and coats hung up. Both our lawyer and the procurator had gone out to welcome the new arrivals, and we were left on our own for some minutes, aware of the noisy clock on the wall.

Finally, the door opened and in walked two men. One of them was Mr Elsie, but I didn't recognise the other. We had been expecting one man, not two, although the fact that Mr Elsie had not come on his own didn't surprise me. Mr Elsie was blond, of medium height, very freckly and extremely worried looking. We shook hands and he smiled hesitantly. The other man, tall, grey haired and about 50 years old, introduced himself as a representative of the United States Aviation Underwriters. His name was Alfred Maroni and he looked a lot less anxious than Mr Elsie – and considerably less friendly. I instinctively felt he was at the meeting to get rid of me as fast as possible. He also assured us that he spoke not a word of Italian, despite his obvious Italian ancestry, but during the course of the meeting it was evident that he was able to follow our comments in Italian quite well.

He started the meeting off with technicalities, asking me where I was born, where I lived, if I was resident and for how long in Italy. He wanted to know if I had bought my ticket in Milan or London and what my job was. These were all questions we ourselves had looked at over the months in an effort to find out where we could sue Pan Am, and I should probably never have answered any of them, saying that these issues were not the reason for this meeting.

He fired off the questions with a rapidity that belied his laid-back position. Long limbed, he had slipped down in his chair and had one leg off the floor, his ankle resting on the other knee. I was sitting rigidly upright, physically ready to defend myself. As I answered his questions I had the distinct impression that he was scraping about trying to find a technical loophole through which he could annul our, and in particular my, lawsuit. I hated having to defend myself. There was too much adrenalin going into my system for the fight or flight necessary, an over-reaction, probably due to all I'd undergone so far. That was quite a handicap but I was also frustrated with this initial interrogation. I had agreed to a meeting with Pan Am because they had expressly requested it, after the radio and TV interest in my story. Finding out about my ticket had nothing to do with their promise to support me, nor did it have anything to do with a settlement – had they wanted to talk about such a thing. Momentarily, they had stemmed the flow of unpleasant bad publicity by calling this meeting, thus giving us hope, but I didn't like what I was hearing.

I made a comment about the fact that I had believed the meeting was to discuss medical assistance. Picci prodded my leg under the table to shut me up, as he saw from my facial expression that I was far too antagonistic. I realised that I should not decapitate my enemy quite so early on, and Mr Elsie, seeing that I disliked his colleague, stepped in to smooth my anger away, asking us specifically what it was that we wanted Pan Am to do. Mr Napolitani intervened and pulled out an antiquated English that he must have learnt from dusty textbooks way back when English was not compulsory in Italian schools. 'You see, my friends, her unnegateable disadvantages are related to those arguments involving the orthopaedic and neurological aspects of medicine and perhaps the plastic field to put into accordance her bottom of the back.' Presumably he was talking about filling in the missing buttock. 'I'm sure that you appreciate my greatest desire is to see this young lady re-establish her good health of past times. Now you can know what it is that we wish you to do.'

Noble sentiments. Both Americans looked puzzled. Our lawyer then abandoned the flowery speech, following up his plea with a lecture on the inapplicability of the limit of liability for compensation in Italy and going on to cite numerous examples of court cases he'd won. I think they got the message that the Warsaw Convention was not going to be of any help to them. Mr Elsie asked me to be prepared to sign a number of medical records release forms given the numerous hospitals I'd been treated in. They would be needed if Pan Am were to contact specialists from around the world for second opinions. No one raised the issue of a settlement and we dispersed, feeling that the meeting had been worthwhile, as we had seen our lawyer in action for the first time.

Within a couple of weeks I had signed release forms for eight hospitals and received a cheque for $20,000, which Picci had requested from Mr Elsie to help me with living expenses. I was impatient for news and hoped that any specialist Pan Am contacted would have specific experience in dealing with war-damaged casualties. Months of silence followed this meeting, however, and I had to sit on my impatience. Picci insisted that I also start looking for hospitals and specialists for myself, so I pursued different avenues of investigation, going to see a specialist in Paris and different orthopaedic surgeons in England and Italy. Each meeting was highly charged on my part, and I always wept before or after, the mere strain of having to live through 20 minutes of telling the case history sufficient to upset me for the better part of a day. Hope, too, was a flashing beacon always a few steps ahead of me, never losing its intensity.

Most of the specialists were fascinated by the problems I presented and thoroughly enjoyed puzzling over ways of resolving them. Suggestions were made to fix the femur to the pelvic girdle so that the concertina movement when walking was controlled, meaning that I would be able to walk without crutches but not sit or drive or have sex easily (which meant for me at all, when I considered the psychological problems thrown in as well). Putting in a hip prosthesis was risky because I was very young and hip replacements only last for between ten and fifteen years. In my case it would probably degenerate even more quickly given the use it would get from a young person. There was also a high probability that it would be rejected because of the low-grade infection lurking around in the soft tissue, and if it wasn't rejected there was always the possibility of it dislocating because of the lack of buttock, which keeps the bones in place.

Seeing so many people gave me an insight into what the future might hold. It also helped me understand considerably more of my body than I had before and realise that the damage was more mechanical than anything else. In addition, whenever I was in Britain, I had started seeing the psychologist who my aunt had spoken to on the radio phone-in. He was convinced that I was suffering from Post

Traumatic Stress Syndrome, which explained my intensely emotional approach to everything I dealt with, including my relationship with Picci. I would imagine that, at some point in their lives, the majority of people suffer from some kind of PTSS given the very nature of life itself. Whether it is useful to identify it with such an important sounding name is, I believe, debateable. As far as I was concerned, I could have used this diagnosis as an excuse to wallow in self-pity, which might have been unhelpful for my rehabilitation. Fortunately, I wanted to hang on to my pride and continued to deny that anything was particularly difficult for me to manage. Our sessions lasted for a very brief period as I felt they were a waste of time, and how could a man possibly understand a woman's grief over losing her body?

On 13 December 1988, Pan Am were meant to reply to the first summons that had been issued in July, to defend themselves against accusations that their crew had escaped from the plane, abandoning the passengers and leaving them to their uncertain destiny; that there was no emergency help once the hijack was over, and so on and so forth. For that initial hearing, Picci went along to the courts with Mr Napolitani's procurator. There he met the lawyer acting on behalf of Pan Am, Mr Gallo.

Despite the date that had originally been fixed, the hearing was adjourned to the following March because the defendants asked to study the citation further. Picci took the opportunity to scrutinise the judge and was a little worried that he seemed so young. Would he be mature enough to handle such a big case? Mr Botti was more concerned that Pan Am was immediately interested in quantifying my injuries and suggested that it would be a good idea for me to be looked over by a medical examiner with that purpose in mind, even though Napolitani had already requested compensation in the initial claim and put a figure (which I thought was extremely low) into the acts. At the time I had thought this was just an amount that had been necessary to get things going and would later be amended accordingly after further examination. Unfortunately in this instance, however, I gave the impression of being very together and only slightly injured as I went about my daily activities. This fooled many, including, so it seemed, Mr Napolitani. He had not written into the citation the request that my health be looked after by Pan Am, as he said that he felt we had come to these agreements verbally in the meeting we'd already had with Pan Am.

The legal firm acting for Pan Am was based in Rome. The man in charge of the case was a certain Mr Bianchi, who was using Mr Gallo in Milan as his procurator. By chance, Mr Napolitani knew Mr Bianchi very well and they were respected colleagues. I expressed my concern to Mr Napolitani that this might compromise litigation but he assured me that their association could only work in my favour, as he was familiar with the way this man worked. I wanted to believe him but felt apprehensive all the same given my ignorance of the whole legal world.

I was so unsure about everything, having no experience in such matters. We wondered if it might not be a good idea to hire another lawyer, who could explain legal jargon and give us a panorama of our options so that we were not entirely in the hands of just one person. This may sound as if we had no faith in our lawyer, which was not the case. We really just wanted to have a second opinion on the direction and strategy the lawsuit was taking. After all, there was a great deal at stake, particularly for me.

20

TAKING CHARGE

PAN AM LOST another plane over Lockerbie in December of 1988. I watched the aftermath, sure in my heart that the crash had been the result of a terrorist attack. My suspicions were confirmed when the news broke from the British Ministry of Transport that there was conclusive evidence that a bomb had been responsible for the explosion. I so hoped that at some point in the life of a terrorist the actions he had taken would boomerang back in his face in some form of divine retribution, thus balancing things out a bit. I also thought of the media and their part in maintaining the business of terrorism, for partner they most definitely were, and wondered if the press were to stop reporting these terrible events whether terrorism would die out.

Picci and I flew to Madagascar for a holiday and we were both a little apprehensive. The fear of terrorism, however, was now accompanied by determination. The Lockerbie bombing for some reason galvanised us into action. Articles on the recent tragedy inspired us to seek help further afield in research I was to initiate once back from our vacation. If anything, the disaster provoked in me a ferment of speculation and a strong desire to know what had gone on in our particular case. Who had negotiated for our lives? How had the flight crew physically escaped and had anyone tried to stop them? I wanted to know why the lights had suddenly gone out and who the person(s) responsible were. Where had the ambulances and doctors hidden and who had been in charge of the external operations once the hijackers had seized the plane? I was determined to uncover the truth but saw clearly that it was going to be a very difficult task. Apart from anything else, I imagined that there were all sorts of people who wouldn't really relish me poking my nose into what had actually happened.

The only help I could count on was that of Mrs Evans, the wife of a medical researcher and librarian of the American Information Library USIS in Milan. She had already assisted me in tracking down the addresses of orthopaedic specialists and medical institutes in the USA with energy and optimism. This next stage was going to be quite a challenge for her, which I was sure she would rise to.

There was still no news from the airline company waiting for us when we arrived home. I was beginning to get worried. Had they reneged on our agreement and decided to string us along until we got fed up, as insurance companies are wont to do? Perhaps it was part of their strategy. I immediately thought of telling our story to the Italian press in an attempt to push home our advantage. It might speed up the medical side, and would also indicate that we were determined. On the other hand, I was reluctant to do this, as it would be a demonstration of a certain mistrust towards the airline company. Then I remembered that we were involved in litigation and Mr Maroni of the insurance company had not hesitated to try to establish whether I had legal rights or not, regardless of my unfortunate physical situation. I didn't doubt for a moment that had they found their loophole, I would have been left high and dry to fend for myself, so we called Mr Botti and asked him what he thought. He agreed about a further newspaper article, but he recommended that we speak to Mr Napolitani before actually contacting the press. I felt sure that Mr Napolitani would not be enthusiastic about our going to the

In the days before the hijack – teaching at a
pharmaceutical company in Milan, 1984.

On holiday in Iles des
Saints, Gaudeloupe, 1985.

Pan Am Flight 073 grounded at Karachi Airport
during the hijack on 5 September 1986.

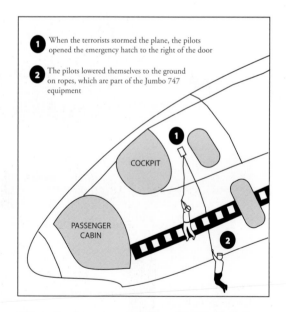

The pilots' escape route from the hijacked plane.

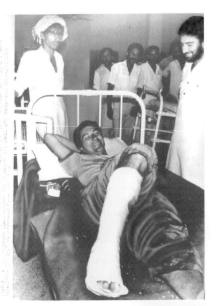

Picci in hospital in Karachi after the hijack.

Picci and his family after his
return home to Italy in
September 1986.

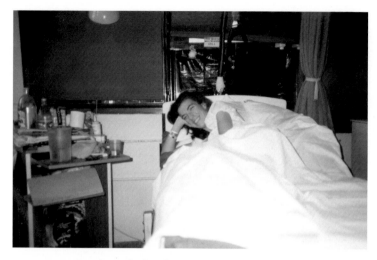

On the airbed in hospital in December 1986.

At home for Christmas, 1986.
I weighed 46 kilos at the time.

My sister Fran with her son
James, Christmas 1986.

My mother, my younger
sister Stephany and me,
1964.

My father, cousin Jane and Bibi at
my aunt Phil's 80th birthday.

Jenny in New York
on my birthday in 1989.

With my brother Greg in
Sydney, Australia, 1992.

The valley in Frera.

Inset: Diego up the wild cherry tree
outside the Rifugio Caterina.

Summer in Frera with Nonna Caterina, Elizabetta and family.

Going to milk the herd with Piero the shepherd high up in the
pastures.

Collecting wild mushrooms
in Frera, 1993.

Me and all the children,
Frera, 2000.

Picci and I at the waterfall
at the end of the lake
in Frera, 2002.

At home in 2004.

newspapers. Nevertheless, I called him and in as delicate a way as possible mooted the idea of publicising the story. He was, as I had imagined, opposed and argued that it wouldn't be a good idea to irritate the airline company when things were going well for me. Despite this veto we took our story to the *Corriere della Sera*, one of Italy's national papers. They interviewed us and wrote a long article about the unfairness of the system, exposing various aspects of the legal problem. We knew that we had acted contrary to his wishes, but we were unable to let our lawyer totally run the way this legal case was to be handled. We had our 'finger on the pulse' so to speak, although we were undoubtedly difficult as clients go for any lawyer. We wanted to follow each step taken and have a considerable say in how things were planned. We considered 'battle' tactics all the time using our heads, often choosing the more difficult routes throughout the lawsuit, but those that would stand us in good stead as we neared the end of the case.

21

RESEARCH

I LOATHED THE centre of Milan simply because parking was impossible. Roads that had once allowed a horse and trap to pass were clogged up with polluted, badly maintained cars belching out greasy black smoke as lights took their time to change. There was hardly enough space for the moving traffic let alone any parking. Those places reserved for disabled people were invariably filled with the cars of able-bodied drivers, or so far away from where one wanted to go that it was better to get a taxi. I could not use public transport. It was one of the after-effects of the hijacking. The thought of standing in such close proximity with strangers on crammed trains or buses gave me claustrophobia. Had I succeeded in getting onto a bus, however, and overcome my fear of being in crowds, I might well have had a severe accident due to lively steering on the part of bus drivers whose fast turns and braking were sufficient to wrench a handhold right out of one's clutch. This had already happened to me a first time and I wasn't prepared to experience it again. I had also once been caught in the doors as I got on a tram, risking strangulation when they had snapped shut on the little bag that was looped over my shoulder and neck. That was a fairly unexceptional way to die and would have been banal compared to the way my life had hitherto gone.

USIS library was in one of those medieval winding streets that meander through the very centre of Milan, and I had to walk there, having left my car near the cathedral, a hot 20-minute trip. Mrs Evans greeted me, asking me how the search for surgeons had gone, and we exchanged news. She was always busy with a queue of people waiting for her help, so I quickly told her what my new plans were. She nodded her head in support, confirming that she'd be delighted to help and then showed me how to work the microfiche machine. I spent an absorbed four hours looking through the main English-speaking newspapers of the period of the hijack, gleaning names cited in any of the articles. Long lists of injured people and American citizens appeared, but of course their addresses were not included. I searched through thousands of typed words, skip-reading until my eyes watered, trying to spot a place of work or study mentioned in connection with any of the victims. Our first hope was that perhaps someone else had looked into the hijack, as pooling resources would have been very helpful.

I wrote down what little there was and stored it in my folder. It felt good to be doing something positive, but, unfortunately, the newspaper reporting was full of contradictions and each paper had used a healthy amount of imagination in their retelling of events. I was amazed that a story could be recounted in so many different ways and saw that much conjecture had been printed concerning the disaster. The picture that emerged from a week's worth of reading was that no one really had a clue about what had actually happened. Reading these articles helped me look at the whole picture rather than just my terrifying ordeal, but it also made me wary. Getting to the truth was going to be very hard.

Some of these stories claimed that a new crew had been on its way to replace the one that had escaped, thus meeting part of the hijackers' demands. They never appeared for some reason, although to be perfectly honest it defied my imagination how a crew might have been persuaded to board a hijacked plane with four armed PLO members waiting for the chance to murder their hostages. It was also reported that Pakistani troops had been about to make an assault on the jumbo to release us, but that didn't reflect the reality when I thought back to our lonely struggle once we'd managed to get out of the plane. The tarmac at the time of our escape had been about as alive as a graveyard at midnight, so the crack troops had obviously still been waiting for the signal to attack from the bushes while we sought freedom. Between America and Pakistan there was much imaginative 'passing of the buck', each nation praising the other whilst trying to pass on responsibility for what happened. The fact that the aircraft didn't get airborne, for example, was reportedly due to the Pakistani forces, who resolutely refused to allow the plane to be moved, and the Pakistani authorities found the American policy of no negotiation decidedly the right one as it meant that the plane was grounded. Pakistan had been host country to no fewer than six hijacks in the past. Rajiv Gandhi, the papers stated, accused the Pakistani authorities of actually encouraging them and President Zia ul-Haq, who'd seized power in a military coup from Zulfikar Ali Bhutto, announced fairly quickly after the hijack that the country's strong support for the PLO would not weaken, although the hijacking left a bad taste in the mouth.

I should have read through the articles in a cool and detached way, but every little word mattered to me, and I raged as I thought of those who had died and those of us who had been so badly injured. Seemingly the US Federal Aviation Administration, a body governing, among other things, the regulations and behaviour of companies in air transport, had sent a letter in the August of 1986 to all American airlines warning them of a possible imminent terrorist attack. This was classified as a 'General Alert'. In June, Pan Am itself had apparently launched an advertising campaign promoting its own watertight security. It was initiated to help deflect the fear of terrorism that had gripped travellers in general. I jotted down the reference, date and name of the newspaper, pondering on how the information might be used in the trial.

On what pretext had the PLO taken over the plane? This in itself never became completely clear, except that the attack was to frighten people and create confusion in the Western world, but one article said they had seized the plane in order to fly to Cyprus to free fellow patriots imprisoned there. Apparently, among the hijackers were three members of Mr Arafat's personal security force and intelligence organisation. None of these articles guaranteed the truth, however, and it was hard to decide which to give credence to, although they all gave me ideas on where to go from there. One of those ideas was the need to find an official document on what had happened before, during and after the event. I needed an impartial and consolidated report, otherwise everything was subject to interpretation and lies that people were ready to tell in order to protect their interests.

From 'Current Policy on Terrorism', a paper from the USA Department of State, I read the report that from 1980 to 1986 there had been 300 terrorist attacks against the airline industry, and in 1986 all of these attacks were against USA, France and Israel. I read the political interpretation and learned how the US saw these acts of terrorism as perpetrated by unbalanced or half-crazed criminals. Seemingly, terrorism didn't occur because of injustices carried out by any one political system to the detriment of another.

I then read 'Policy on Forceful Action against Terrorists', not without some reaction. There was one particular phrase that struck me, and that I wanted to argue about, which said that in the short term the US could face reprisals when terrorists were imprisoned but over time the rule of law would prevail. When would that be, I asked myself. Was it just tough luck on those world citizens who were involved in the reprisals? Didn't they at least have the right to the moral, financial and medical support of the governments involved? At least of those governments who had generated foreign policies that were the reasons for terrorist attacks? Shouldn't there be some international treaty on the treatment of victims of terrorism? Wasn't this terrorist scourge a growing and worrying phenomenon that demanded to be appropriately addressed if the world didn't want it to explode on a global basis?

Reading the papers, I could see that there were many possible culprits in the Karachi tragedy. It seemed that the security forces of the airport were also partly to blame for the way things had gone. It was more than likely that there had been inside help from their personnel. How else could four hijackers have got hold of the uniforms, badges and grey airport van that had been used to get onto the runway? Picci and I mulled over the possibilities of suing the Pakistani airport authorities as well as Pan Am, but soon realised that it would be virtually impossible. The airport was, naturally, state-owned, and it would have been a lost cause, apart from the fact that the Middle Eastern mentality was one that neither of us felt like taking on. All the same, I did write to the Pakistan Bar Association to see if anyone had filed a claim against the authorities. A negative answer eventually came back on a piece of rather dog-eared airmail paper, and even if I had had a vague notion to sue, it was firmly squashed having received the letter, which gave an all too clear confirmation of the difficulties I would encounter engaging with the legal system in Pakistan.

As the weeks passed, Mrs Evans continued her intelligent search for information on the leads I gave her. She became very involved in my crusade and spent much time sending off for obscure microfiches from other USIS facilities around Italy. I was impressed with just how well stocked the library was. On occasion I became very excited about my discoveries and took photocopies of all my treasures, building up a considerable pile of material and a conspicuous debt with the library. I worked hard and my days were full, but reflecting constantly on the events of the hijack did not help me to move on mentally from that tragic episode in my life.

The hearing in March, where Pan Am presented its side of the story, duly took place, and once again Picci went to the courts to see what would transpire. Pan Am defended themselves as best they could, citing all manner of articles which stated that the air carrier was not responsible because the hijacking was due to circumstances beyond their control. I mentally countered their defence as I recalled the measures Pan Am had not insisted on taking despite their own advertising campaign on security. Why hadn't they used sky marshals? An aviation police force that placed armed plain-clothes staff on board flights passing through high-risk areas. At least this form of protection has now been installed and used on some airlines after the 11 September attacks in New York, but it should have been mandatory way back when hijacking first started to become a major problem. At that time all important American airlines could be targeted by terrorist activity. Karachi was listed as a high-threat location and was included in an emergency amendment of the FAA warning the airlines to tighten up security measures. As far as I could see, it was quite an omission not to have placed sky marshals on the plane.

Pan Am also defended the escape of the pilot and cabin crew, who had used a pulley system installed behind the cockpit. It had been deployed for the first time in aviation history on our plane. Clearly it had been designed because hijacks were very much a present reality. I felt that it was right that the plane should have been grounded but not at all professional to leave the hostages on board with no technical expert or flight engineer who would have been able to keep a close eye on the functioning of the aircraft. After all, it wasn't as if all the electrical appliances had been completely shut down. The lights, air-conditioning and water system were still in operation, so there must have been a generator or external battery working somewhere. They would have known that any failure in the supply of energy was potentially dangerous.

Once the initial court skirmishes were over we were beginning to get the measure of the defendants, and as far as we could see, they weren't great strategists. It was after this hearing that Mr Botti resigned. We had frequently phoned him to ask for explanations on various aspects of the case. We were not sure of the agreement that existed between him and Mr Napolitani in terms of work and fees, but because Mr Botti was in Milan it was natural that we tried to talk to him rather than Mr Napolitani, who was more often than not out when we called. Mr Botti had not been happy with his role as go-between, however, and, suffering from stress, handed in his notice.

Our next round in court was scheduled for November and it was our turn to challenge Pan Am and reply to their arguments, but now we had no procurator and had to find a new man who could represent Mr Napolitani in Milan. I had an enormous amount of material to hand over to him so that he could prepare for the next hearing, but I wanted to discuss it with someone beforehand. We set about finding a new solicitor in Milan with anxiety pushing us along.

It was during that period, nearly two and a half years on from the hijack, that Picci saw the scars on my buttock and stomach for the first time. The photographs my father had taken of these areas shortly after my seven months in hospital had arrived in a white envelope ready for the legal medical report. It was lying on my desk in the office, and one day I happened to notice that the seal was broken. I knew what the contents were, but had put off seeing the images myself until strictly necessary and had left the envelope sealed. I was annoyed when I saw it opened, thinking that perhaps the secretary had been curious or had unsealed it by mistake. My relationship with Picci at this time was affectionate, but he was afraid of hurting me and was probably frightened by my disfigurement, unable to either touch or look at the offending areas. I could do nothing to change the situation, feeling deeply ashamed of what I had become. The sadness caused by what I interpreted as rejection was at times profound, so I was shocked to find out when I asked him that it was he who had opened the package. I waited for further comment, but none was forthcoming, except to say they were as he had imagined. I didn't ask him what he thought or how he felt, as it would have caused both of us, for different reasons, much anguish. Some things were so difficult to discuss, and Picci was so private that I knew it was counter-productive to insist on getting answers out of him. Needless to say, the lack of communication and our diffidence was an open wound that had little chance of closing over and healing.

22

NEW YORK

PAN AM TELEGRAMMED to say they'd found a team of specialists in the US ready to examine me and could they fix appointments as soon as possible? I was delighted and wrote back in the affirmative, full of hope for the future.

Bibi and I arrived in New York a month later, on a glorious June morning, slightly woozy from the flight despite first-class treatment on Pan Am. An airline employee met us at the airport and accompanied us to our designated residence, right next to the hospital. Once we had booked in, our chaperone left, telling me that she'd ring in the morning to introduce us to the medical director of Pan Am. We were staying in a high-rise block near Central Park, where the upper floors housed surgeons and medical staff with their families, whilst the lower floors contained small flats that offered accommodation to outpatients and visiting families. We took our bags up to the third floor to rest and have a wash before going out to explore New York and have something to eat.

Over the next few days, Bibi and I were taken round our appointments by a softly spoken consultant whose task it was to coordinate the surgeons. There were three hernias on my abdomen and I was to have plastic surgery performed on the whole area once they had been removed. I had an appointment with someone else who was to look at the gluteal area to see if there was any way that he could cover the missing muscle with soft tissue, and, finally, I was to be seen by the orthopaedic department for a hip replacement.

The plastic surgeon's office was sumptuous, with all his credentials, degrees and awards adorning the walls. The floor was made of parquet with a few Persian rugs scattered around the place. Leather sofas and old-fashioned armchairs completed the impression that one was in the tasteful sitting room of a well-off family, even though just outside the door to the office was the long impersonal corridor of the hospital. Dr Bloom was a pleasant-looking man in his 40s with a large nose and receding hairline. He was obviously doing very well for himself financially, and he was disarmingly informal. He had a gentle voice that inspired confidence, and in the safety of his silent 'sitting room' he drew out my oft-repeated story. He was most sympathetic, exclaiming that I must have been an extremely brave woman to have come through such an ordeal so well and apparently so emotionally unscathed. We then progressed onto the physical examination, where he palpated parts of me, trying to feel where I had the most flesh.

My aunt asked question after question, including whether he had worked on firearms injuries before, to which he replied that he had worked directly on bomb-injured victims. This reassured us that he had the necessary experience. At the end of the interview, he said he thought that he could cover my buttock with a gradual process of tissue expansion, producing extra skin. This could then be moved wherever it was needed. Or he could do a muscle transferral from another part of my body. However, I would first need to go for a week of tests to see if microsurgery was viable on a body like mine. He also wanted to have a consultation together with the orthopaedic surgeons. He made me feel that I'd be well looked after and when he gave me a fatherly kiss goodbye, we left feeling that he was deeply concerned for his patients.

We were up at dawn the following morning and waited outside one of the lecture theatres for a general consultation. Dr Rider, the orthopaedic surgeon, and Dr Bloom, together with 20 or so other orthopaedic specialists, were expecting us. They were all interested in seeing this unique case and had gathered early to offer their advice and experience. This was the kind of thing I had envisaged and hoped for in Europe, but it had never happened.

My aunt held my hand reassuringly after I'd nervously put on a theatre gown and been helped on to a stretcher bed. Dr Rider then explained my case. There were numerous X-rays and medical notes, taken from the other hospitals, illustrating the extent of movement available to me. We worked as a team, him expounding and me performing, kneeling creakily down and wobbling with the exertion, or lifting my foot a few centimetres off the ground and pushing my leg back, where once it had been flexed in the foetal position at the hip and blocked. I was quite proud of my achievements, as many of my British doctors had doubted whether I would ever make such progress.

Various solutions to improve my mobility were suggested and a show of hands given for each one. Soft-tissue coverage was essential for a hip replacement and the options for plastic surgery were openly discussed with the doctors. About 50 per cent of the surgeons present voted in the show of hands at the end of this grand round to perform reconstructive plastic surgery that would allow an orthopaedic hip replacement. Tests had to be carried out and a biopsy made of the internal tissue near the femoral cavity to see if the low-grade infection that had simmered ever since the hijack had gone. The overall plan was ambitious, but if it were done properly I would have a new bottom, which, even if not perfect, would act as a protection for the new hip joint and perhaps be more comfortable for me generally. I would be able to walk well, throwing away my crutches following rehabilitation.

I was excited and at the same time very scared, as the operations were complicated and involved hours of difficult microsurgery, but there were signs during this preliminary approach that things were looking positive for the future. The results from the biopsy taken from the hip area were negative, showing there to be no residual infection left despite the hundreds of pieces of shrapnel still embedded in the region.

Finally it was all over, and a week from the day we had arrived, Bibi and I boarded our plane home, full of news and hope. I had been presented with a plan of action and was to go back to Italy to think about whether or not I wanted to go though with the procedures. On my return, I wrote to the airline company and the doctors in New York accepting their proposals after having discussed the plans at length with Picci and agreeing that perhaps this was the right course of action to take. From then on, faxes, letters and phone calls flew across the Atlantic and the English Channel. Who was going to come with me? Who had time for such a role of responsibility and support? I couldn't stop thinking of the moment when I'd be able to walk again and decided that I'd throw a huge party once I was back on my feet and that I would dance the first dance with my beloved – a waltz. The fact that I had only ever been capable of doing the polka in country dancing, and the man's part at that, did nothing to deter my dreaming and was indicative of the chasm that existed between my own view of the future and reality.

I wrote to the doctors, expecting prompt replies with surgery schedules but received only the date for the hernia closures. Then, on 15 July 1989, I flew back to New York, this time to embark on a journey that was to see me nearly restored to my former physical condition. I hoped to be back home in six weeks' time.

My cousin who lived in California was to meet me at JFK Airport and stay for two weeks while I went through the first operation. Albertina was in her late 30s, full of energy and very passionate about everything she did in life. She was a sensual, lovely-looking woman who had always been on a diet. Meeting up with her after all those years was incredible. She was even better looking than before, having given up her starvation tactics. She flung her arms around me in a warm embrace, smelling of expensive perfume and looking ready to go for a holiday on a cattle ranch far from New York. She was wearing jeans, cowboy boots, a denim jacket with fringes and a large cowboy hat. She bubbled with happiness, expressing her pleasure at seeing me, and I felt lighter and happier just being in her exuberant company. A few hours later we dressed for dinner and took a cab to an exclusive restaurant she knew in Manhattan. That evening we dined on lobster and champagne, celebrating our meeting and life in general. Warmed by the fine setting, and somewhat inebriated, our conversation covered the wisdom of accepting both pleasure and pain that fate strew along our pathway in the course of our lives, for Albertina had had her share of unhappiness over the years. We ended the evening positively radiant with good feelings and joyful gratitude for the lessons we had learnt, but by Sunday I was less willing to open my arms to the experience of Monday's suffering. I had to be in hospital at 10 a.m. for the first of my operations, and, despite the security I derived from being with my cousin, I had twinges of anxiety that picked away at my stomach.

That evening I suggested that we go out for something to drink. We found a bar with tables outside on the pavement and dropped down wearily into the seats. It was 6.30 and happy hour, and the streets were at their busiest on that summer Sunday evening. I was sipping my orange juice and in rather a daze contemplating all that was before me, when I noticed the swaying hips and undulating movement of a young woman as she walked slowly down the other side of the road. I ached with envy at her bodily ease, while strange and sad emotions pulled bitterly at my heart. I coveted the careless coordination of her step, and I compared my lot with hers, burning with the injustice life had delivered. Never would I have her grace of movement and never that smooth unmistakeable swell of buttock and hips – so essentially feminine, so utterly irreplaceable. So much for my accepting both life's pleasure and pain.

As I came round from the first anaesthetic, after the operation to remove the hernias, I saw Albertina sitting by the bed. She smiled her warm smile and handed me the phone. 'Give Picci a call and tell him how you feel.' My spirits were high, and I felt pleased to be over the first hurdle and able to give good news. One down, two to go, even if they were the two most difficult operations. People popped in to cheer me on, including the plastic and orthopaedic surgeons, who were full of jokes and fun. Everyone was so positive. Discharged after about a week, I went back to the residence to convalesce, although my mind was way ahead of my body, which needed rest. I wanted to go off and explore museums, shows and exhibitions, and wander through Central Park, but I had to stay calm.

Pan Am maintained some contact with me through a lovely assistant who came to visit and bring funds, so that we could shop and pay for any extra medical expenses. I was grateful for this help, even though I still felt awkward about asking for money from the airline company.

A week or so later, I went back to have my stitches out and Dr Bloom spoke to me about the next operation. The date set for the microsurgery was 12 August but I asked him if we could make it the end of that month, as I didn't feel that I would have had enough time to regain my strength. He gave me a reassuring squeeze of the arm, which I took as indicating understanding on his part of the importance of postponing things.

The morning Albertina left, and two days before Picci was to arrive, I received a phone call from him telling me that a friend and fellow plastic surgeon of his – 'an amazing guy, great at his job' – wanted to see me. He gave me the phone number and asked me to book an appointment with Dr Tellez. This surgeon was high profile and very busy but said that if it was not a problem with me he would examine me in my apartment at eight o'clock in the morning as he lived in the same block of flats. I agreed to this appointment, unorthodox as it seemed from a European point of view. Dr Bloom obviously wanted a second opinion on the problem, I thought. They really were being exceptionally prudent and I was grateful for all this attention.

The interview I had with Dr Tellez was straightforward, although I found him to be very cool and distant. He reminded me of a thinner version of Clark Gable with his black moustache, and he had an effortless demeanour that is peculiar to the young and successful. He too pinched away at parts of me, muttering as he turned me around, looking at my anatomy. At the end of the examination, I was in for a surprise. He told me that Dr Bloom had asked him to see if a Latissimus Dorsi Free Flap operation could be performed. I asked him to explain what this was. He drew a line down my back to the left of my spine by about two inches and explained that the muscle running from my armpit to the penultimate rib in this position could be excised and connected up to the blood supply around my wound and used to cover up the huge deficit in my buttock. This was a muscle that could be taken away without compromising the movement or strength of the back. He had perfected his technique and this operation was his speciality. Now that he had seen me, he said he felt confident that the surgery could be carried out, and he would be performing the operation instead of Dr Bloom.

Surprised by the change of plan, I asked about his success rate, to which he replied that he had a low percentage of failure for this kind of surgery and that in the case of someone of my youth and fitness, the possibility of a disaster happening was negligible. What about the preliminary tests I'd have to undergo before the main surgery, I asked. He replied that there were none to do. I was perplexed and expressed my concern, but he responded by saying that, in this kind of operation, angiograms were not necessary as they could be risky and didn't give much idea of the blood supply anyway. I was not like the older cancer patients he usually dealt with, so could be excluded from the possibility of failure due to bad circulation.

When he had gone, I reflected on this new turn of events. It was hard for me to be anything other than optimistic, and the doctors themselves were enthusiastic about my health. Everyone seemed to be interested in my progress and people were evidently talking about my case. Pan Am were looking after me financially and had found this group of specialists. They in turn all knew the reasons behind Pan

Am's intervention. Surely this was sufficient to make sure I was treated with kid gloves? The fact that Dr Bloom would no longer be operating on me gave me no cause for concern, and I was sure he would be keeping Dr Tellez informed with regard to my medical history. There were considerable written records and many X-rays to look through, which would keep him busy for a day or two.

With so much to think about, I looked forward to Picci's arrival so we could talk about things together, although I knew he would say at the end of any discussion that '*la pelle è tua*', literally meaning that the skin was mine. He flew in on time, tired from the July rush in the office and overwhelmed by the suffocating heat of New York. We went straight to a car-hire firm and rented a vehicle. I was thrilled to have him with me by my side and could relax. I hadn't realised how tiring the last three weeks had been.

We went to say goodbye to Dr Bloom, who told me he didn't want me flying off to Denver, which had been our original plan, as I was not ready for any long journeys yet, and he asked me to leave him a phone number in case he needed to contact me. He wished me well for the holidays, adding that he would be talking to Dr Tellez and the orthopaedic surgeon over the following days. We left, confident that things were going as well as they could and really looking forward to temporarily forgetting everything and spending time together.

As is often the case, however, if you want something too much, you don't get it. Our holiday to the Adirondacks, north of New York, and my convalescence proved to be oppressive, as I was extremely uptight about the operation to come. I attempted to suppress all signs of my anxiety, which resulted in tetchiness and mutual irritability. We also discovered that the 'Lake District' of New York was ridiculously expensive, and even the ramshackle cabin in the woods we rented cost a small fortune. Unfortunately, there was little to pick or choose from as it was peak season and everything was fully booked.

Despite this disappointment, we stayed in the woods by the lake for a number of days and gradually began to relax. We went for excursions in a rowing boat and tried our hand at fishing. It wasn't the most exciting of holidays, but we knew that I had to have time to rest and really recover before the next onslaught of hospitalisation. It was a shame as we had been looking forward to travelling west in the car and maybe even going to the Rocky Mountains before the next operation.

Our days passed, and I looked at the smooth contour my new tummy had now acquired after the hernia operation. I was so happy with the results and was sure that in a few months' time you would see just a small white line. I hoped and prayed that this was just the first of a series of success stories as far as my health was concerned and knew that the complete rest we were having was doing me good.

A week after we'd arrived, I was called to the phone. Dr Bloom was his usual charming self and told me that the operation was to be done on schedule. I was stunned and asked him what he meant by 'on schedule', to which he answered that the theatre had been booked for 12 August. I said that I didn't want to go through with the operation so soon, as my holiday was doing me a great deal of good and I was recovering well. 'I already told you this before I left for my vacation, Dr Bloom.'

'Well, I'm sorry, Catherine, you see the whole team of specialists, anaesthetists and your theatre team have booked you in on that date and it will be difficult to change things now. The orthopaedic surgeon is also available and wants to look in on the proceedings.' I didn't want to go, but the thought of upsetting all these professional people who were going to do their best to help me walk again was unthinkable. Picci was miserable for me but realised that unless we followed their timetable, we might find surgery scheduled at a much later date. He consoled me by saying that at least it would all be over faster. We packed our bags the following day and motored down in quiet acceptance to the hospital, disappointed with the timing.

At 10 a.m. the following morning, I filled in the many tedious forms requested by the admissions department. There were some unpleasant waits due to the fact that no one had informed them about who was paying for this surgery, and I had to deal with a belligerent young clerk who was rude to me until such time as Pan Am wrote a letter to confirm that they were paying for my entire hospitalisation, which was then faxed through to the administration offices of the hospital.

I was sent along for the routine blood and urine samples, where I cried like a baby. My room was located on the 12th floor and we took the lift up to the reception there. Picci carried my bag along to the single room, fussed about trying to get the phone and television to work and then, depressed by the hospital atmosphere, trailed off down the corridor to investigate my floor. There was a roof terrace off my room that overlooked the Hudson River but there was not a whisper of wind and the background sound was the deep hum of the air-conditioning and hospital pumps going at full tilt. The peaceful sound of silence was nowhere to be heard. Traffic droned in the distance with police sirens screaming and helicopter chops punctuating the air at regular intervals. New York was full of throbbing activity, and the stillness and quiet I'd experienced in my beloved Frera was dreadfully absent.

Lunch came and went, for I wasn't hungry. Picci disappeared to get something to eat and returned in the afternoon to keep me company. I rested a little and waited for something to happen. Different people came in to see me and talk to me: the IV lady, the blood lady, the houseman, the lady who supplied fresh water, the floor mopper, the anaesthetist, a young doctor who wanted to examine me, and, finally, Dr Tellez. They all smelt of disinfectant and gave me the shivers and by the time Dr Tellez arrived I was a tight ball of apprehension. Although appearing calm, I was inwardly suffering recurring attacks of panic that squeezed my entrails in uncontrollable spasms; there was no need for the enema I was given before the operation. To calm my skittish mind, I took a large red exercise book I'd brought along for making notes and stared long at the first white page, not knowing what to write as words seemed by turns theatrical or banal and too self-conscious to be sincere, but in the end I put pen to paper, aware that I was on the eve of another great change in my life. I have since lost that book but have a strong recollection of the content. The moment of writing was so sharp and intense that those feelings and thoughts were sculpted into my memory.

23

THE RED BOOK
AND FAILURE

It's nearly 12 August 1989. They'll be plumbing a piece of my back into the buttock area at breakfast time tomorrow. I've just had a hot shower, and I'm more awake than I've been all day. They came in to set up a drip, but I told them to go away, to do it in the theatre, fewer reminders to excite me. Dr Tellez came in and explained that he couldn't fill in the whole buttock area, as the muscle from my back would not be large enough to cover the entire hole. He said that they could do something at a later date to finish the job. They should have spoken to me about this before admission. Perhaps I won't want another operation. He told me it was not a big problem. Of course it isn't for him, he's not the one under the knife. Fear makes me sweat. I'll have the horrible catheter, the usual IV and they will place me on my side after surgery, as my bottom will be newly covered with delicate tissue, all the paraphernalia that I thought was part of the past will be with me once more.

I just feel so uptight and wish I had been better prepared

this time. The more anaesthetics before operations I have, the more I'm terrified, overdosing on adrenalin. It's not just the fear of hospital that agitates me but also all the other experiences that come back into my head in a kaleidoscope of images: three years of fighting, slowly gaining ground in the rebuilding of body and mind; finding the patience needed to forge a new relationship with Picci; re-establishing self-esteem and my injured ego; walking with crutches up and down mountains; trying to pull this body into good health; and knowing that despite great willpower, the physical results are limited by the damage done.

A few days ago, something upsetting happened in the log cabin on the lake as I started thinking of the procedures I had to go through. I was standing in the bedroom near the window, looking out at the trees. I was barefoot, pleasantly aware of the floorboards warm in the afternoon sun, and watching the dust particles across my vision. I don't know why, but I started to tremble and my body felt like it was going into some kind of overload spin. Breathing became difficult and I began to pant and gulp for air, feeling very out of control. Then emotions of fear, injustice, rage and hatred came sweeping through me in waves of terrible energy. I wanted to scream, to hit things, but most of all I wanted to smash windows, smash glass, smash, smash, smash to pieces anything that would break into thousands of bits. It was the thousands of bits I wanted to see. I ached to be able to exhaust myself in a destructive rampage, knowing that when the storm was over I would have been made whole again.

I did none of these things though. I didn't even scream. I just yelped like a whipped dog, impotent. The animal noises I made were strange even to my own ears. Picci came through with a look of alarm across his face and begged me to calm down, but his presence was of no consequence to me. I was completely alone; incapable of communicating whatever it was that had taken me over. My rage was intense, and I couldn't take it out on anything or anyone except myself. The voice of reason in the background halted such impulses. 'Who'll pay for the windows? What will the owners say? Picci will think I have snapped. What will the consequences be?' Thoughts that dampened my wrath so that I gradually absorbed the anger, sucking its venom back into my system.

Letting go isn't cool but I hoped that so much self-control wouldn't damage me. I still avoid mirrors trying not to think of myself as a woman, longing for some kind of global circumcision to take place within me so that I care no more whether I am male or female. I have spent three years analysing the torture behind the fact that naked I used to be beautiful and now I am ashamed of the mutilation. I've tried to reason away the pain and learn to love my body, diminishing the comparisons. Who'll compensate me for such loss? Once I'm older, it won't matter any more, will it? But now I still have to fight, still have to deal with effects, still have to make decisions. Nothing is over, and no corners have been turned. The nightmares still go on and I have no saintly qualities that can inspire or give me succour. All this is my inner turmoil and of little interest to others. I'm the one who lives with me. I'm afraid to go to sleep. When I wake up, they'll be taking me down.

At six o'clock in the morning, taut as a violin string and ready for action with my glasses firmly in place, they came for me. My heart was beating fast despite the sedative, and I wondered if I could back out of the whole thing. The trolley, after kilometres of hospital corridor, was pushed into a bay with about five other patients all waiting to be operated upon. A fearsome nurse swooped over and pulled off my spectacles, leaving me denuded. I asked her to give them back at least until I was taken into the theatre, but she told me that I should never have been allowed to wear them in the first place. Her sharp reply made my terror escalate, and I thought of jumping off the trolley and running away, but I had no crutches so that was impossible and anyway I wore just a surgery gown that was open down the back. The wait was interminable, and I prayed for something to happen to stop the whole process.

Another nurse came by and fixed a label to my big toe and another with my hospital number was tied around my ankle – making me think of morgues. An hour went by before they came in to get my trolley. Although I could see very little, I was placed near the trays where all the knives and scalpels glittered under the operating table lights and felt shivery knowing they would be slicing away at me. My teeth were chattering as I was placed on my right side in the freezing cold of that room, on a heated plinth rather like a sacrificial altar. Hands did things to me and attached electric wires to my chest. Then the IV doctor took my hand and started to tap lightly on the back just below the wrist, looking for a swelling vein. My veins did the opposite and disappeared. Finally, having fought with all my wits to defy the anaesthetic, I slid off into the land of the unknown, my fate once again in the hands of others.

I was to pick up my red book once again long after the operation, aware that I had to write, but the book had weighed too much and my heart had been too heavy to chronicle the events that were causing such bitter disappointment.

> **23 August 1989 . . . The operation has been an outright failure, but I knew that as soon as I came round. I was lying on my back, which precluded the possibility of a new bottom. There is a very long conspicuous scar running down my ribs from shoulder to waist where the muscle was excised. They couldn't suture it to my buttock and so they threw it away in the rubbish bin. To cheer me up, the surgeon said that he has managed to pull up some of the**

fatty tissue which was my 'dropped bottom' on the left side
and has diminished the old site by a third. I'm sitting in my
hospital bed on tranquillisers and an open wound because,
in expectation of transferring the muscle, the surgeon peeled
off the old skin graft on my buttock. I must now wait until
it is healthy enough to be re-covered, when they will operate
on me again and take a fresh skin graft from another part of
my anatomy.

I remember the effort it took to write those words. All I had wanted
to do was to remove myself from the hospital, New York and America,
but I couldn't because I still needed surgery to put back together what
had been taken apart. Dr Tellez had come to see me when I was still
in the recovery room to give me the awful news, saying how sorry he
was and the disappointment he felt in not being able to do the Free
Flap. The operation was supposed to have lasted only six or seven
hours, but I had been unconscious for at least twenty. None of the
nurses had been able to tell Picci what was going on, and he had
waited, pacing the surgery floor with mounting anxiety, guessing that
there was a problem.

By the time I returned, I was able to talk, although I felt pretty bad.
I had to pull out the sides of my glasses because I couldn't get them
round the cheekbones of my face as I was swollen by about a third and
must have looked like some odd Michelin man propped up on my
pillows. Picci begged me to tell him what had gone wrong, but I was
unable to explain anything. He was furious, already suspecting that a
serious error had been made by the surgeon. He knew that the muscle
from my back had not been attached, and felt that although failure
would have been in some way understandable a few days after the
operation, it was difficult to comprehend how this could have
happened on the operating table itself.

The following day, Dr Tellez and Dr Bloom came to see me
together, perhaps for moral support. They no longer exuded the
previous confidence, neither were they as friendly as they had

hitherto been. Distance yawned between us, and this made me even more frightened. Dr Bloom explained that it hadn't been possible to insert the muscle into the buttock area because it had suffered an embolism and consequently died. He insisted that Dr Tellez's team had worked long and hard to salvage the situation but that, unfortunately, it had all been to no avail. The description of the operation confused me, and I was unable to get a clear understanding as to why things had misfired, but they said that now they knew how the land lay they felt confident that they could do the operation perfectly using the same muscle but on the right side of my back. This admission horrified me, and I listened to them talk, wondering what else I was going to hear while they both appeared to be panicking. At the end of the conversation, Dr Bloom, who was much the more loquacious of the two, asked me what I intended to do. I thought it a very peculiar thing to ask under the circumstances, and the question convinced me something was amiss, but I couldn't let on that I distrusted them and felt they were responsible for the disastrous outcome. I was, after all, very ill in their hospital and although I wanted to get away from them, I knew perfectly well that life wasn't going to be that easy. It was up to them to tell me what they intended doing, as I had a very delicate physical situation that had to be treated. I was in bad shape after this operation, and for the plastic surgery needed on my buttock to be a success I had to get better before going down to theatre again.

The doctors left me with more ideas than I'd had before they came in to talk, and it seemed to me that they both knew there had been a mess-up. Dressings on my buttock had to be changed four times a day, I had a drain hanging out from under my armpit and plasters all down my back. There was a large tunnel going from the buttock scar towards my groin, where they had tried to link up with the saphenous vein. The catheter was in place, although a mere irritant in this latest debacle. Both my legs looked as if they had been blown up by an air compressor, and I was scared of thrombosis given my medical history. As it was, long inflatable leggings were put round both legs and doses of heparin administered during the mornings: nasty burning bee stings but potential lifesavers.

The following day, Picci marched in with pen, paper and carbon copy. He wanted to call the British Consulate about the fiasco but I dissuaded him, concerned not to draw attention to myself. I had phoned Pan Am but no one was available, and all those who'd been involved so far were out of town on business. It was nearly a week before anyone came in to see me. We wrote two letters to the company telling them of the disaster and asking them if they were going to sue the hospital and Dr Tellez. We trusted no one by this time, particularly having seen the way silence reigned when the operation had gone wrong, and as the days passed I too fell silent, knowing that the less I said the more I could perhaps learn.

In the meantime, Dr Tellez told me that he was very tired and had been doing too many of 'these long operations', which felt like a bit of a smack in the face after all that had happened. I had the impression that he had not only been superficial in his evaluation of the case, leaving out important tests, but that he had probably been exhausted by the number of operations he was doing every week. I told Picci what he had said to me and together we wrote another long letter, this time to the insurers of Pan Am asking them what they intended to do on my behalf. By the time Mr Elsie came in to see me, I was quiet and composed. Used to the idea that it had all been for nothing, I wanted only to find out the truth and see if there was any way that I could salvage the situation. I told him that I wished to be examined by firearms specialists and plastic surgeons from other clinics in New York and if necessary around America. He promised me that he would do whatever was necessary. All this was premature as I was weak and hardly in a position to get up and go to other doctors, but I had to do something assertive as vegetating in my bed was killing me and I wanted a professional viewpoint as far as this surgery was concerned.

On about the seventh day, I set off with slow steps towards the bathroom down by the lifts. I wanted to see the damage this time for myself, in the shower. I cannot think why I was prepared to go through so many terrible trials, but it had something to do with trying to accept pain so that it would disappear all the quicker. I had shampoo in my pocket, along with a bottle of strong antiseptic detergent. Once inside the shower, claustrophobically small and painted bright orange, I undressed. The next stage was to remove the dressing, a large nappy-like affair with lengths of adhesive tape securing it in place. As I pulled the tape and started to lift up the white gauze pad, I was sick on the shower-room floor. My knees trembled and I wanted to call a nurse before I blacked out, but something held me back.

Fumbling for the tap, I turned on the shower and swished it all away in a potent jet. I took a deep breath, delivered of the weight in my stomach, and finished taking off the dressing. I stared at what looked like an enormous T-bone steak where my buttock had once been. It looked decidedly off-colour. This rather angry-looking cross-section was a fact of life that could be weighted with any emotional meaning I wished to give it. I felt that no one in that hospital would be sparing a thought for the wound outside work time and that none of them could have cared less for Catherine Hill. Once I'd grasped that idea, I'd be able to move mountains. Taking the bottle of disinfectant soap and pouring some into my left hand, I began to wash the site with care and thoroughness. I'd seen it, smelt it and now I was touching it, not as a dare but because I wanted it to get better. I knew that by keeping it clean and stimulated with water and massage, the granulation of the flesh below my fingers would accelerate. It was clear, too, that accepting the buttock would be much easier if I had an active part in its healing. Even if it felt slippery and uneven, like the feel of a piece of meat when you wash it under the tap, and could have disgusted me, I chose to understand the nature of skin and how it was a little like a waterproof bag into which muscles, bone and organs were packed, and I tried to understand the anatomic configuration of the missing gluteals. I avoided the area where the sciatic nerve passed near the surface, as touching it made my legs buckle with electric shocks, and I was as delicate as I could be. More than any searing pain, I felt as if someone was touching my internal organs, where there was a dull sensation of pressure and every so often sharp tweaks. The epidermis with all those fine nerve endings didn't exist, so, although I felt my own hand touching, it didn't hurt. Slowly I began to respect my body. I felt deep admiration for its tenacity in clinging to life, for the persistent efforts it made to stay well and find harmony. I washed the rest of myself in a kind of ritual of praise. My hair, my arms, my ears and neck were cleansed under the shower, which sprayed down water in abundant complicity.

From that confrontation on, I began to massage the leg I'd so hated, admiring the incredible capacity of the brain which could dull the ache in my bones so that I was not constantly driven by a need to extinguish the uncomfortable sensations. Accepting those things about my body that I couldn't change was a tortuous process and one that didn't come at all easily. That experience of the failed operation held up a certain mirror and, though the reflection was hard to look at, I managed some careful scrutiny, which brought about a long overdue change in my perspective. If nothing else, New York helped me become part of my body once again, and I despised its presence no more.

24

HOMEWARD BOUND

SIX WEEKS WENT by in this transitory stage where the raw flesh of the buttock was exposed to the elements. Picci created a cocoon of love, making me laugh while being as scurrilous and ribald as he could, especially about the doctors. It was one way of hitting back whilst still in the confines of a hospital bed. He was leaving shortly and I would have to stay in New York for at least another month, although we weren't sure how long recovery would really take. Picci suggested that I try to find out what had happened in the operating theatre that day and that I should get hold of a post-operative report. Hopefully, such a report would clarify what had gone wrong.

Francesca, my sister, arrived the day before Picci's departure. We had organised a meeting with Mr Elsie of Pan Am, who agreed, amongst other things, to finance our flight tickets and consultations were I to get second opinions from other doctors in the US. His can't have been a comfortable job – having to bear the brunt of others' desperation, although appreciating his point of view did nothing to alleviate our distress, and solving my problems as fast as possible was our priority. Picci asked Mr Elsie about suing the hospital and whether Pan Am would be willing to do so on our behalf. The reply was neither yes nor no, because many aspects had to be considered and they needed to take legal advice. He felt that it would be a good idea if we started to look for a lawyer in New York ourselves, who would examine the hospital records, thus separating this incident from the Pan Am case. Otherwise, by the time the lawsuit came to trial, he was sure that the hospital defendants would try to lump the injuries sustained in the hijacking and the hospitalisation in New York all together, which would mean that a judge could say the whole problem of damages had already been sorted out and liquidated by the airline company in the trial against Pan Am. So, we decided to pursue the two lawsuits separately. We all hoped that the Pan Am case would be quickly resolved so that there would be no overlapping in terms of time. Finally, the meeting came to a close and Mr Elsie gave me a cheque to take back to Italy for when I was better. He agreed that someone had to provide for me until the case was over and said that it was to be taken out of any final settlement or award. I asked Picci to look after it and put it in my bank on arriving home.

It was wonderful to have my sister at the meeting with me, as she would see how complicated the legal situation was and perhaps word would get around my family that life was not particularly easy for either Picci or me. Hearing these things for herself, Fran would certainly appreciate why I was rarely bubbling over with joy when we spoke on the phone. It was one thing just to listen to subdued comments but quite another to be involved, even peripherally, in the story.

Fran and I were soon ploughing through medical case histories in the research library on the ground floor of the hospital. I was able to walk with the dressings and was very happy to get off the ward, away from hospital odours and boredom, determined to find answers to our doubts. We listed doctors' names and addresses according to the articles they had written, making a series of photocopies. Our work continued for five solid days and on the sixth we spent our time on the phone chasing people for appointments. Fran left for England soon after, and I felt bereft. Seeing her go was more difficult to accept than seeing Picci leave. It felt as if my mother was going away. Somehow there had been so much quiet solidarity with my sister and we had become close during that period. Neither of us was particularly effusive, but the strong warmth was there and I felt very alone as she waved goodbye from her taxi.

Jenny arrived a couple of days later and joked about not wanting to be 'taken seriously' the next time she made a rash offer. She was a recently made girlfriend, but one of the dearest and kindest people I had ever known. She was from New Zealand, and we'd met up in Italy through a mutual friend who'd given her my address. She had flown to Britain looking for work and had foolishly said to me that if I ever needed her, she would drop everything and come. So I'd rung her up from the States and asked her to fly over to New York to look after me. She interrupted her contract as a teacher and arrived after taking unpaid leave for the last stretch of that interminable summer. She was a great cook and marvellous nurse, and also kept me entertained. She insisted on changing the dressings herself because I put the tapes on crookedly, and I was amazed at how she managed to deal with the wound without throwing up, especially as I was so squeamish regarding other people's cuts and general bodily functions. She also put up admirably with my unreasonable attitude to food. Since my experience of anorexia, I was paranoid about what went into my system and quite rigid over what I would eat.

We went for regular check-ups on the progress of the wound and soon it became a brilliant red, a sign that it was healthy once more. Dr Tellez was still away, so we interrogated poor Dr Truman, his assistant. With my red notebook and sharp pencil, we'd go into the surgery and write down explanations of this or that aspect of the operation. Gradually, having asked the same questions in different ways over a series of meetings, we obtained a much clearer picture of what had happened, although I still didn't think we had got to the truth.

Over the following weeks, Jenny and I caught planes to

Washington, Boston and Minnesota for hospital appointments with renowned specialists. It was quite tiring getting back into ordinary life when I was hampered by bleach-soaked cotton strapped to my bottom. I was weakened by the previous arduous operation and, unfortunately, convalescence was something that I could do only when back in Italy. Whilst getting second opinions, it was tempting to ask doctors what they thought of Dr Tellez's work, but I knew better than to probe. Nearly all of them expressed concern that I should not undergo further surgery of such an aggressive nature, and none of them adopted the patronising tones I'd sometimes encountered over the course of my hospital experiences. Jenny's pencil scratched away as she wrote down the answers to our many questions. Perhaps they were shy of people taking notes after such failed surgery, as they knew just what a dissatisfied patient might instigate. We were treated with wary caution, words were measured and a much more conservative hypothesis made regarding future intervention.

Dr Tellez came back into my life and declared I was ready to have a split skin graft. We made an appointment for 26 September, although there was a very definite coolness between us. No doubt his assistant had told him that we had been determined to understand what had happened. I couldn't help feeling strange under his ministering hands and any flow of trust had completely disappeared as far as I was concerned. I rang Dr Bloom and explained my feelings and that I was disturbed at the thought of Dr Tellez operating on me again. I asked him if he could do the plastic surgery and tell his colleague that I would no longer be his patient. His reaction took me by surprise, as, laughing, he said that I was asking him to do the dirty work. Such a turn of phrase was upsetting to hear. Given that he was and had been the coordinator of my operation, was head of the plastic surgery department and, finally, was the person who had handed me over to Dr Tellez in the first place, I thought that dealing with this was the least he could do by way of reparation.

According to the new plans, I was booked in for surgery under Dr Bloom, and this time the procedure was undertaken very carefully indeed. Laboratory tests were carried out to make sure the area was healthy and ready for grafting, and all the pre-surgery exams were performed, regardless of their certainty that I was going to be just fine. I remained on my stomach for five days until such time as the graft was deemed stable. On the sixth day and the day before I was due out, Jenny came to assist in the removal of the staples in the harvest site, which was my other buttock. After all her wonderful stoic help over those weeks, she finally succumbed, fainting flat out on the floor, overcome by the gruesome sight of someone pulling large staples out of the right side of my bottom.

Sick to death of New York, the hermetically sealed windows where not a breath of fresh air came into our rooms, and nostalgic for Europe, we booked our flights for England the following day, despite the fact that I was not really fit to travel. I didn't care any longer and just wanted to go. It would mean travelling in a prone position tummy down, but I thought this was more or less a practical difficulty and as such could be easily accommodated.

Mr Elsie accompanied us to the airport in a taxi, in which I sprawled across the back seat, my face in Jenny's lap. Our conversation was at first formal, but somehow my position was not conducive to stiff niceties and after a while we were talking about Mr Elsie's life and family. He told me about his daughter, who was very ill, and his search to find a cure for her condition. We asked questions about his job and, for some reason, our chat flowed along with great ease. The taxi-driver must have had enough to chew on for the next few months in terms of information, what with Lockerbie, Karachi and the incongruous position I was forced to assume while conversing. Mr Elsie confided in us, telling us of how he had had to talk to the victims' families after the Lockerbie disaster. He'd had to follow through all lines of investigation and represent Pan Am in offering condolences but had not been able to think of anything appropriate to say to these poor people, as the devastation had been so great. Obviously, he was a natural target for anger and accusations, and he could neither give comfort nor defend himself. His had been a thankless, sad job.

By now, the story of the Karachi hijacking was burning in my head. I wanted to know what had happened from the beginning to the end, and if the terrorists were in prison somewhere. He told me that he had been present at their trial in Islamabad. Apparently, the US had asked for extradition but the request had been denied, Pakistan herself wanting to try the criminals. He described his distress at seeing the look of triumph on the faces of the hijackers as they lied their way through the hearings, not even vaguely attempting to corroborate their stories one with another. They were fearless, thinking that their penance would be short lived and within a few years they would be out of prison ready to return to their families as heroes. Mr Elsie, oblivious to the distress I was experiencing, went on talking as if finally he was able to spew out all the sadness and injustice he had had to witness over the years in his job. I saw this man as a fellow sufferer and stopped accusing him in my heart of being part of a system that had denied me my health and serenity. Our taxi drive heralded a new and less formal relationship, as I realised that he was anything but a calculating person, rather he was someone doing his job as well as he could in the circumstances. Perhaps it was this new understanding that paved the way for our future and kept us walking together, either side of a mutual reality: he as a constant witness to acts of terrorism and their long-term effects and I as someone who continued to experience those acts and their hard repercussions.

25

A BREAKTHROUGH

I HAD BEEN back to work part-time from September 1988 to summer 1989, still teaching freelance and doing about 15 hours a week. I continued a previous teaching contract with 3M and went back to my classes in the company feeling a certain embarrassment. My group of technicians, who had been so supportive of my operations in America, had sent a massive bouquet of flowers to me in New York when they heard of the disaster. Now, on my return, they tentatively asked me what had gone wrong and, at first, I found it hard to hold back my tears and behave in a professional way. They were all so kind and understanding, I felt lucky to be surrounded by such lovely people.

Work and research, if not antidotes to the bitterness of the New York period, at least stopped me thinking too much about it. On a late afternoon, at the end of a session in the library, while reading through a bibliography, I saw the heading 'APU Rupture. Karachi Hijack'. I had never heard the term rupture used in connection with our hijacking before, nor did I have any notion of what an APU might be, but I felt it was a good lead. At the Istituto di Ingegneria Aerospaziale, at four o'clock in the afternoon of the following

Tuesday, I sat down to read the article. It had been hard getting the appointment, as the library was not open to the public. Furthermore, I wasn't comfortable explaining why I wanted the piece. Saying that I'd been involved in a hijack was a stumbling block, and I found time and again that I had to explain my story to someone I didn't know. This always proved to be a strain, especially over the phone, but there seemed to be no other way round it.

I was taken down into the vaults of the library and a thin young man who already had the stoop and look of an academic flipped through a volume to find my article. He handed it over and I scanned the index for the page number, missing it twice in my hurry. I started reading, my heart accelerating at every line, while I devoured the words and realised that, finally, I was on to the real reason why the lights and air conditioning had failed on the plane. The presence of the flight engineer, or rather his lack of presence, had, in my opinion, been a determining factor in the final shoot-out. The article revealed the essential part of the story that had hitherto been missing. The APU, or Auxiliary Power Unit, is an external source of electrical power that most aircraft are equipped with, to be used when the plane is grounded so as not to consume its battery. An inspection of the unit showed that a hole had opened up in the cooling duct and this had automatically shut the unit down, interrupting light and air circulation, thus plunging all passengers into darkness and great heat. This had preceded the massacre. How the hole had appeared was not explained, but perhaps more could be discovered.

I felt that this article contained the lynchpin indicating the partial responsibility of the airline company. With laughter bubbling up inside, I thanked the student and went to give the good news to Picci. The next step was to write an explanation on how an APU worked, otherwise the judge would be as clueless as I had been and could miss the whole point of this piece of evidence. My news was great, certainly, but entailed lengthy preparation. Neither Picci nor I were capable of doing this work on our own and finding someone who could write a simplified and coherent description would be time-consuming. We rang our new lawyer Mr Bremmer, Mr Botti's replacement, to whom we'd assigned the case just before going to the States, asking him to phone for an appointment with Mr Napolitani. Mr Napolitani was unable to make it to the meeting but participated in a telephone conference in Mr Bremmer's offices, a method of communication I've always found disconcerting, and he maintained that the evidence of the cockpit crew's escape was sufficient for the judge and that there was no need to go into further detail. I pointed out that the more watertight the proof that Pan Am had placed the lives of the passengers in danger, the better our chances of winning a reasonable settlement in or outside a courtroom. He compromised and agreed to include the APU point at some stage in the case, which he did, at a later hearing.

We also asked our lawyers to make out a fuller written document, which would include Pan Am's invitation to the States to undergo surgery and its unfortunate outcome. As far as we were concerned these details were essential, as we were beginning to formulate a request for damages in our own heads that accommodated both an insurance policy for my future health and a realistic figure for the injuries sustained. The new evidence was vital to the development of the logic of the case, but after the conference call, I couldn't help wondering if all the alterations we had mentioned would be made. Mr Bremmer, noting my worry, said that during the course of the next hearing, he would be speaking to the judge about what had happened to me in New York, because telling someone the story was much more effective than just writing about it.

The day before the hearing, Mr Napolitani phoned to say that he'd be attending rather than Mr Bremmer. My heart dropped down into my boots. Picci had planned on accompanying our new lawyer, ready to spur him into decisive action. Now that idea had to be shelved. I waited for news in the office, expecting the entire morning to pass, but Picci arrived long before lunch, exasperated. The whole thing, for which I had done so much preparation, had taken all of ten minutes. Napolitani had presented our deposition, and exchanged jokes and niceties with the judge and the lawyers for Pan Am. Picci had waited for there to be some mention of the New York experience and the predicament I was now in with regard to my health, but nothing was said and the hearing quickly closed. The letter promising financial help in my quest for a cure signed by Pan Am, although part of the 25 or so documents attached to the court papers, wasn't explained to the judge. We felt that various areas of the case that we thought were immediately important would be treated more urgently if pointed out to the judge as Mr Bremmer had suggested. Picci would have spoken himself but it was already unusual to be admitted to the hearing and, ignorant of his rights as the plaintiff, he felt he couldn't jeopardise our positions by being asked to leave the court. After the hearing, Napolitani stopped to chat with another lawyer he knew by sight, thus quelling the confused barrage of questions Picci had been about to ask. The moment passed and Napolitani clapped Picci on the back, announcing that the case was going very well indeed and that he would be in touch to talk about the next step. Once again, he couldn't stop any longer as he was late for his next appointment.

We discussed the case, and Mr Napolitani, as we drove that afternoon through the cold rain on our way to a medical examiner, trying to make sense of his tactics. Mr Bremmer, our new lawyer, had made us an appointment with an expert from his insurance days, who had said he could examine us both to determine the extent of our injuries and therefore the damages we could claim. Unfortunately, however, through no fault of Mr Bremmer, this meeting turned out to be a complete waste of time as the doctor concerned was arrogant and completely disinterested in my condition. The meeting ended abruptly with Picci and me leaving in high dudgeon.

Mr Bremmer was not pleased by what had happened and went to the opposite extreme of using the services of an autopsy police specialist working at the University of Pavia, who was equally at home with both dead and alive bodies, which was a worrying thought. The specialist was doing his friend Mr Bremmer a favour, having received a long letter from him seeking his help. Mr Bremmer was eager to unruffle our ruffled feathers and, reading between the lines, he must have implored his friend to treat us well. The doctor was patient and considerate, suggesting specialists I could go and see who might help me with certain problems. The report was detailed, with photographic documentation, and ran into the region of 30 pages of type. His evaluation of my injuries amounted to 75 per cent on the Italian point system, while Picci's was 15 per cent. Roughly translated this meant that 25 per cent of my body was still all right. This was great stuff as far as the compensation was concerned but a bit of a depressing thought. Both bosoms were intact along with my right leg and most of my head, except for the memory slips I experienced all too frequently, and the nightmares.

Time was marching on despite the deadweight quality it had acquired. I was working, went for physiotherapy regularly and spent most weekends away with Picci. We were not going through the happiest of periods together. I was more shaken by what had happened in the States than I was openly prepared to admit and was finding it extremely difficult to deal with the possibility that there might not be anything else that could be done to improve my physical condition. I felt very insecure and lucky to get any love and affection at all; once again I was having problems accepting myself.

I became highly sensitive about my physical defects. In Italy, I couldn't help but suffer as a result of the continual barrage of sexually charged images from the TV, billboards, magazines and papers. They can't sell kitchen cleaner without a long-legged mini-skirted beauty with wet parted lips caressing the article concerned. Not that I consciously compared myself to these women, but subconsciously something twisted was going on inside me, and I sought refuge from daily reminders that I couldn't even vaguely compete.

Times were hard indeed that spring. Where once I made light of my problems, I now began to suffer bouts of anger, similar to the hysteria I'd first experienced in New York. Where once I never spoke of the pain I suffered, I would now openly say I hurt, and in moments of physical defeat I would burst into hopeless tears.

The February hearing of 1990 went by, leaving in its wake two sides of handwriting from the judge where he explained that witnesses would have to be cited at some point in the future and that he accepted the request that Picci's case and mine be united in one lawsuit. This was a straightforward procedure that would save paperwork, given that the judicial procedure was exactly the same for both cases.

The judge, imagining that we were near the end of our evidence gathering, had concluded the hearing by appointing a date in October and stipulating it as being our last opportunity to present further evidence against Pan Am. After this date, even if we were to discover that the terrorists had been former Pan Am employees, the proof would not have been accepted as part of the trial.

The problem of the APU had to be resolved between the spring and summer of that year if we were to get an edge over our adversaries. The months marked our dearth of progress and the summer holidays loomed. Lacking in enthusiasm and imagination, we decided to stay in Italy. We were just too tired to do anything other than rest. Perhaps we would find inspiration from a long break doing nothing but spending time together.

26

MADONNA WITH BARE BREASTS

WE LEFT MILAN at the end of July after a very irritable fortnight. The legal case was getting to me. The fact that I couldn't turn over a new leaf and get on with my life was causing me enormous stress. On the journey down to Rome, we had a ferocious quarrel, the most horrible we had ever had, and it didn't clear the air at all, because every day for a week we continued bickering in a series of spiteful eruptions. The slightest thing would set us off: it could be because I slammed the car door too hard, or my driving was too dreamy. It could have been the look on my face or what I had said. I was so confused by his irritation that for the first time I doubted Picci's feelings for me. He seemed really exasperated; I hated my dependence on him and would have done anything to escape from this constant sensation of being in his debt, a millstone round his neck. I just didn't know how to deal with this side of his character, having had no previous warning that he could change from deeply involved and helpful to highly critical and nasty.

I overreacted to any form of criticism, becoming shaky within, to the extent of losing my flimsy self-esteem altogether. A healthy f... off would have been the proper way to balance things out between us and the hostilities would have ceased very rapidly. I have since discovered how to defend myself and can be a bit of a Molotov when provoked.

Picci had started flying lessons, a passion that had always been just a dream until that summer when, fed up with the pressure of fighting our legal battles, he finally decided to learn. He was keen on getting some practice in, before taking his exams in November and blue sky, sleep and his flying lessons with an exceptionally calm flying instructor healed his shredded nerves. We moved through the bad period, although shockwaves reverberated in me for the rest of the holiday. At that time I wasn't used to fighting and was frightened by the feelings Picci had obviously experienced and which had also become unleashed within me. I felt guilty for being disabled and wondered if we both wouldn't be better off with different partners. The thought was miserable to contemplate and I veered away from such tragic meanderings.

During the next three weeks I put on a lot of weight, becoming rotund and curvy. I often spent my mornings at the swimming pool in the town and so became a deep golden brown from sunbathing. I felt rather like one of the over-ripe peaches we gorged ourselves on every day. In fact, the Abruzzi food seemed to be a huge comfort as well as being delicious, and my lack of exercise seemed to add to my lust for sustenance.

Eight days on, and fed up with all this inertia, we decided to hike up Gran Sasso. At 2,915 metres, it was the highest mountain in the Appenines. We set off, following an old sheep trail on a cloudless, torrid afternoon. On the rounded back of the first hill was a gigantic crucifix soaring up into the sky. I was hot and dusty, and sick of the confines and restrictions my crutches and clothes inflicted on me. There wasn't a soul in sight as far as I could see, and so I stripped off my shirt, delighted to do something wayward. Bare-breasted, with my hair loose down my back, I swung up the hill with easy vigorous strides. Loving the sensation of the light breeze on my body, I began to sing at the top of my voice, expressing my immediate joy in being where I was, doing what I was doing. Picci edged away from me, reminding me that others went hill walking, too, and that I was very silly to expose myself in this way. But that only made me sing even louder and I felt wonderful, free and defiant. It didn't really matter what I sang, and I believe even the national anthem got a look in.

I'd worked my way through a fair number of old favourites and was gasping out the diddle diddle dum of 'Rondo alla Turka' when I passed under the cross. The gaze of the old shepherd I nearly collided with was one of utter wonder. He had just completed the same trail but on the other side of the hill, and we met as we both topped the crest. I spun round, tugging a sun top out of my little backpack. Picci had seen the scenario and moved gallantly towards us, ready to engage the speechless man in conversation. I was a little flummoxed, but, decency restored, joined their conversation and just as if nothing had happened we all chatted about sheep. After about ten minutes, we each went our own way. Somewhat mortified but not that much, I followed Picci's disapproving back down the hill.

The holiday over, we were often to wonder what the old shepherd, his sinewy muscles strong and still in good working order, told his friends in the local bar – that he'd seen a bare-breasted apparition, a Madonna with crutches, or the truth. Whatever he recounted would be shot down in gales of disbelieving hilarity. 'Eh, Giuseppe, how much did you drink at lunchtime?'

Picci's reserved flying instructor, Comandante Bruni, had been a commercial pilot of a Boeing 747, in other words a jumbo, and he was now retired. He was still very young and had decided to become an instructor at the airclub in Aquila. We began to ask him questions about the APU, which of course was something he was very familiar with. He already knew about our hijack because he clearly remembered the news on TV and how the cockpit crew had escaped down ropes when they realised that terrorists had stormed the plane.

Over the following days, our conversations with the instructor centred on one topic only and that was the various aspects of the hijack. We learnt how the APU worked and how it was fundamental that the flight engineer be on board to monitor the machine via the cockpit instruments. Were the APU to break down, there was always plenty of warning on the panel, which was a highly sensitive gauge. I asked him what might have caused a hole to form in an oil duct, but he said that there could be many reasons for this. Comandante Bruni then explained the ethical position Italian pilots adopted in a hijack, and, as Napolitani had told us, the last thing they should do was abandon the passengers by running away from the aircraft.

We were lucky that our Comandante was so concerned about our plight. He contacted a friend of his who happened to be a flight engineer called Marco Troisi. Mr Troisi was an aviation engineer and promised to write out a report on the functioning of the APU. We were immensely grateful to be in such excellent hands. He said he would be in touch with us at the end of September with news of how his report was going.

Our holiday ended after a delightful and scenic journey home, where we included a visit to another little airfield with a mad flying instructor who made us laugh with his dry Tuscan wit. We also fitted in a two-day stopover with friends who owned a vineyard on the top of a romantic Umbrian hill near Spoleto. There we caught up on news and had supper in the unconsecrated chapel that now served as a dining room. The only thing that made me a little nervous was the huge bell that was still in place directly over the table and which, had it fallen, would have neatly cut off our heads. It was of considerable size and high above us, magnificent in its sombre grey presence but I wondered about the maintenance of the bell ropes. The walls had been whitewashed and over the wooden arched doorway a stunning stained-glass rose window filtered in the last warm rays of the summer sun. An earthy uneven terracotta floor made the extraordinary chapel perfect, and we couldn't help but converse and behave as if we, too, were descendants of some noble Umbrian family – a rich evening and invigorating encounter that sweetened and boosted our frustratingly fun-impoverished existence.

27

A LAWYER FIRED

ON THE DAY of our meeting in early October 1990, Mr Bremmer was quite clearly bursting with something important to tell us. While waiting for Mr Napolitani, we exchanged essential small talk about the holidays, after which Mr Bremmer, unable to contain himself further, began his introductory speech. He talked about how fascinating this case was for him and that we were exceptional clients, interested in every modicum of detail, conscientious and hard working. (We were well aware of what a nuisance we really were for them.) My courage with the injuries I had was a great inspiration to everyone. Mr Bremmer felt, however, that as I was evidently becoming exhausted by the litigation with the airline company and with it taking up such a lot of my time, wouldn't it be a good idea to close the case as soon as possible?

It took a moment for the words to sink in and when they did I was baffled by his misreading not of my stress level but of the strategy we thought everyone was following. Whatever was he thinking of? Of course it wasn't the right time. We didn't have the airline company in a position of surrender yet. Encouraged by our silence, he continued, saying that he'd been to America and visited the insurers of Pan Am just to see how the land lay with regard to closing the case. I sat listening, wondering why he hadn't told us of his intentions before leaving Italy, as we most certainly would have warned him against doing anything we felt was so rash. Our lawyer, by showing interest in a prompt transaction, had revealed to Pan Am weakness on our part and a need to settle out of court fast with all the compromise that would entail. Mr Bremmer's initiative could only mean one thing as far as I could see: that he was keen to see the case brought to an end. Mr Napolitani would have to agree with this idea, as would we, and we had shown no signs of giving up or wanting to conclude proceedings. I did not believe Mr Napolitani had been party to the idea of this visit and had no idea of what his reaction would be.

Neither Picci nor I said anything, but Mr Bremmer must have caught the chilly waves rippling towards him as he then tried to play down the importance of his meeting in New York, eventually claiming that he had merely 'called in' on the company and had been lucky enough to speak to someone involved in the case.

We told our lawyer clearly that there was no way Picci and I were going to talk about settling our case without having first explained the material we'd prepared regarding the APU. Until every scrap of evidence was lodged with the judge, we would refuse to close the case. We needed valid bargaining power otherwise Pan Am would trample us underfoot.

Anyway, we now had another problem as we had to investigate the financial difficulties the company was in. My cousin, Albertina, had sent me a copy of an article from the *San Francisco Examiner* of 3 June 1990, which outlined the turbulent times that Pan Am was experiencing. The picture that the journalist painted was far from optimistic, as Pan Am's share price had plummeted and they were selling off their Boston, Washington, New York and German routes in an attempt to inject much-needed cash into their coffers. The situation was to become drastic in the new year, but even that small mention was sufficient to start Picci worrying, as their insolvency could make our lives even more difficult.

The doorbell rang and I jumped. As the meeting room door closed on us, Picci and I exchanged worried glances. Compared to our anxious state, Mr Napolitani seemed to be feeling on top of the world that day, handkissing and bowing to all of us, and lavishing compliments on Mr Bremmer's secretary, a whiskery spinster who blushed at such unexpected gallantry. Like some grand impresario, he swept everyone towards the table and with himself seated at the head, paternally asked us all how we were. Picci, slightly embarrassed, opened the meeting, reminding everyone that witnesses had to be found and contacted, the APU evidence and report included and explained, and Pan Am's financial difficulties investigated. He immediately set the tone, and all gaiety ceased as we tried to impress upon our lawyers the sense of urgency and worry we no longer wished to rein in or check. Mr Napolitani listened with the necessary attention and gravity. He, too, expressed worry about the financial problems, asking Picci if he had any information about Pan Am's financial situation. As yet, the only thing we had to go on was newspaper reports. We agreed to try and get hold of something official in terms of proof, to show they were heading for stormy waters, although neither lawyer was able to suggest from whom we could get more information. Last, but by no means least, we talked about how to include the APU evidence.

The meeting was adjourned and I was given to the end of October to do my research. By then all the information and new elements would be gathered and a final court document made out and submitted. I groaned inwardly because it was all back on my shoulders. I was the one who had to do the work and procure all the information. Mr Bremmer didn't look very enthusiastic either and seemed unsettled that instead of things drawing to a close they were burgeoning, becoming ever more complex. Mr Napolitani had dismissed the news that Mr Bremmer had met up with the insurers as being of little consequence, although how he really felt about the initiative was anyone's guess.

That month I worked as if there were no tomorrow trying to follow up the necessary references, witnesses and reports, but I was still way behind target by the time the documents were due. Our fellow passengers, those we knew of who lived in Italy, had moved house and were also reluctant to testify, as they were not keen on raking over painful memories. Anyway, I think they had settled within the Warsaw Convention, as only one of them had incurred serious injury. Other passengers, living elsewhere in the world, were pursuing their own battles for compensation, and at that time finding out who they were and what they were doing was time consuming and not useful to us. I would not have liked to meet any of my fellow injured either, as I could not have coped with listening to their stories of suffering. My experience had been bad enough and there were many others who had been as brutally wounded if not worse. We did get in touch with one person from Germany and someone else in England, but neither was doing any better than we were. They were waiting for lawsuits to start either in their own country or in the States.

Witnesses such as the pilot, flight engineer and head of the Federal Aviation Administration at that time were hard to find addresses for, and I was often obliged to put down those of their workplaces. The time needed was enormous, and I spent whole mornings and afternoons on the telephone. It was a gruelling period, as I had to obtain results and time was against me.

Over-stimulated by all this research, I'd also come up with another idea, which was to try to prove the 'nexus' between the lights failing and the terrorist shootout. Given that everything we said about Pan Am had to be backed up by evidence, I thought that a psychologist's study on terrorists and the effects of stress on them would support the claim that it had been the breakdown of the APU which had led to the violence. By then, both Picci and I were convinced that we had to corroborate everything that we said not only with witnesses but also with professional reports. I contacted my psychologist from the hospital in London. Would he be prepared to write something about the effects of stress on hijackers and the effects of sudden changes in psychological tension? He was interested in the connection I was trying to make and felt it worth studying, but was reluctant to do anything for me because he felt that it was too heavily geared to a court case and therefore not impartial enough. Another psychologist I consulted got cold feet and pulled out when I told him I needed a report for the Milan courts.

With the feeling that I was getting nowhere fast, I decided that the best thing to do was get hold of the written hearings from the trials of the terrorists in Islamabad in an attempt to see if they themselves confessed to killing people because the lights had failed on the plane. What I knew about the hijackers and their fate was minimal, but, since talking to Mr Elsie, I imagined that records of their trials would be held somewhere in archives in Pakistan. As regards their sentences or acquittal, I didn't know what had happened.

The search for such documents was a long shot, and I had my doubts about being able to obtain such delicate information, but I wanted to try everything I could. I was still hoping to find the complete report made out by the Federal Aviation Administration or the FBI on the hijacking, and I was very keen on having Mr Bernard Leak, a former high-ranking employee of the FAA, as a witness. From what I had read, he had been very puzzled over the way the Karachi hijack had been handled, and security in general. I wrote to the FAA asking for his whereabouts and was sent his address and phone number. He was now running a consultancy firm for aviation security. Miraculously, I managed to speak to him after much phone filtering and was able to ask him if he could help us by acting as an expert witness at the trial, obtaining documents or finding out facts. I wanted him to get hold of an official report on what had happened during the hijack. He was prepared to help, but it was obvious that his services would be expensive and he offered to fax me a copy of his tariffs.

Picci and I decided, in view of the fact that we just didn't have time to collate all the necessary evidence for the date of this hearing, that we should ask the judge to postpone it, giving him clear examples of where our difficulties lay. Mr Troisi had been delayed in writing out the APU report due to work commitments, and he too needed another month or so. I had also received the tariff sheet from Mr Leak and was somewhat shocked by how much he cost. For the time being, we stalled, unsure of how to proceed, particularly as I was waiting for a letter from a lawyer in Pakistan to see if he could get the written trial records of the terrorists from Islamabad. I had read that all five men who had been involved in the hijacking were now in prison, including the man who had masterminded the attack. Initially they had been sentenced to capital punishment but this had later been commuted to life imprisonment, whatever that meant in Pakistan.

Two days after the agreed date by which I had to give the data to the lawyers, we received a reminder by fax that Mr Bremmer was awaiting the names of the witnesses and the APU report. We sent him what we had, telling him that the report was delayed and asking him to send us the amended copy of the new deposition.

On reading his new version, we felt that Mr Bremmer didn't really understand the strategy we wished to pursue, and that he was keen to close the case. We realised that we had reached the end of our road together. However, we still had to ask Mr Bremmer to defer the hearing, as we didn't have all the evidence, reports or ideas completed. We sat up late discussing the best way to go about things and eventually wrote a fax asking him to make a request that the hearing be postponed for six months. I was still convinced that something might yet come of the trial documents and the hijacking report, and we just didn't feel ready to close the door on having new evidence admitted to the lawsuit.

We sent the memorandum the following afternoon, knowing full well that he would not like what we had written one bit. Everything in the note pointed to a long, drawn-out trial, which was precisely what he did not want. With my fingers in my ears, I was ready for the phone to ring and explode in my hand when I picked it up that day. Sure enough, at 7 p.m., the sound split the by now tense atmosphere in the office. Picci was packing up groups of razor-sharp heating elements in the warehouse and I was manning the switchboard. My heart was knocking against my ribs and I felt as if I'd gone to the top of the building and was contemplating flying off. I was a terrible coward when it came to confrontation. I heard Mr Bremmer's voice tremble lightly, 'Ah, good evening, Miss Hill. I'm phoning about your fax sent this afternoon.' I imagined his fury from where I was sitting and felt paralysed by irrational fear. 'Please hold, Mr Bremmer,' I said, cutting him off with some phone disco music. 'It's you-know-who on the phone and I think he wants to strangle us,' I squeaked from the office doorway to Picci. 'Can you talk to him, I'm useless.'

Picci, calm and relaxed, eased up from his taping, crossed the courtyard to wash his hands and remove his overall. He sat down at the desk as I hovered nearby. The cold but extremely polite conversation that ensued took exactly one minute before it caught fire. Picci told Mr Bremmer that it didn't look as if he had exactly sweated over the latest draft. After all the phone calls and the last meeting, why hadn't the material for the hearing been used in the ways we had suggested? Our lawyer was hardly up to the mental gymnastics Picci was so good at under stress. Some people perform well in heated moments and others don't. Mr Bremmer lost this battle and said he would be reconsidering his position about representing us, as he felt there were serious problems over agreement on lawsuit strategy. What annoyed him most was the appeal for a postponement of the hearing. Apparently this was just not the done thing. It was completely unheard of to request such an absurdity, although when we asked for logical reasons why, they were not forthcoming. Picci ended the call saying, 'I shall wait here all evening for a fax indicating that you have altered the rough draft. I must be sure that at next week's hearing the judge receives our requests and understands the difficulties we are having.' The phone was slammed down at the other end and Picci was left holding a dead receiver.

'What happens if he doesn't do as we wish?' I asked nervously.

'We'll have to speak to the judge personally and explain the disintegration of the relationship between lawyer and client,' Picci replied.

Just to make sure that Mr Bremmer did as we asked, we sent a telegram to his office insisting that he carry out our request to postpone the hearing and that he send the document back by fax the same evening. This was fortunately carried out and our trial put on hold for a further six months until spring 1991. A week later, Mr Bremmer wrote and said that he was not sure that he should continue in his position as our lawyer given our evident divergence of ideas. To put us all out of our collective misery, we wrote him a letter saying that we would no longer be requiring his services. It was sad and embarrassing to have to close the relationship with our lawyer, who, as a person, was a very nice man.

Napolitani phoned us up the following day trying to reduce any damage done. He had been concerned that he'd have to represent us in court if we couldn't find another lawyer to do so immediately. He regretted that he had so little time with all his other serious cases to deal with, so he had been somewhat relieved after the hearing to learn that the trial had been postponed until spring 1991.

Although satisfied, we were back to square one in that we had to find another lawyer. Mr Napolitani evidently decided that he could not leave things so much in his procurator's hands by continuing to focus mainly on the aviation aspects of the case and announced over the phone a few days later that he was in Milan for the Azores plane crash trial the following week and wanted to see us while in town. He was the legal representative for the relatives of those who had died when their plane had hit a mountain on the Azores because of dense fog, and he frequently came to Milan to deal with the case. He could fit us in in the evening and would wait for us at his hotel. We were pleased with his decision, as the idea of having a closer examination together of the evidence we were trying to gather was encouraging and hopeful.

28

A LAWYER HIRED

WE MET HIM in the foyer of Residence Manini, a four-star hotel situated quite near where Picci lived by the cathedral. He arrived down from his room rather hot and bothered from having had to use the stairs because the lift wasn't working. He greeted us, saying how he'd spent the entire afternoon reading over our documents in order to reflect on the way we should present the spring hearing. He announced that he was exhausted and drained by the constant effort of helping people. With that, he excused himself for having forgotten to kiss my hand and, bowing deeply, did so, asking Picci if we would accompany him for a meal, as he had had nothing to eat since breakfast. On this particular day of the week most restaurants in Milan were closed, meaning that the choice of a place was limited. We wound up eventually in a drab pizzeria with neon lighting that brought out the careworn pallor of our city faces. Mr Napolitani, ravenously hungry, ate a plate of pasta and mussels, and, relaxing, he talked at length of his life and family. When food had charged up his exhausted state, he was able to see us once again as his clients, and, chiding us, he said that we should have had more patience as far as Mr Bremmer was concerned, yet I felt that he was not particularly upset at having lost his colleague. At the end of the meal, we accompanied Mr Napolitani back to his hotel. He asked us if we had anyone else in mind to act as our lawyer, to which we replied in the affirmative. In fact, we had no one to hand, but wanted to find our own representative once again.

We really were going to have to accelerate things and find someone fast before it was too late, so Picci phoned one of the lawyers who usually looked after his legal business matters and a few days later he was able to recommend someone who would act as a procurator for Napolitani in Milan. Mr Napolitani would still be looking after the aspects of aviation law but all the other areas of the case would be in the hands of the new lawyer, and we needed him to follow our ideas.

An interview was arranged. Mr Bellicoso, the new contender, worked in Via Daino, a tiny street weaving in and out of the huge late eighteenth-century houses from behind Piazza San Babila. I had arrived a little early, eager as ever not to be late, and turned just at the right moment to see Picci come sauntering towards me. I smiled at him. I was never indifferent to his presence, and he always made my heart skip a beat at the most unexpected moments.

The gate clicked open and we went up the flight of stone stairs to the first floor. The door was already open, welcoming us into a small hallway. An antique chaise longue was on one side, with mauve and cream upholstering. The floor was covered by a rich navy-blue wool carpet and everything was in exquisite good taste. It looked more like the entrance to some private art gallery than a lawyer's studio.

Our possible future procurator and 'matador' was big, bald and had rather a lugubrious expression. As Picci went through the story – God, how you could get sick and tired of hearing it – I watched Bellicoso. He smiled frequently from his position at the table, revealing a shiny grey brace that was wrapped round his upper teeth. I had never seen an adult wearing a brace before, and was fascinated. Once more I was getting stuck on people-watching when I should have been listening to what was going on. Picci stated our case clearly, emphasising the need to have someone on the job with punch and who would follow, more or less, a strategy that had been worked out but that called for good written composition.

Six months may have seemed a long time, but in actual fact the weeks flew by relentlessly. We left all our documentation, the files of the trial, the photographs and newspaper cuttings with Mr Bellicoso over the Christmas holidays, as we had more or less agreed to take him on as our new procurator. I was neutral about the whole event, feeling pretty disillusioned with legal and medical professionals. One thing which did satisfy us, though, was that he seemed to feel very strongly about the way compensation should be allotted and he wanted to pitch our request much higher than that initially asked for by Mr Napolitani.

We duly informed Mr Napolitani about our new procurator, and he pronounced that he was immensely satisfied that we had found someone else to act for him in Milan. Our next appointment before the judge was for the beginning of April. We agreed to speak to our new lawyer in January on our return from a much-needed Christmas break to hotter climes, and we would be informing him of the date for a meeting with Mr Napolitani. Our roller-coaster lawsuit was still on course even if it was an alarmingly volatile one.

29

A STRANGE EXPERIENCE

WHILE FLYING BACK from an island in the Bahamas on 9 January 1991, we read in one of the Italian newspapers, 'Pan Am in serious difficulty'. Pan Am was going under like the *Titanic*. The report gave a blow-by-blow account of the company's financial situation, explaining the extent of its debts and blaming the catastrophe on rising fuel costs and the ever-decreasing number of passengers. Financial analysts gave their opinions and felt that the problem lay with the fact that Pan Am's image had suffered a severe blow after the Lockerbie disaster and people were avoiding using the airline for obvious reasons. Pan Am had apparently asked a New York tribunal for protection from creditors through the use of Chapter 11. This was a term used in the US bankruptcy courts whereby any company in financial difficulty could seek refuge and be protected by the law over a certain period of time so that it could attempt to sort out its finances without having to cope with creditors knocking on the door. The news was worrying and threw us back into the state of confusion and anxiety we had experienced before Christmas.

Our holiday had been a mixture of relaxation, romance and hope. We had found a beach-house to rent, homely and full of old curiosities. The island was windswept, with the most beautiful beaches I'd ever seen, and there were very few other tourists around. Our days were spent fishing, with help from one of the men from the village, sunbathing, reading and 'procuring' food from the local people. There were of course supermarkets with imported produce from the States but we were desperate for locally grown fruit and vegetables. Anyway, it was great fun asking the friendly islanders if they would sell us some of their tomatoes, bananas, grapefruit or beans. They were delighted to give us whatever they had grown, and we met families who'd lived on the island since their forefathers had been brought over in the slave trade. Our holiday had done us a lot of good and we were quite happy to be returning home.

Once back, we both slipped into our usual routines. I was teaching and had started doing physiotherapy in the swimming pool at San Raffaele Hospital in Milan. Up until then, I had gone to my local pool, and, despite the embarrassment I felt about my peculiar shape, I had brought my swimming distance up to a kilometre. It took me about 40 minutes to do, but I was proud of this achievement. Then, one day, my crutch slid out from underneath me, and I fell at the edge of the deep end, frightening the pool lifeguards, who asked me in the future to go somewhere that was better equipped to deal with people who had disabilities. I went to my doctor, and he found out that I could go to the hospital. The lifeguards were right, although I hated being described as disabled. I didn't consider myself to be so but accepted that I was a liability for others.

My astral chart was moving on, and the long and physically harsh part of my life's journey was easing itself behind me, although I wasn't particularly aware of any change at that time. That year I was involved in relaxation classes which used methods that brought me back to my experiences in the philosophy school of my youth, with less involvement in terms of time and energy. The exercises we performed in every lesson were repetitive, requiring little thought, and helped me to establish contact with a quieter and kinder me. What was most important was the fact that I looked forward to the weekly classes, letting my overcharged mind and body fall into gentle rest as soon as I lay down on my floor mat. On one occasion I had an experience difficult to place in the pattern of events in my life, and certainly not something I could identify in the evolution of an inner life. That life was left very much up to itself. I was far too caught up in the legal case and the problems of looking after my body to give much space to spiritual enlightenment. The experience I underwent, however, was indicative of the intense loneliness that accompanied the years of fighting.

That evening I had gone to the shoe menders to ask if the old man who worked there could customise my shoes. He had to build one of them up at the heel and cut off a part of the heel on the right, so that there was a four-centimetre difference between the two. It was already dark and lightly raining, so I had nipped into a bar to get a hot drink before going on to the relaxation class. I was also hungry and bought a bag of crisps, which I hurriedly ate whilst waiting for the rain to ease off. When it did, I went out to the car and, with rather a greasy feeling about me, drove to the gym down by the canals where we had our course. I was late so didn't even have time to wash my hands, and I distinctly remember feeling a bit dirty from the wet day and crisps, and wishing that I'd washed my hair that morning.

I crept into the room and sank down onto the only mat left free, immediately falling under the spell of Silvana's voice inviting us all to feel a heaviness throughout the body. Breathing properly from my abdomen was easy, and I concentrated all my attention on the simple instructions given, grateful to be able to enjoy a better feeling than that of being tired and worn. Nothing very special transpired during the mantra sounding, or neck and back exercises. I was just very happy to be doing what I was doing, expecting absolutely nothing to happen at all.

During the guided dream we were to walk through a beautiful meadow with flowers, in sunshine and warmth. Hardly a problem to visualise such a nice picture. We were told to go up a hill and see a temple. I saw a mini Parthenon with the sun's golden rays reflected on

Cotswold-coloured stone. She suggested we enter the temple. I walked between two columns, which suddenly became small, grey and marshmallow-like in consistency, and I was having to push through squidgy walls. I was able to get through, but it felt as if I was walking in a huge intestine. Finally, I emerged into the body of the temple, where everything was dark. We had to look for an altar at one end and identify a light that was to illuminate part of the temple. Space grew as the walls left me in a fraction of a second. I saw a light that seemed to come from the very centre of the space near the altar and it grew. Nothing further was suggested, and we were left with whatever was going on in our imagination.

The light for me took on the form of a person, but it seemed to be more a geometrical figure without features or hands. It was transparent and very luminous. The figure moved towards another person, which was myself, and gently wrapped it in its embrace. The arms enfolded, not in a bear hug but in a way that was utterly safe. I remember looking over the being's shoulder as I laid my head to rest. I was filled with solace and was aware of the words, 'at last, at last, I'm home. This is what I've been waiting for.' There was warmth and security, and it was as if I'd come home after a terrible journey of being lost and exhausted. The being then dissolved into my own body, and I felt filled with light and blessed.

After the session, Silvana usually asked us briefly how the dream had gone. I was not eager to relate what had occurred and hardly thought it worthy of comment, not because it had not been extraordinary but because I was already so far away from it in my reality of sitting on the floor knowing I had an hour's journey home, after which I'd have to cook supper and mark books. My turn came, and I started just to briefly describe what had happened but got no further than the first few sentences. I was overcome with tears and a desire to let all my tiredness and human frailty drop away. It was as if I'd been hit with a cannonball of energy, and I couldn't deal with it. My tears spent and the story told, Silvana explained that I had probably met my own self, or a higher consciousness that exists eternally in all life forms. That was a beautiful thought, but I was less sure of putting names to things or of identifying experiences which I knew nothing about. I can only say that this strange episode made me aware of life's heaviness and the burden of my particular earthly existence that I'd been feeling over the last few years. Fortunately, I had never realised quite how lonely I had been until the embrace of that geometric figure.

After that, nothing changed in any thrilling way except for the fact that I became progressively conscious of the mediocrity of my own ability to manage life. I had also had a glimpse of something that made me wonder and desire peace with all my heart. It was to teach me something about compassion for those who suffer in our imperfect human condition.

That evening as I drove home, I was content in my world and utterly relaxed. Years later, I recounted this experience to Picci, something that was difficult to do and meant giving something to someone that was charged with intimacy and more psychologically precious than many other experiences. I finished the story late one night, and it had the effect of uniting us in the most loving and tender of ways I can ever remember, despite the fact that Picci was not the kind of person who was touched by revelations of incomprehensible ineffability. I'm sure the power of the love I had experienced in 'the temple' returned to us through the telling.

30

THE HUFF

MEANWHILE, THE SUPERFICIAL stuff of dealing with life was still going on and we were daily uncovering more and more of the flimsy structure of Pan Am's tenuous existence. The chain of luxury hotels they had once owned had been sold some time previously, as had the famous Pan Am building in Manhattan, New York. Articles appeared in the papers describing their glorious past and then their slow inexorable nose-dive in sad detail, as routes were sold off and jobs were lost. After the third or fourth piece of dire news, Picci sent various cuttings together with a note to Mr Bellicoso suggesting that we ask the judge to do something that would protect our interests. We agreed to meet up to discuss the next step, terrified of Pan Am disappearing before our very eyes.

At long last, the report on the APU was ready and we sent it on to Mr Bellicoso with a note detailing what Mr Leak, the airline security consultant, could do for us and his fees. Perhaps our new lawyer would suggest how Mr Leak might help us. It was agreed after due consultation that Mr Bellicoso would send in an emergency request for a sequestration of Pan Am's assets on 19 March, first faxing it to us so that we could read it and make sure it was as we wished. This was a crucial moment. It arrived and showed that great thought had been given to the problem, although we believed certain things needed to be straightened out and put into a different order of priority. Twelve pages as we saw them were good, but perhaps a little too long. Of course, we were open to discussing the matter and being persuaded otherwise, but our first impression was that we all needed to sit down and simplify the text together. On our part there was no animosity, and we were very pleased that so much effort had gone into the preparation.

We phoned Mr Napolitani early the next day to ask him what he thought of the emergency request from Mr Bellicoso. Confusion reigned. He had no idea what was going on and had not received the copy via fax, nor was any meeting possible because time was short and Mr Napolitani had not a moment to spare to study what his colleague had written. We went into yet another complete panic and were suddenly horribly aware that the message about collaboration just hadn't got through to our new lawyer and he must have been quite convinced that he was dealing with everything in Milan. Many people let their lawyers take over any litigation procedures and work out the strategy of the case in complete autonomy. I imagine few clients show the interest that we did in our lawsuit. Mr Bellicoso can't have been used to so much participation and must have been stopped short by what he could only see as interference. After much sighing, Mr Napolitani said he'd come to Milan on the afternoon flight to sort out the situation, making us feel uncomfortably in his debt.

We now desperately searched Milan for our other lawyer, leaving messages one after another with his secretaries. Finally, at half past five that evening, he rang from his car phone, which crackled and hissed down the line as if he were in some part of Outer Mongolia. He was clearly very irritated and said that it was most inconvenient for him to have to come to a meeting, particularly as the request was already typed out and waiting in his office to be taken to the judge in a few days' time. At our insistence, he agreed to drop by at a colleague's address at seven that evening. Living far from Milan, he was going to have to phone his wife and tell her he wouldn't be back for dinner. He was far from happy that we had disrupted his plans.

We were all there long before he turned up, and when he did arrive he was very upset. Quite convinced that he'd done a good job, he had no desire to change anything and was extremely put out by what we had to say. He was unable to accept the simple but to us important modifications. Mr Napolitani was also against including the APU evidence this time as this hearing was an emergency appointment and there was still another hearing in April to go through.

By 10 p.m. we had defined the request much more clearly without having changed the actual content. We thought it was more logical and read smoothly, but Mr Bellicoso was visibly offended. He continued to be silent and remain aloof as we studied and modified the rough draft with Mr Napolitani. All in all, the sum requested for me was in the region of $1 million, which included a deposit for future medical treatment and compensation for my ordeal and the physical damage that was not likely to be rectified.

This was a modest sum by American standards but an absolute fortune in the European courts. We wouldn't stand a chance of getting that kind of money, even if I was convinced that my injuries and suffering could never be adequately compensated for. Picci, too, was sure that this sum was not realistic in terms of what we could expect from an Italian judge. His request for compensation was pending as he felt it was less important than mine and needed a special report to be made out by a medical examiner chosen by the courts. Fortunately for Picci, he no longer suffered any pain or limp from the injury to his foot, and the only remnants of the grenade blast were tiny pieces of shrapnel that looked like little black moles embedded in his shin. There was also a larger piece under a tendon that was trapped and would have caused more damage had it been removed. I, too, would have to be examined by someone appointed by the judge but only when we were nearer the time of a verdict.

Mr Bellicoso's feelings had been hurt over this episode and he wrote to us to say that this was not the way he liked to work. I replied to him, explaining as best I could why we were so fussy over particulars. I told him that it wasn't that we wished to offend or give cause for argument, but we as clients were in a unique position of thinking about the case constantly and were therefore inclined to seek the best strategy over even the smallest detail. Our involvement inevitably brought us to examine all aspects of every problem. I was trying to calm him down, as I just couldn't face another huge blow-up with the legal profession. The issue was dropped after I'd written, and Mr Bellicoso seemed to be mollified over the upset.

We had other problems to get to grips with that we hoped might be faced together with Mr Bellicoso. Right at the beginning of our relationship with him, we had asked if he had a colleague in America who specialised in medical malpractice, as we were interested in taking out proceedings against the hospital in New York and Dr Tellez. We asked him to find out how much time we had before the statute of limitations was up. We had been told that it varied from state to state but that it was from two to two and a half years. We wished to know exactly what the period was in the state of New York. He'd returned from his Christmas holidays having spoken to a friend who had shown interest in having us as clients. He had given Mr Bellicoso a tariff sheet and told him that the limitation was two years precisely for that particular state – so we would have to hurry. The operation had been carried out in the summer of 1989 and we were now in March 1991. That gave us five months in which to take out proceedings.

The morning of the hearing I stayed in Picci's office giving the secretary a hand, answering the phone. This meant that I was easily accessible, so that if Picci needed anything I could bring whatever he wanted from the office to the law courts. I waited anxiously to hear the outcome of the hearing. All three men, Picci and our two lawyers, went into the courtroom, and the emergency request was submitted. The Pan Am lawyers were also there, having been contacted by the courts, and a photocopy of the request was given to them as well.

They shook their heads, saying Pan Am was in fine financial fettle. The judge spent some time reading the draft before nodding his head and fixing a date within the same week for Pan Am to make some kind of counter-offer. They would have to disprove our claim that they were facing financial ruin.

We insisted on Napolitani coming to the subsequent hearing, as we wanted him to put up a fight if the defendants tried to persuade the judge not to accept our request to go ahead with sequestration. We needed him to make the judge act fast. He agreed to come to the hearing but first asked if we could all meet up at the Residence Maninni to sort out precisely how we wanted the hearing to go. We were delighted, so we invited him to dinner on the date we were due to have our meeting and, with great cordiality, he accepted the invitation.

31

CLOSING IN

IT WAS 8.30 in the evening and there was still no sign of our friend. Half an hour passed as we waited, our conversation becoming more desultory and lacking in enthusiasm as time moved on. At the reception desk of the hotel, I enquired as to the whereabouts of Mr Napolitani and after a little searching through the diary, the girl on the desk found his booking with a note that indicated that he was delayed because of a meeting.

At about 9.45 we were walking back to the car from a café, by way of the main road, when all of a sudden I noticed a familiar little figure ahead of us, strolling along with a group of people and holding forth on something. Clutching Picci's arm, I whispered loudly that our lawyer was just in front of us. Without a word, we hurried our pace so that we might hear what he was saying. He certainly hadn't seen us and was far too busy expounding to the group of people he was with to turn around and see if there was anyone he knew behind him. We caught the drift of conversation about a hearing that was going to be held the following day in the Milan courts. This must have been the group of relatives involved in the Azores crash. They soon turned the corner and we hurried on back to the hotel by a faster route.

Why didn't he just cancel appointments instead of wasting our time, we wondered. We sat in the car outside the hotel to see what would happen next. He arrived all by himself, walking quickly into reception with his briefcase tucked under his arm. I was terrified he'd shoot upstairs before I'd got my hands on him first, and I'd have felt even more of an idiot than I had been feeling all evening. It was surprising the speed I could walk at when I was angry, and I almost ran across the square, barging into the foyer with Picci just behind me at the ready lest I trip and fall. Napolitani had just finished saying something to the receptionist. He pivoted and registered what must have been quite a look on my face, and immediately broke into his dazzling smile of welcome.

'Why didn't you just cancel the appointment?' I blurted out.

'I'm so sorry about the delay, but I gather you've already been told.' He turned to the girl, 'How fortunate for me that this lovely young lady passed on my message. The flight was delayed and, what with the meeting, I was unable to phone you in the office.' I was about to remonstrate, but Picci put a warning hand on mine and took over the conversation. With a less menacing tone Napolitani felt safer and the imminent row was avoided. He invited us downstairs to the bar for a nightcap.

That evening, Picci was able to work towards our objectives, while I was just plain bloody livid. It wouldn't have helped us understand anything about the following day had I let my anger explode. I would have ruined the trial's sequence by perhaps forcing our lawyer's hand, thus ending the legal relationship with him. Elucidating the plan for the following day, he informed us that he would be clarifying our position with regard to compensation by explaining to everyone that I still had a lot of treatment, and possibly unforeseen problems, to go through. He said he would insist on having a court order for sequestration and that he would verbally anticipate the subject of the APU in order to throw light on the real cause of the shoot-out. He assured us that this new piece of evidence would without doubt persuade the judge that Pan Am was partly to blame for what had happened. Napolitani then launched into a thoroughly realistic enactment of what he would say the following day with stage effects of indignant fist thumps on the table and accusing wagging forefingers. I'd never seen him quite so worked up. The task of defusing my anger had been a difficult one, but somehow he'd managed to make up for the wasted evening despite our not having eaten and his lateness. Furthermore I had drunk a double brandy and watched an incredible display of how Napolitani managed to eat a pound of peanuts single-handed whilst acting out the mortal blow he was about to deal Pan Am. This was great theatre, with the brandy helping to ease my stress level.

I closed my eyes that night with a feeling of tired achievement, believing that we'd finally understood Napolitani, who was going to fulfil our every wish right down to the last detail.

The next morning, I tied my hair in a long plait down my back and wore little make-up. I had begun to realise that making the best of myself did great things for my morale but disguised the real damage that had been done to my body. I wanted to give the judge a balanced impression without minimising the difficulties I actually had.

The day was beautiful and I noticed the buds on the trees and the blossom just beginning to flower. The ceaseless cycle of nature put the Carati–Hill versus Pan Am case in perspective, although it didn't make me turn the car around and go home. I was simply allowed to extend my attention to things other than just the court case, and I drove along in sweet serenity, slowing down when I saw Picci waiting for me on the corner. He, too, was dressed formally, and was wearing a suit, which made him look very distinguished. This indeed was a rare occasion, lending due importance to the hearing.

I parked the car and we went into a sumptuous bar to have breakfast. It was jam-packed with court clerks, secretaries, lawyers and judges, all talking as loudly as possible to be heard above each other's din. Picci asked me what I wanted, aware that I was a little nervous, then he settled me down at a table to have my croissant and tea. He put the crutches out of everyone's way and told me to eat up and relax. However hard Picci sometimes was on me, with little time or inclination to indulge, he was always there when I needed him. His constant presence was the way he showed how important I was to him, and, true to his maxim, actions not words were what counted in the long run. Indeed, as far as reliability is concerned, in all the time we have been together, he has never once let me down.

The lift in the Milan courts was very large and old. It was so slow that one could easily miss a hearing waiting for it. No one knew what commands it obeyed as it went up and down to different floors, stopping at some and missing out others regardless of the buttons pushed. It was tiresome in the extreme, but we had to take it as there was a stream of people rushing up and down the stairs and there was a risk I'd be catapulted backwards.

The hearing commenced at 10 a.m. The judge, phlegmatic in the extreme, waited for everyone to find chairs and seats, which proved to be hard given the number of people in the room. Both our lawyers were with us, and there were two from Pan Am's side along with one or two other stragglers who wanted to know the outcome of this hearing.

Mr Gallo opened the proceedings by saying that I had nothing to fear as far as Pan Am's financial situation was concerned. In his view, everything was going very well for Pan Am, so well in fact that they were restructuring the whole company to accommodate new routes and special trips. He sounded very confident, despite the fact that he had no actual documentation to validate his statements. He didn't need any. If we wanted to prove the contrary, we had to give evidence ourselves that they were in trouble.

At this point, Mr Napolitani gently asked Mr Gallo if Pan Am were in Chapter 11 of the bankruptcy courts in New York. Mr Gallo didn't answer directly but replied that unprofitable business was being sold off to provide capital for new projects. He pulled out of his briefcase a newspaper with a full-page advert selling cheap fares. 'You see: no business that was really going bankrupt could afford to have such expensive advertising campaigns.'

He waxed very lyrical over Pan Am's radiant future. The judge, however, cut across the loquacious lawyer, quietly asking him if Pan Am were willing to make a goodwill gesture and leave something as a deposit in the Chancery. I wasn't particularly happy with the way the judge was dealing with Pan Am, as I felt he should have been far more drastic, even despotic, demanding that they pay a certain sum immediately. Mr Gallo sat back, pursing his lips as if searching for something to say that might be tactful given that I was within hearing range. 'Now, as we see things, we feel that a gesture of goodwill has already been made to Miss Hill when we paid for all her medical expenses' – there was a long pause – 'I mean, of course, the USA bills.' I was grateful for the clarification but would have loved to explain the results of all the money spent, of how the surgery had failed in all its lurid detail. Gallo continued on course, strengthened by the lack of resistance, expressing his surprise that we'd even thought of asking for a deposit given the fact that in the original request for damages – and I felt my heart sink at his words knowing what was coming next – Miss Hill had only requested $200,000 as total compensation, a sum that was considerably more than was appropriate given the injuries and the generosity hitherto shown. It was also considerably less than the ridiculous current request of $1 million. He crashed on with his arguments. 'Let's face it, the hospital bills have almost exceeded that sum [$200,000] alone, so this young woman really has already been very lucky indeed and should not even be thinking of asking for further compensation.'

Had I been alone with this man, I would have got up from my chair and rammed him in the balls with my crutches sufficiently hard to prevent him engaging in any sexual activity for the rest of his life. Why was no one getting agitated? How could everyone listen to this rubbish and not jump up in fury as I wished to do? My eyes were filling up with tears of injustice, but I was not allowed to speak. Gallo's, to me, fatuous and unpleasant voice grated on until the judge himself was irritated and switched off the noise. 'I understand what you are saying but believe differently and would like this woman to be protected in the future by a deposit.' He looked around to see if there was agreement.

Gallo dug into his box of tricks once again, pulling out a letter written by the insurers of Pan Am. He read it in a big loud voice so that we could all benefit at the same time. The sentences rolled out for the length of a page and there was a suitable silence when Gallo had finished his reading. A clerk was called and copies distributed to everyone.

I could bear the situation no longer and asked the judge if we could have a break. I wanted to know why my lawyers were saying nothing and why indeed they seemed to be letting Gallo get away with so much. Everyone shuffled outside and, along with Picci, I urged Napolitani into a corner. It was clear that on receipt of the request for sequestration, Pan Am's lawyers had contacted Pan Am in New York to find out what they should do next. This was something they hadn't predicted. Pan Am had got in touch with the insurers, who had sent a letter explaining their position. This insurance company addressed the letter only to the Pan Am lawyers, advising them of the policies covering Pan Am. In this letter, it stated that the limits of liability greatly exceeded the sum sought by Catherine Hill in her protective order and that, regardless of Pan Am's future, the insurance policy would respond to Catherine Hill's claim. Napolitani was overjoyed with the letter, and, pulling his white handkerchief out of his back pocket, declared that he was terribly relieved. Picci and I were not relieved at all. Our bargaining position seemed to be completely wiped out because now the judge would probably waive the need to sequester if the insurers were able to pay in lieu of Pan Am. The possibility of sequestering the airline's assets, our real objective were Pan Am to refuse to make a financial deposit as a goodwill gesture, appeared to be vanishing fast. Pan Am would have been in a difficult position if we sequestered, as they would not be able to sell their assets to other airlines. We could have dictated our terms for a settlement if they wanted us to reverse the situation. All we could do now was hope that the judge would order Pan Am to make a deposit. This might convince them to settle the case and perhaps we could show them that my injuries were worth more than $200,000.

When we took him to task, Mr Napolitani reluctantly agreed that the letter was hardly collateral and that there was definitely something strange going on with Pan Am. Apart from anything else, the insurers should have addressed the letter to me and Picci. We insisted that he speak to the judge about our fears for the future, urging him to be extremely resolute over wanting some kind of deposit, and, if necessary, he was to ask for a court order for sequestration if Pan Am were unwilling to cede. Our lawyer was not prompted into energetic action, yet he didn't appear to want to contest any of our arguments either. He seemed absorbed in thought. Picci and I had already discussed the possibility that the insurers could well have stepped in to confuse the issue, and were afraid that if judicial pressure were taken off Pan Am we'd have very little bargaining power left. The dangers were mounting around us as we tried to push Napolitani into doing as we wished.

Back in the courtroom, Mr Gallo was the first to jump back into the non-existent fray, and I had to bite my tongue not to interrupt him and ask the judge if I could speak. He said that he would like more time to consider a suitable reply regarding the whole issue and formulate a way of compromising in this situation, giving a written answer. He was, in my mind, just playing for time. When Napolitani finally countered Mr Gallo, it was just a little too late, for the judge, having heard no undue clamouring, had granted the Defence's request. It all happened so quickly that our final remonstrance was completely useless. The APU question was quickly introduced by way of the work manual, which the judge accepted pending a full authenticated translation, and we awaited a new date for discussion regarding the matter of the sequestration.

Perhaps the judge hoped that by giving Pan Am time, we would come to some agreement and settle the case before he had to order further measures. Nobody seemed to appreciate how urgent the situation was. It was precisely this hanging around that eroded our patience, as, in the meantime, it seemed more than likely that Pan Am would disappear off the face of the earth, with or without the insurance company. Whilst everyone else was protecting his or her interests, we could be left high and dry shouting into the four winds when all was over.

The hearing ended, and Mr Bellicoso headed off down the corridor with Mr Gallo. They were talking about his new offices near the court, but we were wrapped up in our depressed thoughts about the way the hearing had gone. We walked towards the lifts with Napolitani, who chirpily said how well things were going. We expostulated, saying that our request was taking too long and that we'd played into Pan Am's hands, but Napolitani said he was sure that things were moving at the right pace and, anyway, the judge was as convinced as we were about the necessity of safeguarding our future compensation. He then assured us that we'd have our answers by the next hearing. Picci asked him to speak to Mr Leak, so that we could have further conclusive evidence against the airline company and said we'd be getting documentation on Pan Am's financial state of affairs. Our lawyer nodded his head and adroitly changed the subject. He pounced on the first thing that must have been worrying him, a seemingly philanthropic concern over those suffering from Aids. We had reached the lifts and pressed the call button, knowing that we'd be waiting for perhaps five minutes for the elevator. I couldn't wait to get out of the court and away from the lawyers. Everything seemed to be going against us, and this period seemed darker than any before. We were so near and yet so far from reaching our goals. The Pan Am lawyers appeared to be trying to deliberately put a smokescreen over Pan Am's financial difficulties, and we had to give conclusive irrefutable evidence that they, as a company, were in trouble.

We needed something in writing from the courts in New York that proved Pan Am had filed for Chapter 11. What the document might be, we had no idea. Everything was postponed until June for a final discussion about the sequestration order. I would have to work fast to get hold of a document from America. Another problem that had to be dealt with was the fact that no one knew what Chapter 11 was and what it entailed. Once again, we'd have to find an expert in both American and Italian law who could explain this situation.

We were having to spend enormous amounts of time and money chasing up specialists and getting them to write simple but explanatory details, and May was literally racing by. I obtained the address of the bankruptcy court through the financial report we had, and, finally, the appropriate paperwork came through via a frustratingly long route that nearly saw me getting on a plane to New York just to cut through red tape. It arrived two weeks before we were supposed to appear in court and I quickly organised an appointment with Mr Fuoco, a lawyer I'd found through the American Trade Offices. We explained our business, took up an hour or so of his time and asked him to make out the Chapter 11 description. He was willing to do so, but he had to talk to Napolitani and make sure that what we needed was something he could do, although he probably only wanted to vouchsafe this work and check that we weren't wasting his time. He gave us his card, advising us to get Mr Napolitani to phone him as soon as possible. All the wheels were in motion. Napolitani was contacted and he promised us he'd phone that very evening. We left things for a week, until my uneasy feelings could no longer be suppressed. I rang Mr Fuoco's offices to ask whether the report on Chapter 11 was ready yet. I was put through to Mr Fuoco himself, who coolly responded that he had yet to hear from Mr Napolitani. I was thoroughly embarrassed, as I'd told Mr Fuoco that this was quite an urgent document that we had to have as soon as possible. It seemed as if either we'd been remiss in not telling our lawyer, or that our lawyer did not agree on this strategy. We wrote Mr Napolitani a telegram that evening and rang to say that his behaviour gave us to understand that he was not in favour of going ahead with any sequestration. With apologies pouring down the phone, he told us that he'd had unbelievable problems in the last week or so. He also begged us to remember that he was completely emotionally involved in our case and would do everything to see justice done. He informed us that he'd already rung Mr Fuoco the evening before and sorted out the problem. He'd forgotten, however, to tell him that the hearing was on the Wednesday of the following week. It was Friday morning and when I phoned Mr Fuoco to see when our report would be ready, his secretary told me he'd already gone down to his family home in Tuscany.

Picci and I left for Frera that weekend, exhausted by the turmoil and stress of the last few days. I had tried to get in touch with Mr Fuoco throughout the day but the maid had said he was away hunting. So, Saturday evening saw us driving back down the mountains to find a phone box. Miraculously, our huntsman was in and with great kindness told us that the report would be ready and waiting for us in his offices on Monday morning. Once more life seemed worth living.

The house was empty and we celebrated our good fortune by having supper on the terrace under a setting sun. Pasta with a fresh tomato and basil sauce and a bottle of sparkling dry white wine was a soul-restoring meal as ecstatically we rejoiced in one more hurdle overcome.

32

A COURT ORDER SERVED

PAN AM'S LAWYERS, despite our bits of paper, refused to pay any form of deposit, arguing that the financial state of the company did not warrant such precautionary measures. Napolitani protested that they were in huge financial difficulty, substantiating the point by pulling out document number 1 of the New York bankruptcy courts. Mr Fuoco's letter with the report followed and was given to the judge as evidence that Pan Am was in deep trouble. The judge studied the financial reports for about five minutes. Taking off his glasses, he spoke directly to our lawyer as if he'd only just understood something. 'So it would seem that Pan Am really are in the bankruptcy courts. They filed on 9 January of this year . . . Is that correct?' We nodded our heads vigorously. 'And this letter from Mr Fuoco seems to indicate that those in Chapter 11 are in some kind of financial difficulty – they are unable to meet their debts?' Ah, finally our work was paying off! The judge had begun to get the idea and appeared to understand the very real difficulty we were in. Looking straight at Mr Gallo, he asked him if he was aware of this grave situation. The lawyer managed to side-step this embarrassing confrontation by producing from his briefcase yet another missive from the insurers. He read the letter out loud and we learnt that Pan Am and the insurance company would be arriving in Milan imminently to see if they couldn't come to some agreement with us over settling the case.

The moment of insecurity for Gallo was over. The judge smiled indulgently, evidently pleased, and looked over at me for an approving smile. I couldn't give him one, however, for I was dismayed by the news. Pan Am were coming over too soon. At this point we still had no leverage and whatever might be on offer in terms of compensation was bound to be far below what I was willing to accept. I had begun to see the road of sequestration as being the only way I could obtain any reasonable sum.

Napolitani practically clapped his hands together in excited anticipation of closing this court case that had gone on for long enough. Even our serious Bellicoso broke into a metallic grin – at the prospect of getting rid of us, I imagined. Everyone was happy except for Picci and me. We were willing to talk to Pan Am only when they had something to lose if they didn't talk to us. So far, they hadn't been pushed into a corner. Bad publicity was no longer a threat they would take any notice of if they were genuinely on the road to selling or closing the company. The only thing we had left was sequestration. With such an order in place, had they wanted to sell off their last assets, they would have been unable to do so unless they first negotiated with us.

The judge asked what date the insurers and representatives of the airline were thinking of coming to Europe, to which Mr Gallo responded, 'in a couple of weeks'. I was perfectly aware that Mr Gallo had no set date and that this could well be just another delaying tactic. The judge organised a further date in July so that he could learn the outcome of the meeting we would be having, and the hearing of witnesses was fixed for October should the case not be settled. We were all dismissed. Outside the courtroom we witnessed scenes of unprecedented rapture, Mr Bellicoso and Mr Gallo congratulating each other, whilst Mr Napolitani surveyed his colleagues in seraphic beatitude. Picci and I were not participating in the premature party, knowing that everything was stacked against us. The likelihood of getting more than the sum mentioned in the first citation was highly improbable and the company might well have no money or assets before long. We left for the office that morning feeling very down indeed. It seemed to us as though our own lawyers were blind to these considerations and I felt that matters were heading towards a bitter and foregone conclusion.

I rang my family that evening, depressed and extremely gloomy. I hadn't exactly kept them informed of what had been happening with the case, simply because the Italian law system defied explanation of any sort and any attempt would have been exasperating and boring for all concerned. All I wanted was to be comforted and have a shoulder to cry on. Picci's was already wet and, anyway, we were not very good at giving each other understanding and support when we were both in need of it.

Everyone at home was anxious for the case to close, as they knew how much it was costing me psychologically. They were all convinced it had been going on for far too long. When I told them that there seemed no real light at the end of the tunnel, I felt terribly disappointed in myself that I had not come up to scratch and shown everyone how capable I was. There was always this warped desire to do extremely well in any project, and I wanted to do better than what was expected of any normal person in similar circumstances. I invariably ended up feeling terribly alone after these requests for comfort, and it was the same after this particular phone call to my family. I couldn't expect them to identify with what I was going through, as I rarely told them how I honestly felt, and they wanted to give help, rather than just listen.

From the moment we had put in our sequestration request I felt a very definite schism divide us from our legal representatives. The low amount of $200,000 allotted, considering my injuries, as well as the cheerful bonhomie that evidently existed between the lawyers on both sides, made me feel like the one who didn't fit in. Their goal was evidently the same, to win compensation for us both, but the amount, and the way to achieve it, seemed to be different. Why Mr Bellicoso hadn't shown outrage over the sum defied me, considering the updated request of $1 million he'd made to the judge regarding compensation.

Over the last few days of June, we received various dates for when the Pan Am contingent would be coming over. The meeting was repeatedly cancelled and postponed for one reason or another and still had not taken place by the time we had the next hearing before the judge. Picci and I were exasperated and felt that we were being strung along. No one seemed to be taking things very seriously at all. Several months had passed since our original request for sequestration and, although it was almost unbelievable, a cautionary deposit had still not been paid into the Chancery.

The day of 9 July 1991 was one to remember, both for the terrible heat and the fact that the judge finally authorised sequestration of Pan Am's assets to safeguard my financial future. Mr Gallo wrote into the hearing notes that Pan Am and the insurers had had work problems that had prevented them from coming to Italy but that a meeting date for 15 July had been fixed. We were thrilled that the judge had had to issue the authorisation for sequestration, as it was just what we wanted in terms of power.

Picci suggested, 'If we write a telegram to both our lawyers ordering them to go ahead with sequestering Pan Am property, they may well find some expedient for not doing so. If we write the same thing to the secretary of the Italian Bar Association as well as our lawyers, they won't dare fail to carry out the sequestration. They may well hand in their notice and have a near nervous breakdown, but it will be more than their life is worth to procrastinate over this one. I'm sure that even if we don't explain to the Association why we are including them in this problem, the mere fact that they know there is a pending court order will be sufficient to jump-start Napolitani and Bellicoso.' I agreed, and Picci said he'd phone both lawyers later that afternoon to find out exactly how one went about carrying out a sequestration. What had convinced us totally that this was the right thing to do was the fact that Mr Napolitani had given what we regarded as unclear and unsatisfactory answers to the questions he'd been asked. He had initially tried to dissuade Picci from going ahead, but, on hearing how quietly determined he was, changed his approach and urged us to wait until the outcome of the meeting with Pan Am. He pointed out that we might well settle the case at that point and it would be a dreadful waste of time for both sides to have to undo the damage a sequestration would cause, not to mention the cost we would incur. At the end of the conversation, Picci felt sure that he was on the right track but we decided to await the outcome of the meeting even if only to placate our lawyers.

Picci phoned another legal adviser who had nothing to do with the case to ask what was required to perform a sequestration. Apparently there was a time limit in which to act: a month from the date of issue. Our lawyer had not mentioned this rather important detail. Soon we would have to ask the judge to renew the order. Two or three mornings later, we sent the telegram to our lawyers and the Association to initiate procedures with bailiffs for the sequestration. Both of us were certain that the phone between Milan and Rome would be engaged for a considerable length of time as our lawyers compared their degree of shock and exasperation.

That evening I received a call from Mr Elsie of Pan Am, who was supposed to be coming over for the meeting. We had a very agreeable conversation, although I said absolutely nothing to him about what was happening in Italy as regards the case. It was quite obvious that he had not been told of recent events and I certainly wasn't going to explain to him we had a sequestration order out, at least not over the phone. Once we had met up, it would be a different matter. I felt enormously protected with this simple weapon. If there was a threat of blocking bank accounts, seizing property and maybe even a plane, we had a wonderful bargaining position. At the end of the phone call,

Mr Elsie concluded by saying 'Oh, Catherine, I am actually phoning you because I wanted to tell you personally that neither my insurance colleague nor I can come over to Italy. Unfortunately I have an ear infection and a work schedule that makes 15 July impossible. I'm sure we can arrange another date sometime at the end of the month.' He told me that he had already written to the lawyers in Italy cancelling the meeting.

Picci and I found out the bank account numbers of Pan Am's current accounts in Italy and we tried to see if they owned any property in Milan or Rome, only to be told that everything, including the chairs they sat on in the ticket offices, was leased. We did our best to prepare ourselves for the time when the bailiff would go out on our behalf to freeze their assets. We also waited for the phone call from one of our lawyers to say that the meeting for a possible settlement had been cancelled. It arrived the evening before the appointed day, but we were told not to worry because the Pan Am lawyers had agreed to come up from Rome, in lieu of their clients, and they'd been instructed on how to proceed.

33

THE SHOWDOWN

THE SECRETARY OPENED the door at ten past four and showed us into the meeting. We were extremely jittery. The lawyers were all there, including an older man in his 70s, looking slightly squashed and defeated, who sat at the crystal table. We were introduced to him: 'This is Avvocato Bianchi, head of the legal studio representing Pan Am and who we've obliged to come to Milan at the venerable age of, how old are you sir?' Napolitani bellowed into the old man's ear.

'Seventy-two,' the gentleman replied.

Mr Bellicoso hastily ushered us into a little side room as we nodded fleeting good mornings to Mr Gallo, who, less than relaxed, returned our salutation, tight jawed and with a tense smile. 'We wish to talk to our clients for a moment, please,' whispered Napolitani as he closed the door. I waited nervously once inside, as Picci took up his post behind me, exuding formidable animosity towards our two lawyers and solid support for me. They positioned themselves in varying attitudes of worried consternation as they set to work

That little preliminary meeting took about ten minutes, but it ruined whatever agreement might have been possible with Pan Am, as we found ourselves involved in an unpleasant confrontation with both our lawyers. They were furious that the telegrams we had sent ordering them to carry out the sequestrations of Pan Am's assets as indicated by the judge had also been sent to the Italian Bar Association. Instead of waiting until the end of the attempt at negotiation with Pan Am they had decided to show their disapproval beforehand and this was most unsettling for me. I defended my actions, telling them why I had lost my faith in them as my representatives. This of course didn't go down well at all and led to further recriminations.

Mr Bellicoso concluded our lively discussion by saying that his interest in our case was waning somewhat, as the whole thing seemed to be turning into a bit of a farce. He said that he felt he was wasting his time and that his position as our lawyer was one that he wished to review. My fear turned to ire, and Picci, who had remained in complete silence all through this charade, finally spoke.

'I'd like to remind you both that Miss Hill's condition is very fragile, and this sort of conduct towards her could be very damaging.' There was silence as the two lawyers thought about what they could say in response to that. 'I suggest we change the tone of this meeting and move on to the real question in hand,' Picci concluded.

He was so clear and concise, and I appreciated his detachment from the situation. It was of no benefit to me to have to go through a fight before a moment of this kind where I would be deciding on my whole future.

Everyone must have been listening to us through the thin partition as our voices rose and tempers frayed. Napolitani, seeing that he was getting nowhere, decided to abandon the problem of the telegrams, and instead he'd try dealing with the crux of the matter head on. Once again, he talked to me rather than include Picci in the conversation, despite the fact that we were gathered together to discuss his compensation too. I was clearly the easier one to deal with. 'Miss Hill, I think we shall be very fortunate if we come away with a settlement of $150,000 today from Pan Am.'

There it was in all its disappointing revelation: the amount the lawyers felt I was worth. I was disgusted that he was prepared to settle for such a paltry amount.

He continued, 'As you know, the judge only awarded that amount with regard to your sequestration limit, so I really think you should be most careful about refusing such a generous offer.' Napolitani watched me as I silently called him all the names I could think of in my head. Finally, his temper snapped too. 'Well, what were you thinking of, Miss Hill?' and he banged my file down on the table.

In a voice that belonged to another woman, hard and determined, I stated my conditions: 'I will not settle for less than $1 million.' It sounded as if I was yelling across the room. There was new uproar as Napolitani threw his arms into the air in horrified affront.

'But these are dreams,' he shouted, 'just dreams.' I glanced at Picci, whose mouth was a hard line as we waited for this display of Roman passion to die down. I plunged into a further announcement, rather hoarsely, but the lawyers were no longer listening to me, caught up as they were in this new and to them disturbing prospect. Dismissively, they gathered their files together. We made to leave the little room, unprepared to face the opposition. Before opening the door, Napolitani paused: 'Naturally I will be seriously considering handing in my resignation in the light of Miss Hill's loss of faith.' So now both our lawyers were about to abandon us. It was news I didn't need to hear in a showdown situation. I felt as if I were standing on a precipice and for a split second the idea that our lawyers were probably going to drop us like some noisome refuse caused a sensation of physical vertigo. Was I throwing my last chance to salvage the case out of the window, or were they playing games with us? I had felt manipulated by many people for a long time now, and this thought jump-started my reasoning faculty. It was better that I respect myself and fight for justice than bend to the will of our lawyers, who seemed so keen on closing a deal with Pan Am. The moment of insecurity passed, and I felt strong and clear headed. So I'd lose these two lawyers. So there'd be even greater problems to cope with. Hadn't we lost two solicitors already? Wasn't it better to face these kinds of inconveniences than acquiesce to a mean, unjust compromise that I would regret for the rest of my life and for which I would suffer never-ending rancour? Yes, fighting was much better than succumbing and we were not going to give in now.

United in our cause and in our determination to do this our way, Picci and I stepped into the main room ahead of Napolitani and Bellicoso. It was pretty clear that the negotiation was going to be a wash-out. The previous shouting match slipped more into perspective, but the meeting, as anyone could have predicted, turned out to be a fiasco. Mr Napolitani appeared not to have the wherewithal to regroup for a changed situation and so had to stumble through. I caught Picci's eye. He looked as nauseated as I felt, forced to listen to what seemed to us a lot of waffle as Mr Napolitani asked his colleague how he'd managed to come to Milan despite the heat and his age. It was after this that Picci decided that there were, by now, no holds barred. It was time to respond in kind. He tilted his chair back a little, rocking in relaxed assurance. 'I think at this point it would have been a far better idea had Mr Bianchi stayed at home in Rome as he is quite clearly far too old to take part in a meeting such as this.' Clear as a bell, his voice rang out.

Astonishment registered on everyone's faces and I cringed inside, as I knew what was coming next. Picci wouldn't spare the feelings of the old man in the interests of charity or good manners. Picci coldly continued, saying that anyone who practised their profession should be capable of all the necessary aspects of that work, including travelling to and from the '*forum competente*'. Apart from everything else, he demanded whether it was really to be expected that the injured party, badly disabled – he looked over at me – travel to Rome when the lawyers involved in the case were all able-bodied individuals with no disabilities to speak of? He then invited everyone to proceed with the negotiation.

Still air and a very audible bluebottle became the focal point of attention as Bellicoso, beside himself with discomfort as the host of this aborted meeting, twisted his wedding ring round and round his finger. Napolitani was trying to swallow his by now burning tongue and stood there looking as though he wished he could disappear. Bianchi rubbed his hands together in dazed distraction. The meeting had long got out of hand and I began to feel that marvellous sense of release from tension as the giggles threatened to take me over. 'Well, since you have managed to get here, how about telling us what is on offer for the Signorina and myself.' Picci removed a bare right foot from his shoe, and flexed his moist toes in the air. I hadn't his nerve but admired his style as everyone watched the foot in horrified fascination through the crystal table. Turning casually to a by now goggling Bellicoso, I imagine not used to the ways of such forthright clients, Picci continued: 'By the way, I think your secretary should take the minutes of this meeting.'

Bellicoso, in an effort to deal with this latest insult, and they were coming at him in rapid succession, responded with all the force he was capable of mustering, replying that in confidential meetings it was not their practice to take minutes. It showed a lack of trust and disturbed the intimacy of professionals working. 'Ah, I see, you'd rather not have anything down on paper, very interesting,' was Picci's laconic comment.

Mr Bellicoso looked more and more ill at ease. I was myself very keen on getting out of those chambers as quickly as possible, but the play had to go on to its bitter end. Bianchi, aware that he had to do something, pulled together what little dignity he had left and began the closing speech he had prepared. Pan Am's lawyers decided the best offer they could make was for the sum of $150,000, which they believed most generous in the light of the injuries I had sustained and especially when they were not sure that I wouldn't fully recover.

I knew, as everyone else did, that the failed attempt at the reconstruction of my backside and subsequent failure of the hip replacement plan with all those terrible months in hospital in New York were synonymous with a permanent disability, and I knew that I'd always be walking with crutches. It was depressing listening to these men quantifying the injuries. How do you put a price on the cost of gluteal muscle, 25 operations, including a colostomy, permanent dependence on crutches for mobility, years of pain, destruction of your image as a woman, loss of sexual activity, fear of loud noises, agoraphobia, periods of depression, low self-esteem, nightmares, change of character, yo-yoing weight, etc., etc.? The list could go on and on, and my mind went through a flashback to the long line of events and radical changes that had occurred in my life since the hijack. I watched the faces of the four lawyers in the room, convinced that they had no concept of the pain that I had been through and was destined to experience again in the future. Once again, I felt indescribably alone in the legacy left to me, aware only that with so many of my assets and attributes gone, I was going to have to play my cards very carefully if I wanted to be successful in some area of my life or if I wanted to be respected and keep my pride intact – and this was one of those moments.

Napolitani declared to the Pan Am lawyers in dramatic tones that he would not recommend his clients to accept anything under the value of $200,000. At this point, sick and tired of what seemed to me their shenanigans, I put my cards on the table, expressing my complete disdain for their half-baked solution to what was going to be for me a lifetime of physical pain and suffering in various ways. I calmly stated that I didn't think any of them had the slightest idea of what kind of life I was destined to have with the injuries I carried. Looking at Mr Gallo, I reminded him of how he had made a mockery of my physical circumstances in the courtroom the previous month, trying to minimise the extent of my injuries. I hadn't expected him to identify with my misfortune, but he could have spared me his appraisal at least. Concluding, I told them that none of them had enough imagination to realistically quantify my situation in terms of money so I would give them a figure, below which I was not prepared to accept closing any deal, and also set some conditions that had to be met. First, I requested that a sum of $1 million be paid to me for the injuries I had sustained. Second, that an insurance policy be taken out in my name to cover surgical operations, treatment, drugs and medical costs that I might incur for the rest of my life, and third, that Mr Carati be amply compensated for the injuries he had suffered. Also, he was to receive a sum for all the time lost and expenses incurred whilst pursuing this case and looking after my interests. I waited at the end of my list to see what effect this had had on the rest of the people in the room.

There was an expression of uncomfortable politeness on everyone's face, except for Mr Napolitani, who seemed very embarrassed at my mad request. It must have been pretty awkward for him if he had led the Pan Am lawyers to believe that we might be disposed to sign on the dotted line for $150,000, the sum he felt was reasonable, and thus secure a successful conclusion to the Hill–Carati versus Pan Am case. Mr Bianchi shook his head in bewildered disagreement and Mr Gallo tapped his pencil on the crystal glass table that was by now covered with greasy hand-marks. There was no way any discussion would ensue on the proposal or even a counter offer be made.

I was exasperated and Picci was fuming, as he had known this to be a travesty right from the beginning. He was anxious to get back to the office, as his people needed him in the workshop. We considered the 'discussion' over and were determined to leave as soon as we had dealt with the next issue. 'Would you be kind enough to inform us whether or not Pan Am intend paying $150,000 as a deposit into the Chancery?' Gallo didn't know what to say, even if it was in their interests to pay the sum. The fact that we had dared to play our hand differently might have confused him and he replied with a sharp, 'No!' Picci formulated the question once again, to be absolutely certain that everyone heard the negative reply we were getting and he received the same answer. Of course not. It was perfectly ridiculous that Pan Am should pay. They had already been more than generous towards me. Picci stood up and declared the meeting closed, despite the fact that we were not the hosts. But so many things had happened and so many rules of etiquette been flung to one side that it didn't seem to matter any more who was doing what. He announced that, as from the following day, our lawyers would be proceeding with sequestration and the impounding of Pan Am property. They glanced at each other and Gallo shrugged his shoulders.

Everyone got up from the table and prepared to leave, while Napolitani rushed to his old colleague's side and helped him up out of his chair. They all gathered around the old lawyer from Rome to help him put his coat on in the hallway, say their goodbyes and no doubt commiserate on the failed mission. It was a relief for us to know that our lawyers knew how we felt and would have to carry out the sequestrations. At last we had them in our hand, for they couldn't do much to avoid, delay or forget the by now inevitable court order issued to impound Pan Am property. Mr Napolitani returned and avoided any kind of contact with us, verbal or otherwise. We all awaited Mr Bellicoso, hearing the door close, while Napolitani gazed at the walnut bookcase that lined one of the walls and meditated. His hands clasped tightly behind his back and his whole body in taut appreciation of the titles on the shelves, he ignored us totally.

Mr Bellicoso had obviously had time to pull himself together, and he behaved as if he were in total control of the situation. Addressing those of us left, he started to pull the loose ends together of the work that we now had to do, saying that he felt it his duty to see through the practicalities of the sequestration even if he found it hard to believe we had come to this. He glanced over at Napolitani, seeking support while declaring that he disagreed totally with the way Mr Carati and I had behaved in his studios towards our guests.

I certainly hadn't realised this had been a party. I couldn't deny that 'form' had gone out of the window, but I thought our own lawyers were the cause of that and had started off the afternoon themselves in this way. Mr Napolitani had retrieved his coat by this time and was busy struggling into it. Waiting for a suitable pause in the comments being made, he shifted the entire responsibility for what would be that final mission on to the broad shoulders of Mr Bellicoso. Turning to us with a radiant smile he said, 'I trust that you will be more than happy with such a skilled lawyer dealing with this last practicality. He is one of the best, as this meeting has quite clearly shown in the way he handled the representatives of Pan Am. Unfortunately, I have a case of considerable urgency in Rome and must get back to brief my clients, and, much as I'd love to stay, there is sadly so little time. Bellicoso, my very dear colleague, I want to thank you from the bottom of my heart for your work and for taking this aspect of the case off my desk. I do have so many needy clients in this period. Please don't hesitate to call me for consultation if necessary.' With that, he shook Mr Bellicoso's I imagine rather limp hand and, shouting hearty goodbyes to us, left. As the front door shut on Napolitani, Bellicoso's facial and body language were more than eloquent. Muttering, he turned heavily and prepared himself under our merciless gaze to complete the paperwork necessary to fulfil the sequestration formalities. Our unhappy Mr Bellicoso must have felt utterly trapped and regarded us with a pained expression as he buzzed for his secretary to come through and finally take notes.

34

PUTTING OUT ATTACHMENTS

PICCI AND I continued to talk about the consequences of what had happened in the disastrous discussion with the lawyers, nervous of the direction we'd decided to take, so evidently in contrast with the views of all the professional people who apparently knew better. It was a bit frightening, striking out on our own, but we were convinced that putting out attachments or impounding Pan Am property was our lifeline. At about 9 p.m., Mr Elsie phoned from the US to find out how the afternoon had gone. I had half expected him to call me, as he had said that he would be getting in touch to see what had happened. I made it very clear what I thought of his lawyers, and explained that, no, we hadn't made any settlement whatsoever, given the ridiculous sum of money on offer. There was a long pause before I launched into an indignant diatribe about the fact that Mr Gallo and Mr Bianchi had adamantly refused to deposit the money ordered by the judge. He listened in shocked amazement and said that he thought he'd given instructions for the money to be paid into the Chancery. Full of apology, he asked me in more detail what had been going on. I filled him in to the extent that was useful to me, which was practically the whole story, and judging by the sound of his astonished comments, it seemed that he was completely in the dark, having more or less left things up to the discretion of the Italian lawyers. I told him that there was now a court order to put out attachments and that our lawyers were intent on securing assets – a very small white lie after all, but one that was perhaps sufficient to get things moving. He rang off, saying he'd be looking into things. In the meantime, he asked me to persuade my lawyers to hold back for just a day or two. I said I'd try my best, but it would be difficult as they were really keen on carrying out the court order. Another slightly bigger white lie. I was overjoyed by Mr Elsie's request because it confirmed that he really didn't want Pan Am's assets frozen, which meant that we did. Just before he put the phone down, he suggested that we meet up to sort things out properly. This request was what we'd been waiting to hear for months, and it had come from him.

It was now going to be a race against time. There were about 16 days left in which we could impound property and block Pan Am's financial assets, so our strategy was to push ahead as quickly as possible. The new day dawned and Mr Elsie phoned yet again to reassure me that he was working as fast as possible to get the money. I could feel him getting in a very worried state down the phone, and so soothed him as well as I could, although I was laughing inside as I thought of the way the tables had turned.

I intended to accompany the bailiffs while they carried out the sequestration process, so that I knew exactly what was going to be sequestered and if necessary intervene. We had been told that these people were notoriously obtuse about what was to be attached and tended to choose things that were easy to quantify in terms of money, often impounding objects of insignificant value. I wanted to find assets that were valuable, both to the running of an airline company and in terms of money, so in preparation I went to investigate what Pan Am owned at the airport outside Milan from where the transatlantic flights departed.

I drove down to the Central Depôt to catch a coach out to the airport feeling wonderful. At last I was doing something assertive instead of succumbing to everyone else. I felt free of lawyers wanting to hold me back and full of a sense of adventure. The morning was as radiant as I was. The still heat of the past few days had been washed away during the night by a heavy thunderstorm, and the sky was clear and blue. I hoped to arrive in time to see the flight loading up with its cargo before it left for New York so I could take note of the vehicles and general equipment used, and get some ideas. I was pleased to see that I had got there in time. Everyone was busy with the impending flight, and no one took any notice of me hanging around. Once I'd got a grasp of the full layout of the offices, I went along to the terrace restaurant and watched the aircraft fill up first with cargo, then with baggage and lastly with passengers. I watched it slowly move off towards the runway while thoughts on the preposterous mission I was on bubbled in my mind. I smiled to myself and, finishing my orange juice, got up to catch the coach back to Milan. I felt terribly audacious and laughed at my own daredevilry, while the thought of impounding a Pan Am flight gripped my imagination. I could just imagine the stewardess asking everyone very politely to leave the aircraft and wait for further instructions. There was a technical hitch and the flight was delayed. How exquisite my enjoyment would be at seeing people come off a plane because of my request. Finally, I would be the cause of inconvenience and the proverbial boot would be on the other foot. For sure, my imagination was running away with me, and it would be highly unlikely that something of such magnitude would happen, especially if we were assigned an afternoon bailiff. We'd have to engineer the expedition to coincide with the flight departures in the morning, and, even then, sequestering a plane could be illegal.

I returned home having expended the nervous energy that was storming through my body in the hospital swimming pool. Just as I turned my keys in the front door lock, my phone rang. In the panic to get in, I tripped over the cat and my shopping fell all over the floor. It was Picci, as I had imagined, who was very worked up, demanding to know why I hadn't phoned him. 'Where have you been? I've been trying to get you since four o'clock.' Apparently, Mr Bellicoso had been on the phone asking us to stay the sequestration, as Bianchi and Gallo were doing their best to deposit a sum which corresponded to the amount the judge had set in the court order. Unfortunately, they needed two days to get things moving with the banks.

I started to laugh. 'So, at long last they're jumping instead of giving us the finger. Why should we do them any favours? I feel completely disinclined to help any of them. I can't be bothered any more. They've had months to make up their minds, and they have waited until this moment to do something. I'm very sorry, but I'm not interested.' Picci was delighted that I was as resolute as I seemed to be, but he had wanted me to make the final decision given that I was the one most affected by the case. He said he could hardly wait to call Mr Bellicoso and give him the bad news.

As a post scriptum, he hurriedly said, 'By the way, your first expedition is tomorrow morning in Milan. You have to go to the Pan Am offices, their agents and their two banks. Everything is fixed for nine o'clock. You must go to Bellicoso's offices, and one of his underlings will accompany you to the law courts.'

The phone didn't stop ringing that evening. The lawyer himself called, given the negative response he was getting from Picci. He tried as hard as he could to dissuade me from taking such drastic action. I couldn't see why he was getting so upset about everything. Now here he was at eight in the evening the day before I was due out with the bailiff, doing his utmost to convince me not to pursue the course of action I was set on. I tried to tell him that it was in my best interests to go ahead with it, as I would have greater bargaining power, but all he could say was that I was foolhardy and not thinking clearly. Finally, I told him that there was nothing further to discuss and that I would be coming to his offices the following morning to go to the courts to pick up the bailiff. As I said goodbye to him, his parting shot was that the sequestration was my responsibility and that it had nothing to do with him. He hoped I realised that I was doing something that was totally against my interests, to which I replied that I believed I was doing the exact opposite.

Picci rang me an hour later to tell me that Mr Bellicoso had asked him to send a faxed letter saying that we intended going ahead with the sequestration of any assets despite the fact that Pan Am had given us a particular bank account number from which we could sequester the sum of money stipulated by the judge. Picci just wanted my approval which of course I gave before he sent out this missive.

Things were happening at the speed of light, hitherto unknown in our laborious and frustratingly tedious court case. Rather exhausted from all that was going on, I retired that night and cuddled my much loved but scratchy cat as I thought of the morrow and what it would bring.

Mr Kruger, the bailiff, was a handsome 40 year old with blond hair, a bushy beard and devastating blue eyes. He was tall, a little distant and, contrary to what we had been told to expect, very professional. We agreed to go to the various places in Milan in Mr Pasquale's car. He was a very young graduate learning the ropes in Mr Bellicoso's offices. He looked rather cowed and seemed happy to be doing something that was a little different from the usual running around.

To begin with we went to the tiny offices on the seventh floor where Pan Am officially resided in the centre of Milan. They had chosen the expensive part of the city where all the other airline offices were also located, but once inside the building I realised that, apart from the address, there was precious little to recommend the place. It was dusty and neglected. The lifts were slow and old, and the floor numbers hard to see because of the absence of tiny light bulbs behind the lift floor panel. We knocked on the door of the offices and went straight in. Looking at the discomfort on the faces of the people in there, I had to remind myself sharply that I had chosen this path and was determined to follow things through to the end. The so-called director of Pan Am was not really a manager but just an employee in charge of the offices. He was young, round faced with round glasses and listened to the court order with his eyes popping out of his head. There were three rooms, which housed a few tables and chairs, and one or two desktop computers and printers. On the walls were a few posters from the airline's better days, when the company had represented America and all it stood for.

Surprisingly, the young man got a grip on himself fairly quickly and asked the bailiff, Mr Pasquale and me to all take a seat. He arranged the chairs around his desk and then excused himself, going into another room presumably to phone his superior in Rome for instructions on what he should do. I looked round the bare office, which showed every sign that whoever inhabited it was not going to be around for very long. I half imagined seeing removal boxes piled high in one corner with 'handle with care' written across them. I was beginning to get the real feeling that Pan Am were seriously closing down, and, despite my antagonism towards them, I felt a twinge of regret that such a world-famous name was, in all probability, shortly to be no more.

'Well, there isn't much here to impound,' murmured our bailiff as he got up to peer into the other offices. The young man came back to his desk and with a wave of his arm gave us the all-clear to list those things that were possible to sequester down on the court order paper: eight chairs, three tables, two IBM computers, a coffee maker and a fax machine. Was that really all? The offices themselves were rented and the carpets and light fittings were part of the furnishings. Thin pickings indeed. We left, having asked if the agency that sold Pan Am tickets was on the fifth or sixth floor of the same building. I was hardly thrilled at what we'd found and wondered what else there would or would not be in store for us.

At the next port of call, Mr Pasquale and I were invited by the manager of the agency to remain in the hall of the offices. He seemed to be very angry and closed the door with a certain deliberateness that made the young law graduate and I exchange glances. I couldn't resist the temptation to listen to what was undoubtedly being said to the bailiff and so got up quietly and stood by the door to see if I could catch the gist of the conversation. The acoustics were not at all in my favour, and added to this was the slight language barrier. However well I spoke Italian, it was still a second language and stood up badly to any kind of sound distortion. Mr Pasquale assumed a more active interest in the adventure when he saw how I wished to hear what was going on. He directed me to the chair and took my place. He looked as if he was able to follow what was going on better and was able to relay that the agency had instigated court proceedings itself against Pan Am over some problem concerning reimbursements of tickets sold. Unfortunately for the owner of the agency, however much he ranted and raved, there was little he could do to prevent the sequestration of the earnings from the tickets, and as he angrily showed us out of the offices, our bailiff confirmed what we'd heard. The sum of what had been impounded, though, was still a fraction of the sum indicated by the court order.

Next stop was the bank in Piazza della Scala, a busy chaotic junction, so Mr Pasquale and I stayed in the car whilst the bailiff went into the bank to put a block on the accounts. Our Paul Newman of a court bailiff was not long in returning, and as he opened the car door, he shouted that we were very lucky, as the bank had been closing just as he slipped in the main entrance. Mr Pasquale changed into first gear, and we moved out into the main stream of traffic. 'All finished?' I asked.

'Yes, everything has gone very smoothly. I've blocked both accounts, so there should really be no problem at all now, and we can all go and have a well-earned lunch.'

'I don't suppose the bank told you how much money Pan Am has in the accounts?' I asked, to which the bailiff shook his head, saying that it was not possible to disclose those details.

'It's much better that you don't know how much is in there anyway because it means that you have the right to go on impounding assets precisely because you have no figure. How do you know when you've reached the required sum? – You don't, so you go on until there's nothing left to sequester.'

It would be up to Pan Am to fix an emergency meeting with the judge to release the items that were in excess of the amount requested. They had to demonstrate the various values and get the judge to take off attachments that went over the amount. What with the August holidays fast approaching, there would be little chance of any judge being available, let alone the one dealing with our case, so it looked as if Pan Am was going to be blocked for at least two months. This was just the kind of pressure we wanted to see them under, particularly if the company was selling off its assets. I was delighted with our morning's work for not only had we done what we had set out to do but we had also been lucky enough to have been assisted by a very scrupulous and knowledgeable bailiff.

We drove back to the courts to drop off our tall kindly friend. Mr Pasquale discreetly offered him a tip, which was apparently the custom, but it was politely and firmly refused. I wanted to give the man a hug and kiss, for, apart from his astonishingly good looks and efficient work, he had restored my faith in Italy's state system. Not everyone working for the government was willing to be bought or sold.

That evening, with my swollen legs pointing towards the ceiling because of the heat and stickiness of the day, I went over the morning's drama with Picci. Because everything had gone so well, and with the information the bailiff had given me, we decided that it was time to involve our reluctant Roman in the sequestration. Picci wrote a telegram with instructions to impound the bank accounts and assets belonging to Pan Am in Rome. Despite Napolitani's delegating at the end of the meeting in Milan, he was still going to have to deal with this part of the case.

Mr Pasquale picked me up at 7.30 the following morning outside the offices. We had a long drive ahead of us and our appointment with the bailiff from Varese was at 8.30 at the police station in the town centre. Mr Pasquale had resumed his cool manner and we spoke little on the way out. I just hoped that he was going to feel inclined to help if necessary and that he had not been given instructions to the contrary. It was quite possible that this round of attachments wouldn't be so easy.

We arrived in plenty of time, stopping off first to have breakfast. The police station was actually also the courthouse, a modern structure with beautiful gardens in front of it. We went up to the first floor and asked for Mr Rossi, our bailiff for the day. No one seemed to know where he was. We waited in the corridor and observed the bustle that was going on around us. There were different courtrooms going off either side of the length of the corridor. In the huge central part of the building were the police offices, the traffic department and the financial police headquarters, the equivalent of our tax inspector offices. People came and went with sheaves of paper, policemen paced with radio transmitters bleating out incomprehensible messages, while administrative staff chatted on the stairs as they passed each other on their various errands. I had butterflies and a very sore pair of thighs, for the only place to sit was on a modern mesh bench that was nice to look at but uncomfortable to sit on when dressed in only a light cotton skirt. The backs of my legs were being spliced up into lots of neat little two by two centimetre squares.

It was now 10 a.m. and my agitation had turned into cramps. I was also getting a headache because of the heat and nervous tension. It was frustrating knowing that the Pan Am flight would be leaving in an hour or so, and we would no doubt arrive just in time to see it take off. How I wished Picci was around. Mr Pasquale didn't fill me with confidence, as he couldn't know my rights. I wondered what would happen should the appointment fall through and gazed in depressed resignation down the stairs watching an elderly man with a large wodge of files make his way up to the first floor. He came towards us, extending his hand.

'Hello, I'm Mr Rossi. I'm very sorry I'm late, but I got delayed by another case.' He was a small individual of about 62, but he looked older because he had a stoop. He reminded me of an old-fashioned kindly shopkeeper, the sort who wore a brown overall and thick-lensed glasses and who helped you get your sweets over the counter when you were small.

Climbing into Mr Pasquale's little Fiat, we set off for Malpensa, Milan's international airport. Mr Rossi spent the entire journey telling us of his imminent retirement, his lack of funds, his grandchildren, gallstones and the new car he wanted to buy in September when he would be finally saying goodbye to his job. It was almost as if we were all off on a company-paid day-trip to the seaside, and when we finally got to Terminal 1, I was desperate to get out of the vehicle and give my ears a rest.

Leading the way into Departures, I practically ran, with my crutch threatening to shoot out from under my feet on the slippery new ceramic floor. I got to the corridor upstairs and, hardly waiting for the two behind me, knocked on the door of the Pan Am offices.

It was almost as if Mr Lorenzo was expecting us with his kind greeting and gentle expression of quizzical curiosity. He was very softly spoken, reserved and distinguished looking. I was immediately drawn to him as a type, struck by a funny thought that, on the whole, I liked the Pan Am contingent much better than those who were working for me. I felt this man was intelligent and reasonable, decidedly more so than our playful bailiff, who gambolled through his job like an overgrown puppy.

Without breaking for a minute to get ourselves comfortable or introduce his group, Mr Rossi reeled off the typed script in an incomprehensible and fast monotone, as if pronouncing some kind of incantation. Following this, a long list of office equipment was noted. From the office with the usual filing cabinets, seats and computers, we wrote down other things: 100 cases of champagne, cases of 12 bottles valued at $5 per bottle; 500 cases of white wine, six bottles to each case; 300 of red, again six bottles to each case; and 80 bottles of brandy, each with their relevant wholesale value, one boarding stairway, two maintenance vehicles and three or four airport cars – the items went on.

I then asked the manager if there were any spare parts for aircraft in the workshops, thinking that there must have been certain things stored for ordinary maintenance. I was told there were spare engines, which actually belonged to the company, unlike the aircraft, which were leased. Mr Rossi was quick to point out that he wasn't sure that he could impound spare parts and so it was better not to consider this alternative. He looked ready to finish his work for the day, so, turning to Mr

Pasquale, I asked him what he thought. I knew full well that the young man would have even less of a clue than Mr Rossi, so I got up from my chair and asked everyone to wait whilst I made a phone call, asking Mr Pasquale to come out of the office at the same time. I knew that by sequestering a spare engine I would cause considerable annoyance to Pan Am and perhaps get them to negotiate in more of a hurry. I realised that directly grounding an aeroplane was not possible, but indirectly I could cause logistical problems. I phoned Picci and asked him what to do. He told me to phone just the person I didn't want to have to consult but about the only one who could give me an idea.

I nervously rang Mr Bellicoso's office. Mr Pasquale had suggested I speak directly to the lawyer as I knew what I wanted to do and he was only there to chaperone. Bellicoso came to the phone and listened to my question. I simply asked if I could impound spare parts of the aircraft without infringing any laws that would then boomerang back in my face. Mr Bellicoso coolly informed me that any decision regarding sequestration was entirely up to me and that if I wanted to impound property I could, but that it could have repercussions on the trial of an unquantifiably damaging effect. I said that I imagined that to be the case, but was it illegal? I didn't really get a yes or no, he simply advised me to desist from pursuing this path.

No longer feeling able to fight, I put the phone down and leaned back against the wall by the phone booth. I had no time to discuss the decision to be taken. I certainly didn't want to be cited by the airline company but at the same time was aware that sequestering a spare part was considerably better than sequestering champagne. I felt extremely vulnerable and very disappointed, surrounded by men and not one of them would help me. I turned on Mr Pasquale, who emerged from behind a pillar like a scared rabbit. With tears in my eyes I gave vent to my dashed hopes in a rather incoherent rant. I was beside myself about the injustice of what was happening. Mr Pasquale was looking at me as though I was a little deranged, and clearly my outpourings were those of a stressed woman and one that needed to be calmed down, but the last thing I wanted was a man's understanding support.

Seeing the hopelessness of the situation, I blew my nose and muttered a few obscenities under my breath. Very crossly, I then told Mr Rossi that we would not be impounding spare parts. At that moment I loathed Bellicoso. I was annoyed with men in general and disillusioned with them as human beings, but I was even more exasperated with myself for not trusting my instincts, or screwing up enough courage to go it alone.

The journey home was silent, as I mulled over what had happened. I walked into my apartment, suffocated by my own swirling thoughts and violent emotion. I opened my bedroom window, which looked out on the flat gardens. Every shrub and bush was in late bloom, and the air was heady with summer smells. A warm balmy breeze moved the curtains gently, and I put my hand out of the window to touch the dry, spiky grass. I loved my home, however simple it was, with the tranquillity and green park surrounding me. I felt soothed by my flat, and I had lovely neighbours, discreet and welcoming, ever ready to listen when I came back tired after a day at work, always there to help if there was a problem. Giulia, my very pretty neighbour, made coming home easier, and I felt that I had a family who cared for me and liked to be kept in the picture regarding the events that happened in my life.

That afternoon, I sat down in my wicker armchair with a cup of very strong tea and reflected on the way the day had gone. All things considered, we had made our mark, and I was extremely glad that I had attended the putting out of attachments and not left things up to Mr Bellicoso's office and the bailiff, although I was smarting from the self-criticism of not having had the courage to sequester an engine. Provided that Mr Napolitani had done his bit, too, and proceeded in Rome, we would wait and watch for the next phase to unfold. If I judged correctly, it wouldn't be long before I got a phone call from Pan Am.

I pulled my bag out from under the bed so that I could pack for the weekend and searched for my scratchbag cat Tigger, who'd gone outside for the afternoon and showed no sign of turning up. Picci was coming to pick me up and we'd be leaving for Frera after supper.

35

SETTLEMENT

THE NAME TANZANIA has a marvellous sound, especially the way it is pronounced in Italian: exotic, adventurous and fiery. At last it had looked as though we were going to visit Africa after years of tempting stories and descriptions from Picci, whose love for the continent grew with each passing year that he hadn't been back. The visas had come through at the end of that July for the August holiday period and we'd had our jabs. I'd bought maps and a guidebook, and had drawn up a tentative itinerary for a gentle trip. But it was obviously the wrong moment in my life to be heading off to this particular part of the world. Events changed our plans once again, and we found ourselves heading back across the Atlantic.

Champagne and orange juice were served as we plopped down into first-class Pan Am seats which could have accommodated two of us, they were so huge. We were offered a vast assortment of papers to read. A stewardess carefully put my crutches in the compartment over our heads and lodged our extremely tatty baggage at the back of the cabin. I was very excited by the latest happenings and relaxed back into the soft and well-worn seats. Impressed by all the deference offered by staff, Picci asked me if I thought that there was a chiropodist and massage service available, but he wickedly had second thoughts as he checked out the stewardesses, deciding that first class on a Malaysian airline was much more his thing. Admittedly, the youngest stewardess must have been in her late 40s, and all the others were held together with cosmetic glue, but they were very kind, and I told him to make the most of the flight given that it would be the first and last time he would be travelling first class in his life. 'Not if you get adequate compensation,' he laughed.

Things had been arranged in record time. Only two days previously we had been contacted by the airline company. They wanted to negotiate and as fast as possible so that the attachments could be lifted. Mr Elsie asked when it would be convenient for them to come to Italy and whether our lawyers had already gone on holiday. At that point I told him that we were available for talks whenever they wished, but preferably after the holiday as we were due to leave for Africa within the week and reorganisation of the trip would take longer than just a few days. After a long pause, he asked if we would mind changing our holiday plans and going to the States for talks with Pan Am immediately. I felt Africa zoom into the background of my mind with remarkable speed.

I put the phone down saying I'd let him know as soon as possible. After an evening of discussion, we felt the time had come to see if we couldn't close a particularly stressful chapter of our lives by discussing the possibility of a settlement. We decided that travelling to America was the best solution and called them back to say that we would come. They were more than satisfied and very keen on closing the deal. Remarkably, both we and they were unencumbered by lawyers. Both Mr Bellicoso and Mr Napolitani had handed in their resignations, although they were involved with the finalisation of the sequestration procedures. Similarly, after the fiasco over the sequestration Pan Am were no longer represented by Mr Gallo and Mr Bianchi, so we could all meet up in a civilised way without any third parties present.

From the moment we made our decision, everything clicked into place, from the unexpected availability of Mrs Bianchi, the interpreter who had acted on our behalf in 1989 when I was in New York, and the organisation of who could look after the cat, to getting finances at the last minute. Our tickets, expenses and accommodation were all being paid for and the red-carpet treatment was most definitely about to happen. I thought about our striped nylon bags, dusty from trips and travel, and half-laughed and half-cringed at how our ragamuffin apparel would appear when we arrived. Our bags really were horribly dirty, but, given the fact that we often made trips, it was one way of discouraging baggage loss through theft. They were also squidgy enough to fit in anywhere and we could drag them wherever, without worrying about ripping or spoiling them. Amazingly, they had lasted for years, but all these good reasons as to why we had them wouldn't make them any more acceptable during our stay in the five-star hotel we'd been booked into.

I stretched my limbs. My left leg, even after all these years, was strange, half-numb and constantly filled with the sensation of pins and needles. I largely ignored it, except for when I was tired or damp weather penetrated the bones. Then I reached for the painkillers. I turned to Picci, who was leafing through a paper, and asked him how he thought things were going to go. He yawned and half-nodded to my question but didn't answer, absorbed as he was in his reading. I was well used to his silences. It wasn't that he did it deliberately, but if he thought a question superfluous, he just didn't bother saying anything.

I waited and then lost interest myself, staring out of the window, thinking back to how the whole saga had started. I saw the baggage handlers driving round on the tarmac, the firemen close at hand, technicians standing around ready to wave their flags and watched the catering lorry move away from the plane. It was the same scene, the same activity and the same checks that had occurred all those years ago, only I was profoundly different. I had been pushed and tested to the limits of suffering and was at an absolute loss as to what it all meant and what lesson I could pull out of such shocking experiences. I didn't feel I had learnt anything from all that had happened, except for a few hard facts of life, and I was more bewildered and confused than anything else.

The minutes slipped by, and my thoughts became more practical. I was, in fact, very hungry. The flight was already half an hour late, and with transatlantic hauls things tended to get strung out. I wished I had had breakfast. I sank back into my musings, drifting over the few conversations Mr Elsie and I had had over the phone as we sorted out the travel arrangements. He had been particularly peeved that 'our lawyers' had gone ahead with the attachments and asked me why. I told him that we were sick and tired of Pan Am's lawyers playing silly games over the deposit, shrugging off the responsibility onto Mr Bellicoso. 'They didn't want any more last-minute promises, as they'd had enough from Mr Gallo who seemed more interested in obstructing cooperation than anything else.' I had told him some of the other things that had happened, and whilst I don't know whether any of this had a bearing on his relationship with the firm of solicitors they had hitherto used, I was delighted that they were to play no further part, as I felt they really had been very unpleasant to me.

On and on I pondered over all that had happened, every moment providing memories of the previous five years. It seemed that we were nearly at the end of our adventure, and I couldn't help but re-live certain passages of time that had so radically influenced my life.

I thought back to my father and how our relationship had changed over the years. He'd been my hero as a little girl, the love of my life, and we had been united by a passion for music that often saw us singing old favourites together. When my mother had died, however, I had been on the threshold of adolescence. It was a terrible time to lose a mother, and my father had done his best to bring up his three daughters and son who were all passing, or about to pass, through this period of growing up. Our relationship had ineluctably and painfully changed over the following years, as my teens made me rebellious and his new marriage seemed to me to take precedence over his filial ties.

Then there had been the hijack and he had suffered as only a parent can when they see their child hurt. We had briefly grown close once again, only to experience another breach. He said I was prickly to deal with and I was, but I had many things to cope with and needed understanding. My love for him was constant, but we misinterpreted each other's ways, and it caused me a lot of sadness. I wondered if we would ever build a solid bridge of loving communication. Perhaps in the future, I thought, now that my life would calm down a little, I could dedicate more time to relationships.

The flight was tedious but not economy-claustrophobic. How much nicer it was to fly first class and how very much more comfortable for my leg and bottom. I imagined the cost of the ticket and knew that even if I were to have that kind of money I would never be able to justify spending it in such a way. I was a squirrel at heart.

We were met by a Pan Am official at the airport who helped us into the hired car and gave instructions to the driver to take us down into Manhattan to The Hutton. The car slid out of the airport precincts, and Picci and I, aching with flight discomfort, collapsed into the slippery seats and cool air conditioning. I examined the papers I'd studied on the plane and, with a feeling of intrepidity, asked the driver if he wouldn't mind stopping off at the Federal Aviation Administration Offices, Building 111, just past the Travel Lodge Inn, before taking us to our hotel. I was about to collect my 'last card' in case I was forced to use more persuasive methods of convincing the insurers. I needed documentation supporting a new piece of evidence I had found out in the spring of that year. What with all the comings and goings of lawyers, the date of the final gathering of evidence had been postponed once more, and I was still in time to submit extra proof. I was already in touch with a certain person at the FAA, who I had cultivated though painstaking letters and phone calls. The organisation itself tended to be shy of answering strange questions posed by people they didn't know, but I had had a rare stroke of luck and accidentally been put in touch with someone who was a kind and very enthusiastic lawyer. His name was David Graham and he was one of the assistants to the chief counsel at the FAA. This had come about after I had contacted someone in the Airline Pilots Association, asking him to help me with some research regarding Pan Am's situation. My letter was addressed to a Mr Baldwin and explained that I had in my possession a report issued by the Italian Trade Commission in New York that divulged the financial situation of Pan Am and also included a history of litigation. There was one paragraph which revealed that in the August of the year of our hijacking, the FAA had requested nearly $2 million from Pan Am to settle allegations that it had operated aircraft that had not adhered to maintenance standards, or had failed to act upon FAA recommendations and flown aircraft that were in an un-airworthy condition. This, as I understood it, meant that our APU evidence could be backed up with circumstantial proof. Bad maintenance of the APU could have been the cause of the rupture in the cooling duct. Of course, I'd have to try and trace the actual APU and look at records of its maintenance, but perhaps I would be able to, once I'd let the judge know what I was trying to achieve. I thought that if I let Pan Am see that I had this documentation, they might be more pliable when we started talking about how much Picci and I were worth in terms of compensation. Of course, on looking at the FAA records, the fact that Pan Am had paid the $2 million did not constitute admission that the allegations were true, and there was a qualifying statement made to that effect, but presumably the amount agreed upon cut short lengthy legal procedures that could have culminated in heavy sanctions. I had asked Mr Baldwin to give me the name of the department and person who could give me further help on the matter within the FAA. I was after a copy of the FAA Inspection and Findings with the subsequent fines. Miraculously, I had been given the name of this young lawyer, with whom I'd had interesting and helpful conversations by phone. I had rung him to say I'd be coming over to the States in the next few days. Would he be prepared to have a talk?

Mr Graham was expecting me, and we greeted each other like old friends. I had not told him of my involvement in the hijack, as I hadn't wanted to alarm him or suddenly find myself being given the cold shoulder, so when he saw me walking with crutches he asked me whether I'd sprained my ankle. I had to laugh, and in doing so I suddenly found myself letting go of much of the tension that had been mounting over the last few weeks. Of course, I enlightened the puzzled man, who was sufficiently shocked at my confessions to wonder if I was making everything up. Gradually, however, I calmed down, and he too realised that what I had to say was far from a joke. He was transfixed by my story, and as soon as he understood why I needed the documents, he wasted no more time. Within a half hour I had a copy of the initial FAA letter listing all the alleged infringements on the part of Pan Am, a copy of the settlement agreement and the copies of payment instalments. All were signed and certified by the FAA.

I left the building waving my precious file at Picci who was slumped in a tired heap in one corner of the immensely long limo. 'I gather you were successful,' he said, grinning at my pink cardboard file. I squeezed his ear lobe. This, I explained, would give credibility to the possibility that the APU had failed because it was just too old or badly maintained for the job – too many service hours. This knowledge gave me more power, and I felt that now we were going to be better equipped psychologically to face the insurers and the Pan Am representative.

An hour later we were trailing behind a porter carrying the awful bags up to our room. We gave him a huge tip because of our exhausted state and collapsed onto the beds before going down to have something to eat. The Hutton was a vast place, a mausoleum kept at refrigerator temperature. The room was actually cold, and I had to look in my luggage for the only cardigan I'd brought with me. I hadn't bargained for American air conditioning, which could literally induce flu symptoms if you didn't have something warm to put round your shoulders. In the central foyer, which was also part dining room, mezzanine and reception area, there was a fountain that shot five metres into the air and had twelve mini-fountains spurting round a vast pool. The water was icy cold and, with its continual flow, rise and fall, caused a merciless draught of wind which moved round the tables in the dining room in chilly wafts. We had decided to have something to eat there as neither of us felt like going out into the bold sunshine to look for a place to dine. We should have ventured out, however, as the two occasions we ate in the foyer were sufficient to give me a summer cold and hacking cough.

Although we had just arrived and felt exhausted, we were in a lighter frame of mind. Picci's irreverent sense of humour had me in stitches and he was at his best when he was feeling very tired. A languid relinquishing of control seemed to release his more sardonic and wicked side. A small orchestra was intermittently playing old favourites which came and went in volume with the moving current of air some way further down the room, and I shivered while we waited for our server to arrive. I watched them move in amongst the tables with their white cloths over their arms and hoped that one of them would come over to us. We sat there for ages because of a shift change, which then brought us face to face with an incredible lookalike of Mr Bellicoso. Both of us were tickled by the similarity and joked about how he'd chucked in his career as a lawyer to become a waiter. We were unbelievably silly that late afternoon, wondering if we could create a bit of fun with washing up liquid surreptitiously squirted into the fountain that was beginning to get on our nerves what with the noise and wintry blasts of cold air.

A clerk came over to our table and gave me an envelope containing a warm welcome from Pan Am and the news that Mr Elsie would be ringing at eight o'clock that evening. Well, I supposed he would just have to wake me up because I was dead on my feet and it was gone midnight for us. We tottered off to bed, past thinking about any strategy or what our plans were for the next week.

I suppose Mr Elsie must have called me, even if I have no recollection of the conversation, because we met up briefly the following day with his personnel manager, a quiet kindly lady. The main meeting was to happen on Tuesday, when the insurance people would be available. We all sat down after slightly over-excited greetings and skirted the awkward subject of compensation by becoming engrossed first in the menu and then in the family concerns of both the Pan Am representatives. Picci was always more fortunate than I in that he used his ignorance of English as a way of getting out of talking so that he could people-watch. I picked through the salad I had ordered, uncomfortable as I was balanced on the very loud pink love settees in the mezzanine area that were just a fraction too far from the low table on which we were trying to eat. All references to the purpose of our visit, or, indeed, the common ground we shared, were carefully avoided, but it was what remained un-alluded to that occupied all our minds. Everyone was courteous, but it was with some relief that we went our separate ways after lunch, they back to the office and we to stretch our legs in Central Park, working off the excitable speculation surging through our strained imaginations.

The negotiation was a match that we wanted to win. I so wished it was possible to read other people's minds, as knowing what Pan Am's financial limits were would have helped considerably in calming me down. We were at a significant disadvantage in that we were emotionally involved and unable to defend our position from a psychological distance, while Mr Elsie or anyone else in the meeting would not be depending on the outcome for a better life. Skateboarders dodged round our sedate amble as I watched my feet take a slope. I had always tended to watch my feet even before walking with crutches, and I recalled various occasions when I had ended up apologising to lamp-posts on my way home from school, living as I did in my imagination, but now being forced to keep my eyes glued to the ground made me resentful from time to time, and I pulled Picci over to a bench so that we could watch what was going on without the risk of my tripping over. It was a trial having got this far to still have to fight. I knew we were into the home-run but was so painfully aware that we could still come off badly.

Picci was unusually quiet, except for commenting on the fact that we should try to organise our holiday. The meeting would be over by the following lunchtime, so we might as well decide on what to do after that. I felt his lack of enthusiasm thickly coat my thoughts. When he was unsure, he tended to be pessimistic. I had not even thought about where to spend the other 28 days or so of August because our visit represented the end of a certain world as I knew it. We moved on, poked into action by the realisation that unless we hurried we would not get to the travel agent in time and certainly neither of us wanted to hang around in the city more than necessary. Our schedule was to include two or three days in New York, first to settle the case and then to start on a search for a lawyer there who would be interested in taking me on as their client to pursue the case against the hospital and surgeon who had operated on me in 1989.

We had declined the help of Mr Bellicoso's colleague as his fees had been a little too expensive for us, and we hoped to find someone who would work exclusively on a contingency fee basis. The first place to start would be a look through the Yellow Pages, to find someone who dealt with malpractice cases and make an appointment to see them.

Later, jetlag, anxiety and the obsessive background noise of New York's collective 24-hour functioning, won over sleep. If only we had been able to open a window and switch our air-conditioning system off, but the windows were sealed. We should have drunk a bottle of thick red Californian wine to take the edge off such an important 'eve', but we were too jumpy to let go, fearful that alcohol would blunt our wits the following day. By the time we had dropped off, after having discussed at length strategic alternatives, it was two o'clock in the morning and the consequent late rise had us rushing about the hotel room like two blind old moths as we got dressed and tried to remember what we'd agreed upon during the night.

We met Mrs Bianchi, our interpreter, as arranged in the lobby of our hotel by the lifts. She was a portly but very Italian-looking lady, elegantly dressed, with fine black eyes and beautifully cut hair, thick and gleaming. She sat beside me on the large leather bench after our initial greeting as we waited for Picci to come back from the bank. He'd had to change some money so that we could pay Mrs Bianchi at the end of the day. We were pleased to see her, and she us, after a three-year silence. She asked after my sister Francesca, whom she'd met, and made positive noises about how well I was now looking. The last time she'd seen me I had been green and very ill. I had walked with unbelievable slowness and was mentally shot to pieces. Quite clearly I had made a significant improvement as she continued to exclaim how she had hardly recognised me. I must have looked even worse back then than I had imagined.

We went off to have a cup of coffee together so that we could fill her in on the story so far and tell her the purpose of this meeting. We all ordered thick espressos and a croissant to perk up the grey matter. When we told her that we'd come to New York to try to arrive at some sort of agreement with Pan Am, she clapped her bejewelled hands together in optimistic joy and charged us both with a great many '*auguri*', getting up from the table to come round to my side and plant a powdery kiss on my cheek. 'We're not there yet,' murmured Picci.

At quarter to ten, it was time to make our way to the Pan Am offices, which were in the same vast complex that housed the hotel, the underground station and the skyscraper called the Pan Am building. I had the same sensation walking in the cavernous halls of this place as when I had gone into the dinosaur section of the Natural History Museum in London as a little girl. I was dwarfed by immense space. I felt a little like David in the Goliath story, at long last about to walk into the great powerhouse of those who had been my adversaries for so long. I, who had been ignored in the beginning and had stamped my foot for attention via the British press and the BBC, was about to see justice done, and I felt proud that after this tremendous battle the last word might just possibly be ours.

We got out of the lift on the ninth floor and looked about us. There was no one to be seen and the surrounding silence was disconcerting. Getting to Pan Am's offices reminded me of how Alice must have felt when she followed the White Rabbit down the rabbit-hole. There were numerous anonymous brown doors which didn't look grand at all, and what was really odd was that literally no one seemed to populate this floor of the building. Eventually we found a door with a small, quite unobtrusive nameplate to the left saying Pan Am World Airways Incorporated. We knocked and went in. The place was fairly desolate with a brown threadbare carpet that took the place of the sludge green linoleum of the external corridors. Office dividers separated one area from another in what seemed to be a huge open space. No one was there to greet us or even seemed to know who we were, and so Mrs Bianchi, buoyed up by the crusade she felt she was on, asked a young man if he would tell Mr Elsie that we had arrived. He casually pointed down to the end of the room and said, 'If you follow your nose, you'll see him in Mrs Arbuthnot's office. He should be there.' We thanked him, noting the informality and feeling somehow disappointed. So this was what happened when a company was dying. My spirits were dampened by the fact that the offices of Pan Am were actually rather drab. They smelled of cheap old carpet and human odours, stuffy despite the temperature, and the last vestiges of any myth surrounding this grandmother of airlines fell away, revealing the unhappy reality of a company in deep trouble.

The first person I saw in the office was a minute but exquisite Indian girl, who introduced herself as the secretary I had always spoken to when calling Mr Elsie. She was immediately welcoming, saying how pleased she was to finally meet me after all these years. She radiated her pleasure and offered coffee to everyone, apologising for the polystyrene cups and instant granules. We were a long way from Italy, and I accepted the cup and put it to my lips just as Mr Elsie came through the door with a 'Hi, everyone, good to see you. Welcome to Pan Am. Mr Popomodus, who will be taking the meeting on behalf of the insurers, hasn't arrived yet, but he'll be here in about five minutes.'

Evidently Mr Maroni was unavailable, and I found myself quite relieved. Mr Elsie then invited us through to the meeting room. We squeezed past piles of grey files and a photocopying machine, rounded a corner and were then led into a very small airless meeting room without any windows. The ceiling and walls were made of hardboard. One wall was lined with files, and there was a computer sitting on the end of the table. There were about six chairs in the room, and the carpet was blue but threadbare all the same. My heart was beginning to beat extremely quickly, and, with a cold coming on, I felt uncomfortably hot in such a small space. My head was feeling prickly, too, and a nervous sniff had started up.

Mr Popomodus arrived after some ten minutes of small talk: thank heavens for Mrs Bianchi, who was quite in her element. The insurance man sat down after hearty handshakes with all of us and placed his litre of coffee just out of reach of hand movement. There was more conversational small talk, as was the requirement of such meetings, until a natural lull in the chat suddenly focused everyone's attention on the central matter. I was beyond coherent participation, with a thud thud thud going on in my bosom that drowned out even my thoughts. Mr Popomodus was very tall and well built. He was the classic American affluent businessman. He had big pouty lips, fleshy wobbly cheeks and a lunch tum. He was used to the good life. Mr Elsie looked more ill at ease than usual. I didn't imagine that leading a company through bankruptcy was very satisfying, and the more I studied the poor man, the more I realised he was in fact near exhaustion.

Mr Popomodus explained his role as being that of liquidator of Pan Am's financial obligations. He asked us how we wanted to pursue the meeting. We said it was up to him and that we were there to listen. So he began explaining that their objectives were to lift the sequestrations or attachments in Italy, and we confirmed that ours were to settle the case for both Picci and me. At first both Mr Elsie and Mr Popomodus thought that we were only there to discuss the possibility of closing the case in Milan and that we had very little autonomy in actually coming to any agreement because we were not represented by any lawyers. This problem was soon sorted out and the situation clarified. By this time we were terribly sympathetic to each other's frustrations and were on each other's side. This had to be the strangest of situations.

Mrs Bianchi was far more interested in what was being said, wanting to contribute to the general negative attitude concerning lawyers, than she was in translating for Picci. I was aware that she was leaving things out and loosely interpreting, but saw that her presence served as a buffer and gave us time to collect our thoughts. Besides, Picci understood a great deal of English even if he didn't talk. I could tell that he was really nervous and imagined that he felt the huge burden of not failing in this meeting. My financial future was at stake here.

'Well, Miss Hill and Mr Carati.' Mr Popomodus' gravelly voice took on a more serious tone. 'Your attachments have certainly caused us some problems. We can't honestly understand how all that got so out of hand, but, anyway, if it's helped to get us all together to sort out Catherine's very big difficulty, then I suppose that's a good thing.' He rubbed his hands together and looked at Mr Elsie, who was pulling at a whisker or two of his moustache. 'It's about time we all had a talk, don't you think so, John?' Mr Elsie nodded, and I thought what a shitty system we lived in when innocent people involved in hijacks or other misfortunes had to scream their heads off and attack before anyone would do anything to help. Mr Popomodus knew exactly how much people had to fight, for this was a scene he saw every day. I carried on smiling, my facial muscles in unhappy tension. Picci mapped out his response. He started by giving a few definitions and the reasons for the sequestration, the way it was rationalised and what this signified in an Italian court. He was also able to explain how the attachments could be lifted, what the time span was and what steps would have to be taken to unblock all these assets. He similarly confirmed that things would be a little hard to shift over the August period, as this was the classic month where everyone went on their annual holiday, particularly in Milan.

Mr Elsie pulled at his moustache a little more insistently. Seeing the tension mount somewhat, Picci softened the blow by explaining that an emergency amendment would be possible with a different judge provided they could find a lawyer in Milan. Naturally this would also depend on our settling the case. Mr Popomodus sighed as he rubbed his nose between thumb and forefinger. 'Perhaps we should then discuss how we can close this case. As far as we can tell, Mr Carati, the amount that the judge decided as a deposit was the amount that you would have probably won had we not agreed to meet up here in New York.' My stomach fell down to the first floor of the Pan Am building, and I felt myself change colour. Disappointment and fear paralysed my thinking apparatus.

'I believe you have been misinformed about what the deposit was actually for,' replied Picci, who was gaining more control by the second. 'You have to realise that that sum was only a part of Catherine's future provision for medical care. Our request for financial help was based much more on the problems she's going to have as she gets older and the difficulties she will meet as her body, which is at the moment in its prime, falls victim to time. You do realise that to date she has had 25 or so anaesthetics, and that of those 25 about 15 have involved major surgery. Any one of those operations would have laid any of us up for weeks on end. You can all imagine what this has done to Catherine's future prospects, where in all probability she will undergo further treatment of a similar nature.'

I was watching the insurer's expression closely. He was getting into difficulty because the discussion was beginning to move into the territory of human suffering and tragedy, with the subject, me, sitting staring at him, trying to steer his conscience into the higher financial bracket. He cleared his throat and started off on a different tack.

'Now, of course that was a starting sum, and we are the first to agree that the deposit asked for by the judge hardly reflects the extent of Catherine's injuries [Picci hadn't said that but the interpretation was correct], but we feel that what with the amount we have already paid out to Catherine in terms of maintenance cheques, I think the sum amounts to, let me see, umm, $100,000, with something extra for her health care . . . ' He was referring to the New York operation and paused to think.

With great patience, never losing his measured tones, Picci, as if he hadn't heard what Popomodus had said, introduced the problems of finding medical expertise to help me walk again. 'As I'm sure you know, Catherine would like to walk again without a crutch one day. In her present state she will never be allowed such a luxury – walking – something we do without a thought but without which our lives would become extraordinarily difficult, I'm sure you agree.' There were wary semi-sympathetic nods from the two men and vigorous ones from Mrs Bianchi. 'You must understand that it is no simple matter finding treatment and medical knowledge of the highest calibre. You will remember the operations in New York.' The skewer went in and both Mr Elsie and Mr Popomodus squirmed on the end of it as the failure of the summer of 1989 was brought to all our attention. Pan Am, of course, were not responsible, but unpleasant memories were attached to the incident.

Mrs Bianchi was adoring Picci from her interpreting seat and relishing his words as she translated. She was after all part of the Pan Am–Hill–Carati history as well, albeit only as an observer. Seeing the opposition waver under his meticulous logic, Picci drove home his point, explaining that in all probability we would win the case in the Italian law courts. He also emphasised the fact that there had been no compensation limit at the time of the hijack. In other words, it was up to the court to decide on a suitable sum of money once it had been proved that Pan Am was partially responsible. I wondered how we were going to be able to swing it.

'I feel we could offer perhaps $500,000 dollars. What do you say to that, Catherine?' Mr Popomodus swivelled his large eyes round to where I was sitting and smiled. I naturally didn't smile but decided to say something myself that might help clarify the degree of mental anguish I was in. I also clutched the FAA documents concerning the monies Pan Am had had to pay out in August of 1986. This in an unconnected way gave me strength.

'I know that Picci will feel bad about what I have to say, but I must let you know of the misery we have had to go through.' I was about to confess something that was extremely private and embarrassing. I took a deep breath as I began to speak. 'I have not had an intimate relationship since the hijack on more than three or four rather desperate occasions, due to the fact that I experience great pain and as a consequence avoid the activity.' I was suitably scarlet. 'I am also convinced that, even were I able, my shame over my body would make the act a travesty of what it is meant to be. [This was just dreadful.] I hope you understand that this is only one small area of my life that has been changed for the worse.'

It was awful having to spell out for these people what kind of difficulties we had had to circumnavigate, for even though our lives were not completely celibate, the hijack had massively undermined our intimacy and this had been a huge area of distress for me. I had never been one to talk about the agonies in my life. I had always tried to make little of them. Now it was in my interests to reveal them.

'Can we quantify that in terms of a small sum of money? Can any of this pain be quantified in financial figures? I do not believe that it can, but what I do believe is that by at least taking the pressure off having to earn a salary, by having the equivalent of a health insurance policy and a pension, you will be going a long way to helping me resolve practical problems. If you help in this way, I'll be able to start tackling the psychological difficulties so much more effectively, and, no, I don't think $500,000 will be sufficient.'

By this time I'd completely forgotten the FAA allegation, caught up as I was by the emotional drain. My body was damp with perspiration with the effort of having dragged out into the open such a personal aspect of our lives. Mrs Bianchi was a picture of aching sympathy, which embarrassed me even more as she listened to what I had to say. Picci picked up where I had left off, and his voice gathered in strength.

'Our request was for $1 million but we are fully aware that you are not considering this kind of figure. Might we not reach a compromise?'

We all knew that by American standards our request for compensation for the kind of injuries we'd had was a pittance, but in Europe we were probably in line or asking for more than we would have been awarded in a court of law.

'Let's say that our two compensations together could be placed at $700,000? I have hardly been touched compared to Catherine, and so I want to give her the compensation you will be paying me. Please be generous. She has suffered more than any of us could possibly understand.'

Mrs Bianchi had tears in her eyes. Mr Elsie was clearing his throat a little, and, after a considerable pause, Mr Popomodus finally answered.

'Yes. You know, Miss Hill and Mr Carati, I think that we'll be very happy to pay you this money. Yes, I think that will be just fine. I admire you both enormously, and I hope that this will take away just a little of all that you have been through over the last few years.'

There was a split second of silence, and then Mr Elsie jumped up from his chair ready to embrace the insurance man, delighted he'd erred on the side of largesse. Mrs Bianchi didn't know who to hug first and was waylaid by having to look for her tissues. Picci had a quiet smile on his face, and I felt extremely wobbly and unable to grasp that it was actually all over: the trial, the lawyers, the hearings and the anxiety. I was swooped up in a bear hug by Mr Elsie, who kept saying to me, 'Well done, Catherine, well done.' He shook Picci's hand, and Mr Popomodus came over and wished us both well, too.

After a suitable amount of celebratory back slapping, we lurched out of the stuffy meeting room supporting each other. Lunch was booked in a beautiful seafood restaurant, and, after further congratulations, we all went out for a large celebration. For two hours, compliments flew, jokes were made and everyone behaved with wild gaiety. It was hard to believe that we had got almost what we wanted, and without any lawyers.

Typically, I came down with a cold in one staggeringly huge sneeze at the table. My eyes filled up and I felt as though an army of tickling ants were trudging through my head. I kept shivering, wondering if it was my state of health or this unbelievably shocked state of mind. I was thrilled that we had decided to risk the wrath of the gods when we refused to accept the $150,000 offered to us in the unsuccessful meeting in Milan, but only wished they had been with us to see what we had been able to do without them. We had actually increased the amount enormously by going it alone. What was so comforting was that both Mr Popomodus and Mr Elsie were good people, and it occurred to me that perhaps things needn't have gone this far.

After so much stress and struggle, Africa would have to wait because it would take too much travelling to get there. We decided to go off down to the Caribbean for a rest and give our sorely tried brains the necessary time for things to sink in. The handing over of cheques and signing of release papers would be done on 26 September, when we'd all had a break. Both Mr Elsie and Mr Popomodus would come over to Italy to deal with the actual transaction, and in the meantime the attachments would be lifted. We were given a very reassuring signed letter explaining the deal, and it had been signed by the United States Aviation Underwriters. There was no possibility that this agreement was not final, and it was with awe and some reverence that it was tucked away in the documents case purchased for the occasion and slipped into the tartan rucksack.

We turned in early that evening, tired from the lack of sleep the night before and the excitement of that day, but before going to bed, I phoned my father and then my beloved aunts in England, announcing proudly over the phone that we'd 'slain our dragon'. I heard the pop of a champagne cork in the background and cries of happiness as the good news was passed round at a lunch party my aunt was in the middle of giving. 'Our love to you both, my dears, our love to you both. Enjoy your holidays and don't worry about ringing everyone else up, we'll be thrilled to do it for you.' I put the phone down, smiling at the genuine happiness our triumph generated. We got into bed, and our heads aching for sleep touched the pillow. I sneezed again and then fell headlong into sweet and dreamless unconsciousness for the first time in many months. Picci murmured something about having no more dragons to fight and how it felt strange, and then he too closed his eyes and was off.

36

DANCING IN THE SEA

WE FLEW DOWN to Turks and Caicos two days later, having thrown all our clothes in disordered bundles into the bags. For some reason, Picci was upset after the case had been settled and was subdued. I was puzzled by his manner. After all, wasn't this the end to the legal torture – an end we had both wanted? His withdrawal confused me, and, as usual, I thought I'd done something to cause it, but I knew better than to push him for explanations, hoping that time would reveal the problem.

The journey was strenuous, with changes from one plane to another, and the effort of claiming baggage in record time temporarily pulled him out of his strange mood, even though we didn't really talk, each going over in our minds the curious, and at the same time for me marvellous, meeting we'd had two days before. I watched the string of Bahamian islands pass by as we flew 30,000 feet above the sea, and I wanted to be happy, but there was a nagging worry as to why a coolness had come between us. I would far rather have exuberantly celebrated, but Picci was not that sort of a person, and, anyway, I could feel that there was something he was afraid of. I only hoped that he wasn't trying to find a way to end our relationship now that he'd safely secured compensation for me, a prospect that made me very agitated. I'd just have to sit the problem out until he felt like talking.

Quite possibly we were the only tourists arriving on the island that hot month of August. There were few people who disembarked and, as the door of the plane opened, it was fairly apparent that the islands were better suited for winter vacations. The heat was oven-like, hot and humid with the tarmac shimmering in the bright noon light. We scuttled into the shade of the walkway to Customs like two discovered crabs. One or two taxis were parked outside in the shade of the only two trees, which looked more dead than alive, dried out by the sun's rays. We asked to be taken to the nearest hotel in town.

The streets were deserted with not a soul in sight. Everything was hard baked and bleached white, with flurries of dust and sand that blew up momentarily only to die down as quickly as they had started. I watched the scenery slide by in disappointment as we drove along the white roads. We so badly needed to relax and this arid desolation made me feel like the Ancient Mariner. The sun was an ugly mustard yellow ball that hung menacingly in the sky, and the sea was as dull and black as a sheet of metal. I hoped that this was only a short spell, for such heat surely could not last. We had three weeks ahead of us, and the thought of staying in a similar climate was too draining for words.

We installed our belongings in a seedy hotel, one of the few apparently open, and were generously given the largest room, which was unfortunately positioned under the corrugated iron roof. We went down to the reception area to ask if we could have lunch and were offered fried fish and canned beans, which demoralised us even further. Having eaten, we sat about under the veranda awning waiting for the heat to ease off, reading, as it was the only thing we could do, our conversation having long since petered out. Two litres of water and ten chapters later, we looked at our watches. It was four o'clock and we were very bored and not a little morose. The temperature was going down and a gentle breeze had started up. No sooner had it become cooler than we went to get our costumes to go for a swim. At least we might try to freshen up in the sea and perhaps shake off the terrible mood that had crept stealthily into our hearts.

The only accessible beach for me, however, was in fact the nastiest of places. The sand was not sand but mud and squelched up between our toes, while the sea was of blood temperature and very murky. It was low tide and we had to walk far out before it began to get deep, not the kind of refreshing dip we had hoped for. It felt as if the sewage system was active in that particular bay, and although I didn't see any toilet paper or worse float by, I felt unhappy in the water. We came out of the sea feeling unclean and even more disconsolately we walked back to the hotel, dreaming at least of a cold shower. This wasn't possible either, however, as water was rationed because it hadn't rained for months, and you could only have a shower between certain times in the morning and evening. We had to hang around, salty, sticky and feeling dirty.

That night, we decided that should the following day be as bad as this one, we would get the next plane out to a different island away from this humid but desert-like atmosphere. Predictably, the day after was as bad if not worse, because in the heat we hadn't been able to sleep and had spent the night whacking ourselves and the walls to rid the place of mosquitoes. As agreed, we went to the little travel agency to find an alternative.

The island we picked was a stone's throw from Turks and Caicos. In fact, it was part of the island group but far better developed in terms of tourism. So we bought tickets, got ready and left that same day. Although the sun was as hot as the day before, the vegetation and beautifully landscaped gardens on the second island provided welcome shade and relief from the otherwise flat chalk-like scenery. The hotel we chose had air-conditioning and was well decorated with cool ceramic tiles, small windows and subdued light. Just the sort of place where one could rest and replenish depleted batteries. After a few days' break, we found a very pretty house to rent, overlooking the beach, where we could relax and enjoy our 20 days together.

With such a disastrous start to the holidays, things did get progressively better, and even the sun seemed less fearsome once we acclimatised to the heat. The weather had changed a little and sea breezes blew away the torridness of the first few days. Picci visibly relaxed, sleeping and reading, and I set about getting a tan, tired of the strained face that peered back at me from the bathroom mirror. The problem that had started to scratch at our relationship was one that couldn't be resolved immediately. Picci mentioned his anxiety casually one evening, after a brief conversation that ended with him saying that now I was financially independent and no longer involved with the trial, I was free to go and do whatever I wanted, meaning, I think, that I could leave him. I had known this was a thought that had ridden closely on his back over the past few years, as it was the most obvious thing anyone might think when considering our relationship. 'She won't leave him because he's her ticket to financial security', or something like that. A friend of mine had taken me out to lunch one day and said as much, which had caused no end of distress and led to the end of our friendship. It had been an uncomfortable reflection that possessed me sometimes during the trial, particularly as I knew that without Picci's support and invaluable advice I would never have seen justice done. Certainly, I knew that I would never have received the kind of money I had, or been allowed that luxury of not having to worry ever again, had he not been there.

How could I be sure that my dependence on him wasn't the only thing keeping us together? The way I felt towards Picci didn't seem to have changed, but these situations are hard to work out on a rational level. I certainly hoped that our bond and love for one another would not now fizzle out, leaving the unpleasant realisation that I had been with him because I needed him. The thought was extremely unwelcome and made me feel very unworthy indeed. Picci found it easier to face this possibility, as he had behaved with impeccable morality, whereas it could only reflect badly on me. When he brought it up, I therefore sighed and simply told him that I didn't think this was the reason I had stayed with him. Truthfully, though, I didn't know and was frightened by the possibility of it being the case.

These darker considerations remained for much of our holiday as nasty, fleeting shadows. Now that Picci had spoken, he evidently felt the relief of having unburdened his mind, and his humour came back. To some extent I felt reassured by the happiness we obviously felt from being in each other's company. There was also talk about the next lawsuit. We had found a couple of promising names in New York via the Yellow Pages and had popped into their offices to talk to them the day after our meeting with Pan Am. They were very helpful, although declined to take us on. As Mr Elsie had predicted, there were problems regarding the previous lawsuit. The defendants would try to say that the New York problem had been settled with the Pan Am case, and the lawyers who I'd approached were shy of taking on a case that had an inbuilt problem right from the beginning. Picci was adamant that I sue the American doctor and hospital in New York, convinced that they had messed up the operation through negligence. I was less enthusiastic, tired out by the whole hijacking event and our long legal struggle. I didn't really want to know anything more about lawsuits.

Our conversation never waned, and there was always something to discuss, not least the idea I was nursing to write down what had happened to us. Right at the beginning of the hospitalisation, I'd been urged to write a book on all that I experienced, but I had shunned the idea almost as violently as I had shunned eating. The thought of recalling so much pain and confusion had been an anathema to me and a hindrance in my quest to rebuild my life. Apart from the New York episode noted for posterity in my red book for some indefinable reason, I had refused to jot down a single memory during all those years, convinced that nothing good could come out of something so bad. The moment the case was finished, however, I knew that I wanted to write because I could no longer lock up the memories and keep them at bay. One way of expunging my mind might be to put the story onto paper, and now I had something to celebrate. We discussed the ways a story could be written, and Picci suggested placing it in a romantic context. His idea was in stark contrast to the way I felt it should be portrayed. He could see the book from an artistic point of view, while I wanted to let blood.

The idea of actually writing was what drew me to the activity. I bought a notebook and pencil, and began to scribble. It was a fascinating and wonderful activity, and I spent many an evening recording events and the painful reality I had experienced. Attuned to my own inner cameraman, I began to live everyday experiences vividly. Simple things like swimming, walking and chatting with Picci became acutely pleasurable because I was so aware. I was examining everything from an observer's point of view and wondering how I would describe these normal activities in words on paper. There was a kind of detachment, and I found it to be an immensely enjoyable activity, painting pictures with words. I was a child experimenting with materials for the first time at school and thoroughly enjoying myself.

Our holiday drew to a close. The day before we were due to go home, we'd been fishing. Then, because it was the last afternoon, we thought we'd go for a swim. There was an empty beach in front of the deserted Treasure Island Hotel. There were many of these unsuccessful attempts at tourism, and they were nearly always situated in the most beautiful parts of the islands. This hotel must have been deserted for five years or so. It was disintegrating among the palms, whitewashed, with peeling boards hanging loosely under window frames and off doors. Beach vines had worked their tendrils into and over everything. Old office equipment was piled into corners and upended bedsteads were propped up against the walls. We parked the car a little distant from our swimming spot, as I didn't want to advertise the fact that there were people on this beach. I had no swimwear, but only an old and rather long T-shirt I'd stuffed into the car in case the sun got too much for me whilst fishing.

Walking through the thick vegetation and palm floor was a complicated operation. I had just seen a hairy dead spider that must have been as large as my hand. I was repulsed and fascinated at the same time, spiders having long been my phobia. I picked my way through the vegetation and finally walked down the cracked paving stone steps onto the pink and white beach. Walking on sand was marvellous exercise but extremely hard work. There were two small bays each half a mile long, with the hotel placed in the middle of the two. The crescents of pink were perfect. No one had come to the beach that day and the colour of the sea was extraordinary. One bay was a translucent royal blue and the other transparent emerald. We went for the one that was facing the setting sun. I was drawn to it, seduced by its perfection. Coconut palms provided a scenic backdrop to the wide sweep of the bay, and cicadas were beginning to quieten down. Pre-sunset sheets of light were already smacking the surface of the water.

Wasting no time, Picci and I, holding hands because I was without the crutch, moved down to the water's edge. The tiny pebbles sent searing pain up through my left foot, and I staggered heavily, falling with a huge splash into shallow water. I always felt so clumsy, unable to do even the simplest of things without help. I ignored the waves of self-pity, however, intent as I was on making the most of the last swim of our holiday. Picci pulled out in front of me and briskly swam 50 yards into the sun in energetic strokes. I felt the marvellous healing effect of water. It was for me a benign element, for it calmed, soothed and cradled whereas the land so often exacerbated my difficulties. In water, my weight disappeared and I, too, could be free to move like everyone else, with the added bonus of all my pain disappearing.

I swam into the setting sun, while rays bathed my face, my skin and shoulders in an effervescent tingling shower. The contrast of that intense warmth and the stripping cleansing quality of the cool sea filled me with excitement. I loved those moments and must have lived them to the full as they now provide the images upon which I meditate when I need strength. Picci swam towards me and such was my own happiness that, instead of turning away from him as I would normally have done, anticipating rejection, I waited for him, my head and shoulders above the water. I watched until he was a few feet away and saw that he was observing my face in the setting sun. He smiled and slowly walked towards me. He drew me to him, his hands holding mine. All those terrible thoughts I had about how unwomanly I was hissed vaguely at me from somewhere, and I faltered, almost convinced that I should swim away. But the power of that sunset kept me with him, and he slipped his arm around my waist and kept his other hand in mine as if we were about to dance. He never stopped looking into my face, and, shyly, I looked at his mouth, avoiding his eyes as I was uncertain of what I might see there. He moved me gently round, holding me so that I couldn't lose balance, and we started our dance. I moved on up from his mouth to look into his eyes, afraid yet drawn to read his expression, half of me wanting to be reassured, and the other half laughing, ready to dash my hopes.

Finally, I made it. A strange intense energy passed from one to the other, and it was once again something that was very intimate. The moment, the dance, the sunset and the closeness were rare to have together, and I understood in that dance something of precious value. Dancing could no longer be defined as a ritual to be performed with healthy legs and music. I had danced without any of those requisites. I had danced in the sea. Whilst some needed music, I needed water, for the music I could hear in the wind and the sea and my partner's body. That afternoon I recognised that I could, in fact, do anything in my life, provided I did not ask myself to follow rigid expectations or conform to set assumptions. Provided I was versatile, had imagination and was open to considering everything from a different point of view, I had a chance of doing whatever I wanted, thus finding balance and enjoying a sense of achievement. Imagination was of fundamental importance in getting better, but it was one thing just to know on a rational level, it was quite another to experience such a reality and its curative potential.

We spent our last night holding each other, gently aware that the fears we had both had regarding our love were unfounded. Neither of us was good at unveiling those wonderful emotions that constituted love in intimate confessions. We didn't need to talk about this feeling that all was well, we just knew it and could move on in our minds to the next stages in our lives knowing that any crisis for the moment had passed.

37

ON EQUAL FOOTING

MR SPILLO, WHO was Pan Am's newly appointed lawyer handling this final transaction, Mr Popomodus, Mr Elsie, Picci and myself met in the bowels of the Milan Civil Courts, near the clerk's office, late in September 1991. We had to sign release forms so that Pan Am's property could be given back to them, their bank accounts freed and the money that had been deposited tardily in the Chancery returned. Mr Popomodus signed our cheques in front of us and handed them over with a certain paternal concern, advising me to invest the sum wisely as it was an awful lot of money to deal with in one go. It was very strange, but I cannot honestly say that I was overwhelmed by my new financial situation. It had become a concept that I had absorbed quickly whilst on holiday, as I was only too aware of the price paid. It seemed shocking that a sum had been put on the value of my life, and in my heart I felt that it was nowhere near the real one. I was conscious, too, of the incredible gift Picci had given me, first of all in terms of his solidarity throughout the case, then his relentless pursuit of the final goal which was my financial independence and, finally, of course, the making over of his cheque to me, to pad out the compensation package. They were sacrifices he'd made in the name of love and were to give me much food for thought over the following years.

The actual settlement took at the most three-quarters of an hour, and Mr Spillo was in a real hurry to be on to his next assignment, unaware of what that moment represented for me. The drama of what had happened to Picci and me was quite irrelevant to his life, and it all seemed quite absurd that each of us should be so caught up and at the mercy of life's strange whims.

I had phoned Mr Elsie the evening before in his hotel to say that I wished to take both himself and Mr Popomodus out for lunch once all the official paper signing was over. They had the rest of the day to spare, so had agreed with enthusiasm. Although Picci wouldn't be coming with us because he couldn't leave the office, he had participated in the organising of the trip. We wanted to give them an afternoon they might remember. America was a long way from Italy, and it would probably be some time before they came back, so we thought it would be nice to go out into the countryside and show them how very beautiful Italy could be. I was taking them to Lago Maggiore, one of the most scenic parts of the whole of the lake district. It was a marvellous destination, and the morning itself was one of those hazy late September days, warm and full of colour. How I wished that Picci had been able to accompany us, for I had wanted him to be there for the gentle finale to our involvement with these people.

We set off at about 11 a.m. Conversation at the beginning was a little stilted because, nervous of driving anyway, I was also nervous about having to be guide to two businessmen who I didn't know very well. We also followed the prettier route, which meant that we had an awful lot of winding roads to drive down. We chatted about Italy and the rather hopeless political mess it was in, although I was hardly able to express an opinion in that area as I had been too involved in my own problems to take much notice of an Italy that was steeped in Mafia bloodbaths and political intrigue. I could feel my guests relaxing as we left the grey streets and cheap cement buildings of the industrial outskirts of Milan. Mr Popomodus, being the larger of the two men, sat in the front of the car next to me, and I caught his expression out of the corner of my eye. He was clearly enjoying the drive, and, oblivious to my tension, carried on his conversation, asking questions I answered as best I could and making many appreciative noises regarding the countryside. Mr Elsie was similarly impressed, and they started to talk about how much fun it would be to fly over this part of the world, for both of them were light aircraft pilots. Holidays in Italy were already being planned by one then the other, as their enthusiasm grew with each passing kilometre.

An hour or so out of Milan, we finally reached Stresa, with its old-fashioned turn-of-the-century hotels in pastel colours of yellows and pinks. Few people were around and there was a feeling of stepping into some Impressionist's painting of a late summer's day picnic. I parked the car under a large plane tree near the little pier. The boatman was leaning up against a wrought iron bench with his ticket machine slung over his shoulder and I bought our passage to Fisherman's Island.

The trip across the water lasted about 15 minutes, and we were alone, accompanied only by the noise of the ferry engine muffled in the mists rising up off the lake. I was wrapped up in reflections about the obstacle race that had culminated in such a trip. Their minds, I'm sure, were far away from such thoughts. 'I' was part of their job and everyday bread and butter.

The little boat docked, touching the side of the wooden slatted pier gently, and we wobbled off the boat, or, rather, I did. Mr Elsie held out his arm to steady me as I tried to step over the gap onto the land, and I felt shy being helped by another man. Picci had always been the one who steadied me and held my hand. It was funny, too, this mixture of Pan Am and the insurance company and the men, Mr Elsie and Mr Popomodus. For me, the two companies were identified by the men. They were so very likeable, full of all the strengths and weaknesses each of us could have, and I was amused by such contradiction. Indeed, nothing was black or white, and I decided that deadly enemies should only be figments of the imagination.

On arrival, I couldn't see anything except for the line of boats and two old men cleaning and sorting their fishing nets. There was at once the smell of tomcat, which assailed our senses as we walked up the cobbled slope to the main island road and reminded me of Venice – damp alleyways and scrawny strays. On quick examination, the island housed a very old church and about eight cottages that had once belonged to the fishing community. Their traditional livelihood had long since given way to the more lucrative tourist industry. Boutiques offering garish plastic imitations of the hotels and churches, painted wooden spoons and lace dollies barged into one's consciousness, and I started to look for the restaurant, hoping my guests wouldn't be put off by the awful shops. The rest of the island and its position were really very pretty, quaint and rather eccentric. There were one or two old ladies working on their crochet and wearing black, which seemed to set my guests off in ecstatic cries because it was so obviously an Italian or Mediterranean scene. Even some of the souvenir shops were hastily checked out after lunch.

We rounded a corner ready to go up another slope right in the centre of the houses, and there I saw the sign for the restaurant. Oh how pleased I was, for it was open and things would go smoothly. I'd not been able to book a table, as I didn't know the name of the restaurant. We went up some steps and found ourselves in a large room overlooking the lake. Geraniums were thriving out on the terrace and looked as fresh as if they were the first spring flowering. A vine-covered trellis invited diners out onto the terrace, and despite the slightly cool air we decided to have lunch there. A waiter appeared and offered drinks. Champagne was ordered, for this lunch was another wonderful excuse to celebrate. We chose our main course quickly and awaited our grilled trout and vegetables with growing hunger. The champagne in the meantime arrived and brought smiles to everyone's lips.

We were more or less the only customers in the whole

establishment. Raising our glasses, we each toasted the other, wishing long life, good fortune and good health. We drank, a little affected by the words, which brought us to quietness, and we watched the sailing boats out on the lake to disperse the rather charged moment. That whole afternoon for me felt as if I was in a time warp. Had I been wearing a hat, long gloves and button-up boots I would have belonged to the late 1800s. The soft misty colours, gentle sun, cool air and easy conversation, and perhaps the effect of the champagne, gently coasted the door shut on a part of my life. I was a serene woman that afternoon and enjoyed every minute as it passed, not beset by the tiresome business of always having to think ahead and plan my life.

We had coffee, bought some souvenirs, caught the ferry back and walked amongst the tall trees by the shores of the lake. It was wonderful, and the two men seemed in even less of a hurry to go than I. We sat down on two benches facing the water. Promises were made about visits to the States and further visits to Europe. We were going to stay with each other in our various country hideaways. Cordiality and charm possessed us all, and we wondered why we hadn't resolved the case earlier. I didn't even make a dry comment to myself, steeped as I was in the romance of this Monet afternoon. Mr Elsie asked me if I was going to get married now that things were over, and I murmured something about it being probable. Mr Popomodus wanted to be sure I wasn't going to buy a Ferrari and fur coat and blow the rest on hugely expensive vacations. He was also worried about me telling people about the money I'd been given, because he said that suddenly people would become my friends, and so he did his best to warn me of the hazards by telling me ghastly stories of people who'd spent everything in the first year, falling prey to sharp tricksters and generally losing their heads over their fortune. I did think that it would take a considerably larger amount of money to make me do that but didn't say anything to that effect as he made me promise I wouldn't do anything so silly.

A light breeze sprang up, and I suggested we head back to Milan.

Apart from the natural decline of the day, I was tired out by the benign nervous tension of the trip itself. Reluctantly, they walked back to the car while I felt satisfied that each of us had played our part properly. The journey home was not as brilliant as the journey out. I got lost somewhere on the outskirts of Milan and proceeded to meander in and out of the suburbs looking for familiar crossroads in the dark. We eventually arrived at their hotel around nine o'clock, when I confessed to them that I had not followed the direct road. They didn't seem to mind at all, still suffering from jetlag as they were, and amidst much handshaking and cheek kissing, we bade each other our fond farewells, repeated our promises and went on our way. My car was silent, and I was calm and perfectly happy to be on my own once more, where the noise and clattering sound of my thoughts regarding the court case were finally and completely brought to a full stop.

38

STALEMATE

SHORTLY AFTER WE settled the case, I plucked up the courage to ask my friend whether she could remember where she'd consigned the Ladakhi prayer stones. I hardly expected to see them again, having thrust them so forcefully out of my existence, convinced in some way that they had been the cause of my grief. Hannah, my Irish girlfriend to whom I'd entrusted the precious burden, instead of giving them to a university or some other institution, had left them in their boxes at the bottom of her wardrobe, sure herself of their potential to bring her bad luck were she to transport them anywhere. She was delighted that I wanted them back and in taking them I fulfilled each of our desires.

My doubts had vanished once the Pan Am cheque had been safely invested, and I was more than delighted to have them under my roof, pleased that part of my story was not lost. I already had practical ideas about making them into bookends for my ever-expanding number of reference tomes, but I was also curious to know what the prayers said. Unfortunately, there was no teacher at the Oriental Language University who was expert in Sanskrit. They suggested I went to the Tibetan Centre in Milan, as there were people there who had not only studied the language but were also steeped in Tibetan culture. So, at six o'clock one evening I put a stone into my bag and set off for Porta Nuova. There, in a draughty building full of huge classrooms, I found a Tibetan monk wrapped in his maroon robes, waiting for his students. Quietly, he translated what was written, but warned me that I should really set aside an afternoon if I wanted to understand the full meaning of the prayer. I asked him to give me one or two ideas just to begin with, and I'd take things from there.

The prayer was one used by the ordinary people, easy and short enough to engrave into a stone. One of its many meanings included a request. It asked that the cycle of reincarnation be broken so that the person praying could go back to the source of all creation once his life was finished and not have to suffer the pain of returning to yet another human existence. Yes, I thought, I'd go along with that. My inner world was certainly richer by a thousand times in terms of experience, but I was still without psychological instruments for handling life better, and, what with all the things that had happened to me, I did wonder to what end I'd had to go through so much. The mere thought that I would be coming back to have more of what life had to offer left me cold. I did not want further earthly experiences. This life had already been more than enough.

The financial struggle was over and my physical problems were to a large extent resolved, as far as they ever could be, although I would be walking with a crutch permanently, and I still had pain. This made me very uncomfortable sometimes, but for the most part I was able to live well enough. I continued to push myself to my physical limits, as it gave me a sense of self-esteem that I lacked in so many other areas of my life. I was by now back to working freelance as a teacher in companies, managing my time with physiotherapy and other interests that were important in my daily life, and I gave what I could to my relationship with Picci. That was something I believed in and more than anything wanted to work. But I was about to undergo another period of transition and great pain, and the usual means of fighting were not of any help to me in this new strife.

At the time of the settlement in 1991, Picci and I had spent five years trying to sort out the material aspects of my life that so badly needed putting into order. In fighting so aggressively for justice and reasonable compensation in the courts, and in trying so hard to regain my health, we had left little room or indeed time for the care and attention of my mental and psychological well-being. That aspect was crucial to any future I might have, but it had been the most neglected of all the problems that had arisen from the hijack.

The new walls of my practical existence had now been erected and I was, for a year, happy, basking in the reflected glow of all my money in the bank and the financial security this gave me. I would never have to ask anyone to support me, and I would never experience the pressure of having to find a job with no one wanting my services because of my disability. I had resumed a normal working schedule and felt stronger in my health than I had ever been since the hijack. The swimming had paid off, and I was busy but in a relaxed way. What I hadn't bargained for, however, was that emotionally and psychologically I was in a desperate state. The life-saving goals I'd had up till this point had been achieved, so in the time I'd previously used for pursuing them, I was now doing other things. The lawsuit against the hospital and surgeon in New York were underway, but required nothing like the emotional involvement needed for the case against Pan Am. There was still plenty to prepare and documents to find, but the strategy was very much in the hands of the American lawyers. I didn't need to see the memorandums for the hearings, and certainly felt that I was being taken care of well given that the lawyer's financial fate was completely tied in with mine. If he lost the case, he didn't get paid.

But the easing off of all pressure meant that there was space. Other components of my character started clamouring for attention; the frightened, angry and lonely feelings needed to be addressed, and it was urgent that I start to deal with the questions that began to increasingly pester me. There were unsolved existential problems that

I'd ignored because I couldn't bear thinking about them, but now they were becoming ever more persistent and would pop into my head at unlikely moments. One of the most terrifying of these, for me, was death. It was a blasphemy, a poor joke and a truly terrifying thought. Having been so near death and experienced hell, for I can only describe my experience as such, I no longer felt I could trust anything other than the physical realities and known limitations I could grasp from and within this life. My own knowledge of the 'beyond' was frightening in the extreme. Similarly, the fact that the experience had had nothing of the good or heavenly about it – 'God' wasn't even within satellite distance – gave me nightmares before going to sleep.

For years I had slept with the light on, afraid of the demons that reached out with evil intent to grab me and take me back down into the depths of inferno. Whether what I had seen on board the plane or come into contact with in terms of subtle or cosmic malevolence had made an impression on my psyche, or whether it was the true reality awaiting me after my demise, I had no idea, but the mere fact that I wasn't likely to understand it on any rational level filled me with despair, and I was beyond being reassured. Sometimes I would half awaken and into my mind would come that question of what lay beyond this life, a question which was more of a sensation than anything I could put into words, then I would feel as if I was falling into a vortex where I would lose my name and identity, engulfed by nothingness, to then suffer the pain of loneliness on a scale of eternal proportion. Rather than consider that frightening possibility, I'd jump out of bed, go through into the kitchen, get something to eat and switch on the TV, usually at half past two in the morning. Once I was calm, I would go back to bed and, anxiously, try to fall asleep again.

During this period, the dreams I experienced were becoming very peculiar, full of extraordinary symbols, which, had I understood them, would undoubtedly have revealed much that was going on inside me. I dreamt of monsters, of cannibalism, of killing my loved ones, of flying, swimming with dolphins, burying people in the basements of houses, awful horrible dreams that were frequently to do with death. And, of course, back had come the recurring dreams of my mother, dusting herself down, shaking off the mould as she stepped out of her coffin. Overjoyed, I'd ask her if she was coming back to live with us again, to which she replied, 'It depends.' I'd stopped dreaming of her when I'd got to about the age of 16, but now I was having those dreams once again, and the same feelings of distress and need would engulf me.

Then there were often states of half-dreaming, where I'd suddenly find my consciousness gripped by the frightening memory of the effects of all the drugs I'd been administered. The experiences were unclear but had in some way thrown my mind into dimensions that were not of this world. Those moments of déjà vu were quite simply haunting and deeply disturbing.

Perhaps the most difficult dreams to shake off were those where I was being betrayed. Sometimes I dreamt of embracing a loved one who I didn't necessarily know in real life. That loved one then, on turning his face to me, was the devil incarnate who would mock my innocent affection. The first time I woke myself up with a shout. The second time I'd embraced a child who had been lost and cold in the winter fog. I had been persuaded that this child needed loving, although instinctively I had tried to run away from him. The child was only about six or seven years old. Finally, I was convinced that I should hold him and give him all I was capable of giving. I wrapped my arms around the little body, filled with remorse for having distrusted a young child and been prepared to leave it to its own fate. The child then turned its face to me, and, to my horror, I realised from its glittering and ancient eyes that it was the embodiment of all evil: the devil himself. The shock and sense of betrayal was sufficient to awaken me. That dream stayed with me for a long time, and I just couldn't explain its meaning, for there had to be some significance to such symbolism.

I think sometimes that my sensibilities to external violence were so acute that I may well have been picking up in some way on the cruel things that were happening in the world. I was without the usual protective coating of indifference that most people have, and so I suffered for every small display of ignorance, unable to rise above it and respond to situations in any enlightened way. Some people must have thought I was most peculiar when they saw how exaggerated my reactions were. Once when I was trying to find a place to park the car for a lesson, a large car behind sounded the horn a couple of times as I'd slowed traffic down considerably in my search. I stopped the car immediately, blocking the queue, got out of my car with both crutches, went to the window of the man who had hooted at me and railed against him and his impatience. I'm sure I was quite insulting. He looked at me as if I was slightly psychotic and told me to move my crate of a car otherwise he would do so for me. I parked at the side of the road and shook with anger for about five minutes, expending more energy than I would have used doing that morning's teaching. I had definitely over-reacted.

Outwardly, I carried on, but as we moved through 1993, when I underwent further surgery in July, I felt that my life was becoming very meaningless indeed. I was not following in the footsteps of my brothers and sisters who were married and enjoying normal family lives. I had actually wanted to marry Picci and have his children, but it wasn't happening and there were difficulties in discussing these aspects of our lives. I was not in close contact with my family because we had little in common and their time was taken up with more urgent worries than thinking about me. They had children, and school, books, Cubs, swimming, homework – all the important activities that go with family life. I wanted contact with them more than anything else but felt envious and jealous of what seemed to be the greener grass of their lives. From their point of view, I can only imagine that they felt years had gone by since the hijacking and never imagined that I might still be having a bad time. I had been financially compensated, so now I could move on and get over the whole upsetting incident. I was better, wasn't I, or at least I should have been better after all this time.

I'm not sure how I managed to become so unhappy, but I think that once you begin to slide down the slope of depression, it becomes ever more difficult to climb out of that mental state. There were contributing factors, not least of all the anger and frustration I had had to deal with on my own. I was without religious faith of any description and so was trying to rationalise my anger over what had happened to me by running down all sorts of theoretical alleyways. But the anger was there, and I think it began to get wrongly channelled. I was getting angry with my brothers and sisters, who seemed to have everything they wanted in life. I spat my anger out at my father and his wife for the life I'd had in the past and for their apparent lack of care over my present situation. I had so much resentment towards my family. It was a very insidious and powerful negative force that began taking over. At the same time, they were the very ones I wanted to be loved and understood by.

I was becoming highly critical of people generally, and I became uncomfortably hard and judgemental. I was only aware of the intense pain inside my own heart and failed to see the pain I was inadvertently causing others when I perhaps spoke to my family by phone or saw them when I went for a visit to England. Only now can I comment with considerable objectivity concerning this period of my life. I was acutely aware of the things I said, thought and did in my everyday existence and, therefore, remember everything. I cannot have been poisonous towards others outside my family, for I was normally gentle and considerate. Now and again for no reason, though, I'd lash out with my anger, but afterwards I was always filled with self-reproach.

Ominously, the black clouds of depression became more frequent. I had had them throughout the trial years, certainly, but they were now more lingering and persistent, and I became emotionally immobilised. A word, phrase, or interpretation of a gesture were sufficient to accentuate feelings of loneliness, uselessness, apathy and self-hatred. I stayed in this straitjacket of despair for four to five days at a time, thinking the worst things and pushing myself further and further away from life itself. Indeed, I felt more dead than alive in those periods. It was as if I were sitting on Mars watching the activities of others in a rather malevolent confused state.

Naturally, I spoke to no one about these depressions. They were exclusively mine, and I felt I had to deal with them without making too much of a fuss. But I couldn't. After five days or so, the depression would lift as suddenly and as fiercely as it had arrived, and I found myself able to laugh and see the world from a different perspective. The idea that I should suffer from depression was a confusing one, for I had a naturally sunny disposition and would never have associated a character type like mine as being susceptible to this illness. I now know that depression can strike anyone and that it is a cruel enemy, hard to identify at first and tenacious once it has found its victim. In the past, I had briefly been to see two psychologists, one at the time I had gone to the press in England and the other briefly in the hospital after the failed surgery, both of them men and both very much products of male-orientated Western society. I had been rational, full of jokes, and gave them to understand that I had indeed recovered. At face value, of course, this must have seemed to be the case, and I thought that I had tight control over my external relationship with the world. They would have had to dig deep and with infinite patience to learn of my unhappiness. Even I at that time thought that I was very together about this hijack thing; yes I did have bad dreams, upsetting thoughts and a huge complex about my body, but who wouldn't have had these problems in my position? The psychologists were concerned about the walking, not about the aesthetics when talking to me, telling me that character and personality were more important, which may well have been true, but I wanted to be appreciated for my body and looks as well. As time passed, I began to wonder if I'd ever be happy or if the depression would consume me completely. Picci knew about these periods, but I tried hard to keep away from him when I was down. He asked me what the matter was, but I would distract him by appearing interested in his work. I couldn't talk to him, as I didn't know what to say.

By the time 1994 had arrived I was struggling to cope with two depressive bouts every month. I couldn't seem to keep a grip on myself any more. I could not at that time readily identify the cause of my distress, and all I knew was that I was spinning round in orbit, panicking about where I was going to finally finish up. I would spend huge amounts of time justifying my negativity and hoping that all my nearest and dearest would suffer the same pain that I had suffered over the years. The only person who seemed to understand my inner misery was Bibi. She gave me time and a lot of love, which enabled me to calm down when I was in one of these fits. Either she wrote or we spoke by phone, and her support was unconditional.

In retrospect, I'm convinced that those last two years where I suffered from depression so badly were the final throes of a gestation period – the labour pains before the birth. The chaotic muddle in my head was at its worst during that time and my most unpleasant personality traits were to the fore, easily identifiable and quick to surface. It was almost as if I had done the digging and now all the mental rubbish was there for everyone to see.

October 1994 was the real closing chapter on the hijack story and indeed on the questions and uncertainties I had experienced many years previously. Perhaps October was the month where the key to my future life lay. Unbeknown to me, the last scene of my psychological angst was about to unfold, and it offered as spectacular a stage exit as I could have wished. It suited me well, as I had always loved happy endings. What happened to me was unexpected and a shock to my system.

39

CHECKMATE

I HAD COME back from a ten-day stay in England with Bibi, having spent much time rushing round London looking for a small flat to invest in. I was semi-serious but beleaguered by conflicting desires and looking for a flat was really an excuse for me to feel free. I was in England ostensibly to fill up on my own culture and English customs, to see friends and family. It was something I did every six months or so in order to regenerate my Milan-consumed batteries. It was all very romantic living in another country, but when you wanted to drop by a friend's for a cup of tea, or wished to see a sibling on spec, Milan wasn't the right city.

This time I had asked to see my father, under the pretext of a social visit. On the one hand I needed to keep up some semblance of civility for my own frail emotional world and on the other I wanted to challenge him on a personal matter. We rarely saw one another because of tensions in our relationship, although I missed not having a father close to me. I was a little uptight for the entire duration of my stay in London, because the lunch we were to have together had been organised for the last day. The letter I had written to him was also rather provocative, and meeting up, with or without provocative missives, was always cause for anxiety.

The search for a house in London was symbolic but I was not really conscious of the fact then. I must have seen about eight little apartments in the West End, all horribly expensive and pokey for the price, needing a lot of maintenance, but the freedom I experienced, dreaming of starting my life all over again, was like a breath of fresh air. I just wanted to get away from everything.

I had made up my mind to do this on our previous summer vacation. I had had a whiff of this freedom on a boat coming across the Red Sea from the island of Dahlak and the excitement I had felt in my heart at the prospect of starting afresh was immense. Picci had asked me what I was thinking, for he had caught my wide-eyed absorbed expression. I didn't tell him because it was my secret and not telling him helped me feel free.

My last day in London presented itself, and my aunt had prepared a beautiful lunch for my father and me. He duly arrived and was understandably wary of his oversensitive hostile daughter. My emotions were quick to ignite because he didn't come forward waving an olive branch or confess that he had been miserably at fault regarding our difficult relationship. I was taken aback by the intensity of my feelings and aware that they were far from healthy. After a difficult meal, where I had tried to make a move at reconciliation – but with gritted teeth, because I wanted the new understanding to be on my terms – we parted, not before my father gave me a present. On one of my aunt's chairs, he left my great-great-grandmother's leather-bound Bible. My father was no more religious than I, but it was comforting to have a family heirloom. It was huge and the writing was widely spaced and clear to read. There were also pencil annotations in the margin and a smell of old book about it, and it was in perfect condition.

We had agreed to a ceasefire, although I was not convinced that I wanted an end to hostilities. In my mind, he had not recognised his part in our communication problems, and for me to forgive him I had to have an apology, heartfelt, where he acknowledged his insensitivity.

We left with the promise that I would go to France to see his new house in the near future, for I had not up till then visited him. I was still upset about his imperturbable exterior. It would be absolutely impossible for me to change one bit if he couldn't admit his own area of guilt. I felt so hard, brittle and angry. After he'd gone, my aunt, wisely or unwisely, reproached me about the fact that I'd been so aggressive. Stung by her audacity to criticise, I rounded on her. She'd touched my weak spot, and I struck like a cornered snake. She managed to quieten me down before sending me back to Italy, but I felt very jumbled up and full of hurting bruises.

That same evening after my return to Italy, depression hit before I'd even had time to unpack my bags. I arrived in my home and literally felt as if unhappiness was determinedly putting chains around my heart, shackling me to the greyness of a hopeless life. I could almost hear the rattling and wanted to run, but physically and psychologically it was impossible. As evening approached, I kept asking myself what it was that made me so heavy with sadness. I was literally coming to the point where I could stand myself no more and would have done anything to change my lot. Looking out of my bedroom window that evening into the beautiful fading light, I felt a great wish to unburden my heart of its troubles. I was reaching that watershed situation where you either take the opportunity, or close your eyes and sink back to the place you so dearly wished to leave, saying goodbye to one lucky chance. Without thought, I went down on my knees in front of the radiator in my bedroom and began to say the Lord's Prayer. It was the only prayer I could recall because I knew it by heart. I repeated it, I cannot remember how many times. I used the seat of a chair for support and went over the sentences in my mind until at last they began to present themselves phrase by phrase, slowing down until the awful turmoil inside me ceased.

In the silence, the line 'forgive us our trespasses as we forgive those who trespass against us' became as a huge mural to be studied scene by scene. My mind moved along the words, examining them and listening to them. As I repeated these sounds, I felt as if something was being moved inside me, a great block was turned over in my chest, and I began to breathe easier, feeling physically and psychologically better. Serenity and calmness washed over my body and mind, the like of which I had never experienced. There was the feeling that something enormously good and powerful was within my body and outside me. There was a full silence now and the sensation of comfort grew, a warm glow in my heart area. I was at peace and words of kindness and generosity for my family spilled out of my heart and into my mind. Energy began to fill me, and I felt charged with an extraordinary joy. There was compassion for myself and for everyone else, suffering or not.

When I got up from my kneeling position on the floor some time later, I knew that I had forgiven my family, but most importantly I had also forgiven myself for everything I'd failed to do, couldn't do and for those things I shouldn't have done. The sensation was miraculous. I felt I had been in the presence of something marvellous, that I was not alone and that, if I wished, I would never have to feel alone again. I was clean and purified as if I'd stepped into a new person which was still myself but minus those old worn aspects that were of no value any more.

From this experience and others that occurred at a later date, I found a new understanding of myself. I was radically changed by that experience of forgiveness and, as a consequence, knew that there was a rich spiritual world to be drawn from. The fear that perhaps there was only hell after death had been removed, even if I was aware that a negative subconscious reality existed. I also knew how that reality could erupt into daily actions, corroding and corrupting human life, and that it was important to maintain a clean heart if I wanted to live peacefully.

Since that afternoon all those years ago I can honestly say that I have not experienced depression in any form. I have become aware that I am not some independent entity that has to resolve the burden of its own existence, or be responsible for what happens in life. I have realised that it is the way I deal with how life presents itself that can give me happiness. Reflecting on that experience, I am surprised that the help I so badly needed came from inside me, in my own home. No one convinced me to go and speak to so and so about these problems. I didn't go to the local vicar to ease my distress. And I had never prayed before. In fact, I didn't know how to pray. I had gone down on my knees instinctively, desperate for respite that one initial time. The very fact that this relief came to me from no outside stimulus persuaded me that this experience was authentic and a gift from life's great goodness.

The night after praying, I slept better than I'd ever slept in that house. I felt wrapped up in a cocoon of benevolence and safety as if nothing and no one could ever harm me again. I knew that I'd come home, rather like that strange experience where I had embraced the geometric figure of light and felt the tranquillity of, at long last, being where I was meant to be, but in this second experience the after-effect was concrete and practical. The following day, on waking up, my first thoughts were positive and the feelings of guilt I used to experience were noticeably missing. I was happy and couldn't believe that this had happened to me. That same evening I sat down and repeated the prayer, stilling my mind so that I could express gratitude. I found that I was hugely emotional and cried, finally aware that I'd be alone no more. It really was quite an extraordinary sensation, not dissimilar to falling in love, and although one might attribute this reaction to being that of a person susceptible to strong emotions and a lively imagination, the benefits I was experiencing were tangible. I was also able to sleep with the light off.

In the first few months I had some very strong experiences which filled me with great emotion. Then the intensity stopped and the visionary episodes were repeated no more. A calmer, more down-to-earth kind of praying then went on and has continued to this day. This finale to the hijacking chapters of my life was the biggest surprise to me and an enormous gift that could not have been better chosen.

Picci and I have stayed together, both benefiting from this experience. He has become gentler and more understanding, and I have become surer of myself, able to accept my shortcomings without aggression. I have also removed the pedestal on top of which I'd placed Picci, and in so doing have found I laugh at much in both of us that made me miserable before. I think that the effects of the hijacking, managed by a strong personality such as mine, were not in themselves the easiest of ingredients to deal with. It took a profound and spiritual experience to bring about that alchemy which would help me move beyond.

Many years have now gone by since 1986, and I have seen acts of terrorism in different forms with dramatic consequences, where death and maiming are the usual outcome. Every time there are victims, my heart goes out to those who'll have to deal with the very things I have had to accept and learn to live with, and I always pray that the power of good will stand by them. I also pray that the women of our world, whatever their creed, will have an ever-increasing influence over their men, using their innate sense of justice and nurturing qualities to neutralise aggression, even when they themselves sometimes lead oppressed lives. I believe that they will also need the help of God now more than ever.

On a more personal note, I have to say that in my misfortune I have been luckier than many, not only because the injuries have left me sufficient autonomy to enjoy life but also because I have been given a glimpse of another world and another dimension, not bound by time or space and far removed from a rationale which governs our daily activities. This other perspective helps me to accept what I cannot change and gives me strength to act where sometimes it would be easier just to let things go, and let things go when I harm myself by holding on to them. Without that extraordinary experience of forgiveness, I wonder how I would have proceeded on my way.

The other piece of great good fortune was in having such a stalwart companion who loved me and did not run away when our fortune changed but stood by my side from the beginning to the end. Perhaps for all those who have to go through particularly gruelling circumstances there comes an opportunity, a helping hand to move beyond the grim reality, and it might not necessarily be of a spiritual nature but will resonate with the person and suit their character. Perhaps, too, help comes when we profoundly ask for it and we are ready to accept it. When help came to me, I could do nothing but surrender completely to its great wisdom, and despite the ups and downs that inevitably accompany existence, I feel that I'm a steadier person, anchored to a quiet centre within my psyche that grows as I move on.

EPILOGUE

1996

'Harefield Crematorium'. We passed by the signpost and yew trees on our way to Bibi's house one day on a visit to England, and I was jolted out of my thoughts. 'That's where my mother was cremated,' I said in amazement, never having been there but for that one occasion all those years ago. Picci unexpectedly pulled the car into the gravel turn-off and slowly drove towards the chapel.

'Whyever do you want to come in here?' I exclaimed, surprised that Picci, usually so wary of emotionally loaded occasions, should bring me to a place filled with possible trip wires.

'I think it will do you good to visit this place and find your mother,' was all he was willing to say.

I was curious and for the moment unfazed by what he had done, little imagining what might transpire. With that, he opened the car door and we walked into the gardens behind the church. Everything was as I remembered it: the modern red-brick walls, neat tidy gardens and wide pebbly sweep for the hearses to bring the deceased. Images of that time had been seared into my memory, then buried and hopefully forgotten. Seeing the shiny coffin on the little wheels disappearing through the hatch towards the furnaces while reciting Psalm 23 was the most excruciating moment of my young life, for at 11 years of age, I realised my mother was dead only in the instant that I saw she was about to be burnt. I struggled to put those thoughts to the back of my mind as we searched for her plaque, remembering how, at the end of the service, I had pushed her face, voice and person out of my existence for 26 years, only to be then haunted by the very lack of them throughout my life.

We looked everywhere for her amongst the hundreds of names on the cemetery walls, but she was nowhere to be found, and I wondered for a moment if I had got confused. Then I saw that the offices were open, and, overcome with a primitive need, I went in. The room was large and airy with amber floorboards and furniture of the same hue. There were summer roses in vases, and the windows were open, letting in the scented breeze from the gardens. Despite the location, this seemed a calm and comfortable place, reassuring in its solidness.

I approached the desk, behind which sat a gentleman reading a book, and asked if by any chance Christine Lamb had been cremated there. When he asked me why I wanted to know, I explained that I was her daughter. Looking through the large registry books he had lining the wall, he pulled out the relative year and within moments had found her name. Beside the black ink was a column for the date and additional notes. Next to the date was written 'Plaque not wanted'. The words I gazed at had been written at the time of her cremation, and seeing this script seemed to unlock memories and sensations banished all those years ago. The words regarding the plaque proved how the whole family had collectively thrust this woman from their lives in an act of almost surgical removal. Why hadn't her memory been honoured by an inscription of some sort?

Picci was no longer around, having had enough discretion to leave me alone. My eyes filled, and I felt what seemed to be an internal dam bursting as I walked out into the sunshine of that morning. The distress of having lost my mother was for the first time fully expressed as, sobbing, my tears flowed behind a wall of the cemetery where Picci found me some time later, my face swollen by grief. He put his arm around my shoulder and said, 'I think we can go now.'

My mother often comes to mind these days, and I miss her, especially in situations when I would like to confide in her and ask for advice. I remember small things of her character and phrases she used to say will come into my head on particular occasions, but I don't remember many things we did together as she was ill for five out of my eleven years. Having finally faced the grief of her death, I am at peace with what happened and in touch with a softer, more indulgent aspect of my character. I have gradually and inexorably drawn closer to my father, his wife and my brothers and sisters, and feel their support and love in my life. Their presence enriches all that I do and provides a network of security from which I feel nourished. It is wonderful to find this unity after so many years of feeling quite isolated from them.

2000

I went for an ecco-doppler at my local hospital to try to address a problem I'd been experiencing over the previous year regarding the circulation in my legs. I was asked numerous questions, including whether at any point in the past I had experienced swelling of my ankles and calves. My medical history was complex and all told I'd spent the equivalent of nearly a year in a hospital bed. The only time I could remember such a situation was when I was in New York, when my whole body had blown up considerably after surgery in 1989. To my great surprise, the doctors carrying out the ecco-doppler explained that I had all the clinical leftovers of two deep vein thromboses in both legs.

Despite the quantity of complications I'd had as a result of the grenade blast, I was unaware that DVT was part of that long list, and so I asked the medics how far they believed the episode went back. Their estimate coincided with that terrible experience in America when Dr Tellez had tried to transfer the muscle from my back down to the buttock area and failed. I reflected carefully, thinking about everything that had happened in that period. If the thrombosis had occurred during surgery, there was absolutely no report of the matter in any of the medical records. I couldn't be certain of when or where this particular medical problem had happened, but the missing parts of a jigsaw puzzle began to slip into place and doubts became even stronger regarding the New York experience.

In 1992, Picci had insisted we pursue the surgeon and the hospital for medical malpractice in the New York courts. Just after settling with Pan Am in September 1991, we enlisted the help of a lawyer in Manhattan who was willing to investigate the case and fight it for a contingency fee, should we win. I signed a contract with a very fearsome patriarchal Italian-American who, despite his years, was sharp and wily and who we named 'The Silver Fox'. After numerous depositions and years of collecting evidence, with the legal offices doing much of the work this time, the moment came for the trial by jury and in 1998 I was once more off on a trip to New York. The case was supposed to last ten days, but I ended up there for four nerve-racking weeks, where every day I had to go to court and listen to all kinds of interesting testimony, some of which was way off the truth.

I had a magnificent lawyer, who fought against the lack of clarity exhibited by the defendants. The jury was made up of mostly black women and an Irishman. One of the doctors talked to the members of the jury, implying that understanding the ins and outs of microsurgery was something that could only be done after years of study and certainly not during a trial of this nature. The jury retaliated by listening carefully to everything said and drawing their own conclusions. The doctors claimed that I'd had a thrombosis in the previously healthy back muscle after it was excised and whilst they were transferring it down to my buttock. They admitted that this was most unusual but said it could happen. Apparently, however, it wasn't unusual enough to warrant sending the muscle to the pathology labs to investigate why, or indeed if, there had been a thrombosis. The useless muscle was instead thrown into the theatre rubbish bin. Neither had it been felt necessary to carry out preliminary tests to determine the status of arteries and veins. Other doctors said that I had known what risks I was running by going for such complex surgery and that I'd insisted. They also said that I had been told that I'd never walk without a crutch or support: a suggestion so ridiculous that even they must have realised their mistake. Why would I be going for surgery if there was to be no improvement in my walking?

The questioning and answering went on for days as people came in to give testimony, and thoughts and memories bounced around in my head as I listened attentively to everything, especially what seemed to me to be lies. Finally the lawyers wrapped up their cases and the judge told everybody it was time to make a decision. While the jury was segregated and talked for two days in order to arrive at a verdict, I paced up and down the court corridors in a huge draughty building in the south of Manhattan with ballroom-size lifts and filthy windows. It reminded me of similar institutions back in Europe, and the cold February weather offered pitiful respite from that tense unpleasant period. On Thursday afternoon, the court gathered in wintry gloom at three o'clock to listen to what the jury had to say, and I suffered pre-exam butterflies sitting behind my lawyer. Dr Tellez was not in court. His last appearance had been three days before. He'd looked lost and dejected, and I remember seeing a hole he'd had in the heel of his sock. Usually well-dressed, I realised he was probably suffering the pains of hell, nothing to what I'd been through, but from a certain point of view I didn't enjoy seeing him so morally beaten.

The court officer asked the jury leader for their findings. They were unanimous in their verdict. Both the hospital and doctor were found guilty of medical malpractice, and I was awarded a staggering $7 million compensation. Once the verdict was read out, the court was dismissed and I was allowed to go and talk to the jury members. I shook their hands and embraced them with my lawyer. These wonderful big black women reproached me for not having been a better judge of doctors. They hadn't lived through what I had, though, and perhaps I was no longer a good judge of people or situations. The lawyer dropped me off at my hotel where we said our goodbyes, warning me that the case was nowhere near finished and that the defendants would appeal against the amount of damages as the sum awarded was unrealistically high. I hardly heard him as I nodded my head, desperate to be off up to my room where I could call Picci. It was about 5.30 p.m. in New York and nearly midnight in Italy. He was waiting for me, anxious and tense, expecting the worst and I didn't want to delude him. I told him to get a chair so that I could give him the news. I maintained a sober and rather sad voice, and felt his sympathy as he gently asked me if I was OK. The suppressed laughter made my throat ache.

'We've won,' I whispered.

There was a long silence.

'How much?' he whispered back.

Instead of staying one more night at the hotel, so that I could go out on Fifth Avenue to buy myself a long-promised ring to celebrate, Picci ordered me home the same evening. Once he realised it wasn't a joke and that I had been awarded this enormous amount, he was desperate that I should not be alone with such a massive mental responsibility. The last thing he wanted was for me to be ecstatically out and about on the streets of New York with no one to advise me or keep me calm. He insisted I get a taxi out to JFK and a plane back to Milan immediately, otherwise he would be coming over to get me. I did as I was told, throwing my clothes in my bags and telling the hotel staff who'd looked after me for a month that I'd won the court case, after which I tipped them all. I received many congratulations, hugs and advice on how to spend the money, which I hadn't put a figure to but which had stimulated everyone's imagination.

The receptionist ordered a limousine to take me to the airport, taxis being unavailable because of torrential rain. My bags were loaded into the boot of a very long vehicle with room for at least ten people. The seats were honey coloured and smelt of plastic. The engine was silent and windows darkened, and it felt as if I was in a mobile library, all sounds from the outside world dampened to the point of near silence. Suspended in explosive euphoria, I watched the moving lights of early evening traffic flicker in front of my eyes as we sedately drove off. The city skyline receded as I put my feet up on the seat in front and we headed out towards JFK. I hesitated between choosing the small bottle of whiskey or can of lager, courtesy of the limousine company, eventually snapping open the latter to sip the cool bubbles while enjoying a nirvanic feeling of solitude and well-being. I couldn't have wished for any other experience in that moment. There was something very precious about having to celebrate such happiness geographically far from home, and that exquisite emotion was heightened by the fact that there was no one to share such feelings with.

For the record, the compensation was subsequently massively reduced by the judge, who deemed the original sum far too much for the damage sustained. I could have fought the decision but chose to accept her ruling. It was already something to have seen justice done, and I didn't want to have to go through another trial by jury.

Following that examination in hospital in the year 2000, I was told that I could not have treatment for my legs due to the fact that I had had these thromboses. The risks that my circulation would pack up were high, so I was advised to live with the problem, which at that time was not yet critical. When the situation deteriorates, we will have to think again.

2001

After a period of renovation on an old farmhouse in Milan, Picci and I were finally going to be living together. We had spent five or so years bringing a derelict farmhouse back to its former glory using old materials from demolished buildings, a marvellous team of workmen and a lot of patience. We drove all over the north of Italy looking for fireplaces, old bricks, interior doors, flagstones and ornate stair banisters that reflected the style and period of the building. I had been the first to move into the house, with workmen still on the job, and from the moment I was there, I felt I'd finally reached my oasis.

That was in May. Picci was due to move in with me in November of the same year, as he needed time to organise his business and make family arrangements. On 11 September, at about 3.30 in the afternoon, I was ironing in the breakfast room with the doors on to the courtyard wide open, enjoying the last of the warm summer breeze. Suddenly the programme I was watching was interrupted by an emergency news bulletin. I watched in horror as one of the Twin Towers of the World Trade Center in New York collapsed. I ran to phone Picci at work, who listened in stunned silence to my running commentary. It was as if someone had pushed me over a cliff, and I was free-falling as I reacted to the events that were changing the course of history on a global scale.

Worried sick that something might have happened to my Pan Am friend, I rang Mr Elsie's home in the state of New York and spoke to his wife, asking her where he was. He was supposed to be on his way to his offices in Manhattan, and she was terrified that he was caught up in the general panic and perhaps stuck in the subway somewhere. When I at last got the news that he was safe, he told me that he'd just come up from the underground when he saw people jumping out of the windows of one of the towers as they literally tried to escape a fate worse than death fleeing from the flames behind them. He was devastated and once again asked me why he had always been the one to witness terrorist acts but never been directly involved. We hugged each other telephonically and said goodbye. At least I knew he was safe.

The week that followed was so full of the news of the hijacked planes and kamikaze use of them that I had to switch off the TV. I was on horror-overload. My hard-won equilibrium was near total collapse as Picci reacted in one way and I in another. He became strident against the 'arrogance' of the US, while I shook with anger over the audacity and arrogance of bin Laden. Picci seemed to rage at everyone and everything, and I found his comments exhausting at times as he gave his remedies for fighting terrorism to the newsreaders at supper. I think that he, too, might have been over-reacting to what had happened in New York. The emotions that passed through me in that period were very strong and my mind was occupied with the aftermath such a tragedy would cause. It was hard for me not to cry and relive the moments of desperation I had experienced over the years.

About two weeks after the attack, I was sitting in my studio, wondering where all this terrorism was leading us. Almost absentmindedly, I pulled the lengthy manuscript of _Dancing in the Sea_ out of my desk drawer. I opened the first page, read what I had lived through and decided with fierce determination that I would edit it and send it off to the publishers as soon as I could. This was the only way I could think of usefully using the energy unleashed by the Twin Towers disaster. I, too, had been a victim of terrorism, and despite everything had lived to tell my tale. I hadn't gone under after the experience but had survived by fighting back. It would help me if I made that achievement public and sent one small message of hope out of my personal world to others.

2004

Peter George and I were in touch again. He asked after my well-being and informed me that the sentencing date for one of the hijackers who was caught by the FBI after his release from prison in Pakistan would be held on 12 May 2004 in the US. He would plead guilty to 95 counts of the indictment against him and would be sentenced to the maximum term of imprisonment on each count, some 160 years all told, presumably without appeal or parole. He will seemingly have to cooperate and testify should any of his fellow hijackers be caught by the FBI and brought to justice in the States. The other four hijackers are apparently still sitting in prison in Pakistan.

Peter George was going to America to witness the sentencing of the leader of the terrorists and asked me if I wanted to go. I said no, because the hijackers and their fate have never interested me, nor have I wanted to follow their story apart from needing the documentation of the court reports from Pakistan for the case against Pan Am, which were unavailable to me at that time.

One of the hijackers in Pakistan has written a letter full of remorse for his part in the attack. For me, nothing they can say or do will change their past. I have repaired myself to the best of my ability, and I'm happy with how I've turned out. What the terrorists did and how they deal with their consciences is between them and God. As far as I'm concerned, they existed only at the time of the hijack, after which they gradually became of no consequence, though I am thankful that at least one will be paying an adequate price for multiple murder and grievous bodily harm.

Finally I would like to say to all those who were on Pan Am flight 073 with me on 5 September 1986 that my thoughts and best wishes are with them. I hope they are doing well.